CLARENDON ARISTOTLE SERIES

General Editors
J. L. ACKRILL AND LINDSAY JUDSON

Also published in this series

Categories and *De Interpretatione*
J. L. ACKRILL

De Anima Books II and III
D. W. HAMLYN
New impression with supplementary material by Christopher Shields

De Generatione et Corruptione
C. J. F. WILLIAMS

De Partibus Animalium I and *De Generatione Animalium* I
D. M. BALME
New impression with supplementary material by Allan Gotthelf

Eudemian Ethics Books I, II, and VIII
MICHAEL WOODS
Second edition

Metaphysics Books Γ, Δ, and E
CHRISTOPHER KIRWAN
Second edition

Metaphysics Books Z and H
DAVID BOSTOCK

Metaphysics Books M and N
JULIA ANNAS

Physics Books I and II
WILLIAM CHARLTON
New impression with supplementary material

Physics Books III and IV
EDWARD HUSSEY
New impression with supplementary material

Politics Books I and II
TREVOR J. SAUNDERS

Politics Books III and IV
RICHARD ROBINSON
New impression with supplementary material by David Keyt

Politics Books VII and VIII
RICHARD KRAUT

Posterior Analytics
JONATHAN BARNES
Second edition

Topics Books I and III
ROBIN SMITH

Other volumes are in preparation

ARISTOTLE

Politics

BOOKS V AND VI

*Translated
with a Commentary
by*

DAVID KEYT

CLARENDON PRESS · OXFORD
1999

Oxford University Press, Great Clarendon Street, Oxford OX2 6DP
Oxford New York
Athens Auckland Bangkok Bogotá Buenos Aires Calcutta
Cape Town Chennai Dar es Salaam Delhi Florence Hong Kong Istanbul
Karachi Kuala Lumpur Madrid Melbourne Mexico City Mumbai
Nairobi Paris São Paulo Singapore Taipei Tokyo Toronto Warsaw
and associated companies in
Berlin Ibadan

Oxford is a registered trade mark of Oxford University Press

Published in the United States
by Oxford University Press Inc., New York

© David Keyt 1999
The moral rights of the author have been asserted

First published 1999

British Library Cataloguing in Publication Data
Data available

Library of Congress Cataloging in Publication Data
Data available

ISBN 0-19-823535-6
ISBN 0-19-823536-4 (Pbk.)

1 3 5 7 9 10 8 6 4 2

Typeset by Best-set Typesetter Ltd., Hong Kong
Printed in Great Britain
on acid-free paper by
Biddles Ltd, Guildford and King's Lynn

To
Sarah and Aaron

PREFACE

This book had a long gestation. The idea of writing a commentary on Aristotle's study of faction and constitutional change was formed in the late 1960s during the period of political unrest in the United States connected with the Vietnam War. In the summer of 1971 I discussed the possibility of doing this volume in the Clarendon Aristotle Series with John Ackrill over lunch at Brasenose College. But the time was not ripe. There did not seem to be a market for another volume on the *Politics* beyond the one by Richard Robinson on Books III and IV. Though interest in the treatise increased steadily in the following years, I thought no more about the matter. Then, more than two decades later out of the blue an aerogramme arrived from Ackrill inquiring whether interest in the project had faded. It had not. I leapt at the opportunity to realize late in life (having already lived longer than Aristotle) a dream of middle age.

Now that the project is finished I must acknowledge the help I received with the translation and various aspects of the commentary from S. Marc Cohen, Fred Miller, Jr., Nils Rauhut, and David Reeve. I am greatly indebted to the editorial skill and forbearance of my wife, Christine Keyt, who read many versions of the translation and commentary and whose acute observations about the quality of the writing and argumentation were not always warmly received. The editors of this series, John Ackrill and Lindsay Judson, were enormously helpful. It is sad to realize that six years of correspondence with Ackrill on Greek, English usage, Aristotle, and British and American politics will now necessarily come to an end. Working with him was a belated (and extended) Oxford education, and I shall always be grateful that when it came time to commission this volume he remembered our lunch at Brasenose College.

I am also grateful to the Research and Royalty Fund of the University of Washington for a grant in support of this project and to the University of Washington for a research leave.

D. K.

Seattle, Washington
January 1998

CONTENTS

REFERENCES AND ABBREVIATIONS

Athen.	Athenaeus, *Scholars at Dinner*
Aristoph.	Aristophanes
Eccles.	*Ecclesiazusae*
ARISTOTLE	
An. Post.	*Analytica Posteriora*
Anim.	*de Anima*
AP	*Athēnaiōn Politeia*
Cael.	*de Caelo*
EE	*Ethica Eudemia*
EN	*Ethica Nicomachea*
GA	*de Generatione Animalium*
GC	*de Generatione et Corruptione*
HA	*Historia Animalium*
MA	*de Motu Animalium*
Met.	*Metaphysica*
Meteor.	*Meteorologica*
MM	*Magna Moralia*
Oec.	*Oeconomica*
PA	*de Partibus Animalium*
Phys.	*Physica*
Poet.	*Poetica*
Pol.	*Politica*
Rhet.	*Rhetorica*
Soph. El.	*Sophistici Elenchi*
Top.	*Topica*
Dem.	Demosthenes
Diod.	Diodorus of Sicily, *Library*
D.L.	Diogenes Laertius, *Philosophers' Lives*
Her.	Herodotus, *Histories*
Isoc.	Isocrates
Areop.	*Areopagiticus*
Panath.	*Panathenaicus*
Paneg.	*Panegyricus*
Justin	*Epitome of the Philippic History of Pompeius Trogus*
Paus.	Pausanias, *Guide to Greece*

PLATO

Apol.	*Apology*
Ep.	*Epistle*
Gorg.	*Gorgias*
Prot.	*Protagoras*
Rep.	*Republic*
Stat.	*Statesman*
Symp.	*Symposium*
Theaet.	*Theaetetus*
Plut.	Plutarch
Gr. Q.	*Greek Questions*
Lys.	*Lysander*
Prec. Stat.	*Precepts of Statecraft*
Polyaen.	Polyaenus, *Stratagems of War*
Strabo	*The Geography of Strabo*
Thuc.	Thucydides, *History of the Peloponnesian War*
Xen.	Xenophon
An.	*Anabasis*
Cyr.	*Cyropaedia*
Hell.	*Hellenica*
Mem.	*Memorabilia*
Oec.	*Oeconomicus*

In the case of a reference to a passage in Aristotle, where no work is mentioned, the reference is to a passage in the *Politics*; and where the number of the book is not given, the reference is to a passage in the book that is currently the subject of the commentary.

The *Athēnaiōn Politeia*, the *Magna Moralia*, and the *Oeconomica* are listed above as works of Aristotle even though their authenticity has been questioned. For our purposes it does not matter whether the *Athēnaiōn Politeia* and the *Oeconomica* are from Aristotle's own hand since they are cited only for the information they contain about historical events and Greek institutions. And since the *Magna Moralia* is cited only to supplement references to works of Aristotle of unquestioned authenticity, what matters is that it is Aristotelian, not that it is from Aristotle's own hand.

INTRODUCTION

Equality, democracy, tyranny, revolution, reform—these are some of the topics of Books V and VI. Since they have been major themes in the politics of the twentieth century, and will no doubt continue to be so in the twenty-first, they lend these books an immediacy that is unusual for Aristotle's writings. The conflict between freedom and equality that Aristotle finds at the root of democracy is still unresolved. Some of the causes of revolution that he discusses were operative in the twentieth century. And his description of tyranny fits the modern, as well as the ancient variety: it was even quoted in one of the leaflets distributed by some of the students at the University of Munich in their heroic (and doomed) resistance to Hitler.

Although Books V and VI are relatively self-contained and can be read on their own apart from the rest of the *Politics* (particularly when supplemented by a commentary), the two books fit comfortably into the larger treatise and presuppose many of the ideas of its other parts. The subject of the *Politics*—aside from Book I, which is on managing a household and ruling slaves (III. 6. 1278^{b}17–19)— is constitutions (I. 13. 1260^{b}12; IV. 2. 1289^{a}26, 8. 1293^{b}29–30). A general theory of constitutions is presented in Book III; ideal constitutions are discussed in Books II and VII–VIII; and constitutions that are less than ideal in Books IV–VI. These three books on less-than-ideal constitutions compose a single unit organized by a programme of five questions laid out in the second chapter of Book IV (1289^{b}12–26). The first three are discussed in the remainder of Book IV, and concern the species and subspecies of constitution, the second-best constitution, and the suitability of a particular constitution for a particular people. The fourth, the question of how to institute the various forms of democracy and oligarchy, is addressed in Book VI; and the fifth, concerning the destruction and preservation of constitutions, is the topic of Book V. That Aristotle intended Books V and VI to be parts of a larger whole is indicated not only by the programme in Book IV but also by the particles μὲν οὖν that come at the beginning of Books V and VI. The antithetical particle μέν ('on the one hand') points forward to an antithesis signalled by δέ ('on the other hand'), while the inferential particle οὖν ('then') connects with what precedes. (The particles μὲν οὖν occur, incidentally, in the last sentence of Book VI; but here there is no answering δέ-clause, which implies that the book is unfinished.)

In Aristotle's list of questions the one addressed in Book VI precedes the one addressed in Book V. So one might wonder whether the traditional order of the two books is the order that Aristotle intended. Some editors have thought not, and switched them around. But this is probably a mistake. There are four backward references to Book V in Book VI (1. 1316^{b}34–6, 1317^{a}37–8; 4. 1319^{b}4–6; 5. 1319^{b}37–8). And, furthermore, Aristotle explains why Book V should precede VI: the lawgiver who wishes to establish a stable democracy or oligarchy needs to know the things that preserve and destroy constitutions (VI. 5. 1319^{b}37–1320^{a}2).

As a treatise in practical, rather than theoretical, philosophy the *Politics* has as its end, or goal, not only knowledge but action (I. 11. 1258^{b}9–10; *EN* VI. 8; X. 9. 1179^{a}35–^{b}2; *Met. α.* 1. 993^{b}20–1; for the two kinds of reason, or *logos*, see *Pol.* VII. 14. 1333^{a}25). The usefulness of the knowledge being provided is a theme of Books IV–VI (IV. 1. 1288^{b}35–7; VI. 1. 1317^{a}33–5, 4. 1319^{a}14–15, ^{b}19–23). But useful to whom? And for what? The *Politics* as a whole is a handbook for statesmen and lawgivers (IV. 1. 1288^{b}25–7, V. 9. 1309^{b}35–7). Books IV–VI are intended to be useful to them in dealing with political instability and in establishing or reforming constitutions— but not in overturning them. Since justice (*dikaiosunē*) as well as stability (*asphaleia*) is a watchword of the *Politics*, one might expect Aristotle to have some advice for revolutionaries; but he never explicitly advocates the overthrow even of tyrannical constitutions. One reason may have to do with his audience: the *Politics* is addressed to those in power, not to those seeking power. Another reason may be his idea that political communities are held together by their laws, that people obey the law out of habit, and that to break this habit, as revolutionaries must, is to weaken the power of law and to create anarchy (II. 8. 1268^{b}26–1269^{a}24; Miller, pp. 185–6). And a third reason may be his notion that constitutional change is like substantial change in the animal world: it is the death of the body politic. (Medical handbooks do not ordinarily discuss euthanasia.) But although Aristotle tacitly assumes throughout Book V that faction and revolution are bad and should be guarded against, he does not think they are always unjust. (They are like death, which is sometimes a justly imposed penalty.) He says, for example, that 'those who excel in virtue would form a faction with the most justice of anyone' (V. 1. 1301^{a}39–40), and writes with what appears to be admiration for those who attack tyrants for love of honour (V. 10. 1312^{a}21–39). (See also Miller, p. 305.)

If constitutional change is to be avoided, there is a question about the extent to which constitutions can be reformed. For a modification of a constitution counts as reform only if it makes the constitution better. This seems to imply some standard of constitutional excellence such as the ideal constitution of Books VII–VIII—a true aristocracy in which the full citizens are men of complete virtue (Keyt 1996, p. 141 n. 41). But it has been objected that, on such a view of constitutional reform, radical reform of a bad constitution, as distinct from the replacement of one constitution by another, is impossible. A bad constitution such as a democracy or a tyranny, according to this objection, cannot approximate the best constitution without changing its end, or goal—without undergoing what amounts to a change of constitution (Rowe, pp. 73–4). But this objection may not be sound. For Aristotle apparently thinks that democracy *can* approach true aristocracy without ceasing to be a democracy and that tyranny *can* approach the monarchical ideal—kingship—without ceasing to be a tyranny (see the introductory note to V. 11. 1314^{a}29–1315^{b}10 and the notes to V. 11. 1315^{a}40–^{b}10 and VI. 4. 1318^{b}6–1319^{b}1).

The idea that constitutional reform presupposes a political ideal bears on a problem about the relation of Books IV–VI to Books VII–VIII. The problem is important because the order in which topics are discussed usually reflects the logical order of the topics. If Books IV–VI presuppose Books VII–VIII, we would expect the latter set of books to precede the former set. On the other hand, if Books IV–VI are intended to provide support for Aristotle's political ideal, the traditional order of the books is the logical order. There are a number of indications that the traditional order is wrong. When Aristotle outlines his theory of constitutions in the first chapter of Book IV, the question of the best constitution is listed first, not last (1288^{b}21–4); and he explicitly declares which constitution is best at IV. 2. 1289^{a}30–3. Furthermore, the validity of the claim of virtue, the basis of aristocracy, is recognized throughout Book V (1. 1301^{a}39–^{b}1, 3. 1303^{b}15, 4. 1304^{b}4–5, 10. 1310^{b}2–14,

31–4, 11. 1315^{a}40–^{b}10); and the description of agricultural democracy in Book VI seems to presuppose knowledge of some of the
details of the constitution sketched in Books VII–VIII (see the
note to VI. 4. 1318^{b}6–1319^{b}1). On the other hand, Aristotle's ideas
about the best constitution do not appear to depend in any way
upon his investigation of constitutions that are less than ideal. The
internal logic of the *Politics* thus seems to be at variance with the
traditional order of its books and to favour the placement of Books
VII–VIII before IV–V–VI. The only explicit indication of the order
of the two sets of books within the treatise itself supports this
rearrangement: the last sentence of Book III promises an immediate discussion of the best constitution, and a fragment of a further
sentence appended to the last sentence is a slightly altered version
of half of the opening sentence of Book VII. There are no cross-
references between Books VII–VIII on the one hand and IV–VI on
the other to buttress either the traditional order or the promise of
the last sentence of Book III (though a few references, such as IV.
3. 1290^{a}1–2 and IV. 7. 1293^{b}1–3, are hard to pin down). Given all
that can be said in favour of the order VII–VIII–IV–V–VI, one
wonders how the books ever fell into the traditional order. Well, at
the end of the *Nicomachean Ethics* we find what appears to be a
prospectus of the *Politics* in which Aristotle says that *after* studying
'the sorts of thing that save and destroy cities and the sorts of thing
that save and destroy each of the constitutions' we should 'be able
to see what sort of constitution is best' (X. 9. 1181^{b}15–23). Reading
this, an early editor, like the twentieth-century scholars Ross (pp.
6–7) and Irwin (p. 601 n. 13), may have surmised that Aristotle
intended Books VII–VIII to follow rather than to precede Books
IV–V–VI.

For a good discussion of the relation of Books IV–VI to Book III
see Schütrumpf and Gehrke, pp. 178–85; and for the history of the
dispute about the order of the books see Zeller, pp. 501–5.

Aristotle assumes that his reader will be familiar with the many
historical examples of faction and constitutional change mentioned
in Book V. Since this assumption may not be true of the philosophical reader of today, I have attempted in the commentary to provide
some of the background knowledge that Aristotle took for granted
in his original readers. Though some of the episodes of Greek
history he mentions are shrouded in darkness, we know an amazing

amount about most of them from one literary source or another. I have retold the old stories directly from these primary sources. But I have not written an historical commentary on Book V. I make no attempt, for example, to resolve the inconsistencies between Aristotle's account of a particular event such as the assassination of Philip II (V. 10. 1311^{b}1–3) and other accounts of the same event. That task belongs to an historian not a philosopher. My historical notes are intended to throw light on Aristotle's political philosophy not on Greek history. The reader whose interest in Books V and VI is primarily historical should consult the commentary of Schütrumpf and Gehrke (which, I should mention, appeared after I had written the commentary on Book V).

In my translation, following the policy of this series, I have tried to get as close to the Greek as English idiom allows. I have tried to render key terms consistently and to preserve the Greek word order as much as possible. And since we are dealing with a philosophical text, I have paid particular attention to the inferential particles. I believe I have translated every occurrence of γάρ ('for'), though I have not managed to capture every οὖν ('then').

Words and phrases enclosed in angle brackets (⟨⟩) correspond to nothing in the Greek text. A few are explanatory; most stand for Greek words or phrases that are understood but unexpressed. The numerals and italic letters within parentheses are similarly extratextual. Double square brackets (⟦⟧) signal a problem in the Greek text. Complete sentences enclosed in double square brackets correspond to sentences in the Greek text that seem to be out of place; words or phrases enclosed in double square brackets correspond to words or phrases in the Greek text that probably should be deleted.

The text I have translated is Dreizehnter's, though I have usually followed Ross's more elaborate punctuation. I have departed from Dreizehnter only in the following places:

1308^{a}40: I omit the brackets around πῶς χρὴ ποιεῖσθαι τὴν αἵρεσιν.
1312^{b}15: Following Susemihl, I add μετ᾽ before αὐτῶν.
1318^{b}13: I omit the brackets around μὴ.
1320^{b}22: Reading ἐν ᾖ with Ross.
1321^{a}12: Reading ὁπλιτικὴν with Ross.

TRANSLATION

BOOK FIVE

CHAPTER I

1301ᵃ19 Almost all of the other topics, then, that we intended to address have been discussed. Following what has been said, we must examine (1) the sources of change in constitutions and how many they are and of what sort; (2) what things destroy each constitution; and (3) from what sort into what sort they are mostly transformed; further, (4) what things preserve constitutions in general and each constitution individually; and, finally, (5) the means by which each constitution may best be preserved.

1301ᵃ25 We must first assume as a principle that many different constitutions have come into being because, though all agree about the just and the proportionately equal, they make a mistake about it, as was also said earlier. For democracy arose from those who are equal in some respect or other thinking themselves to be equal without qualification (for because they are all alike free, they think they are equal without qualification), whereas oligarchy arose from those who are unequal in one respect supposing themselves to be wholly unequal (for being unequal in property they suppose themselves to be unequal without qualification). Accordingly the former, on the ground that they are equal, think they are worthy of an equal share of everything, whereas the latter, on the ground that they are unequal, seek to get more and more, for the more is unequal. All these constitutions then have a bit of justice, but without qualification they are mistaken. And for this reason, when either party does not share in the constitution according to the opinion ⟨about justice⟩ that they happen to hold, they form a faction. Those who excel in virtue would form a faction with the most justice of anyone (though they do this least of all), for it is most reasonable to regard as unequal without qualification these alone. There are some, too, who are superior in family and do not think themselves worthy of merely equal things, because of this inequality. For those are reputed to be well-born who have the virtue and wealth of their forebears.

1301ᵇ4 These, then, generally speaking, are the origins and

I

5 springs of factions, from which men form factions. That is precisely
why constitutional changes also come about in two ways. For (1)
sometimes they make a faction against the constitution in order
that they may introduce another constitution in place of the established one: for example, oligarchy in place of democracy, or democracy in place of oligarchy, or polity and aristocracy in place of these,
10 or these in place of those. (2) Sometimes they make a faction not
against the established constitution, but (*a*) intend rather for the
established constitution, such as oligarchy or monarchy, to remain
the same, but wish it to be in their hands. Again, (*b*) they make a
faction over the more and less: for example, they may wish to
change what is already an oligarchy into being more oligarchic or
15 into being less, or what is already a democracy into being more
democratic or into being less, and similarly also with the remaining
constitutions—in order that they may either tighten them or loosen
them up. Again, (*c*) they make a faction with the aim of altering
a part of the constitution: for example, to establish or abolish a
certain office, as at Lacedaemon some say Lysander attempted
20 to abolish the kingship and King Pausanias the ephorate. At
Epidamnus too the constitution changed in part (for instead of the
tribal leaders they made a council, though it is still compulsory for
the office-holders ⟨alone⟩ among the governing class to go to the
25 assembly when an office is put to the vote; and the single ⟨supreme⟩
official was also an oligarchic feature in this constitution).

1301ᵇ26 For everywhere faction is due to inequality, where
unequals do not receive unequal things in proportion to their inequality (for a permanent kingship is unequal if it exists among
equals); for in general men engage in faction in pursuit of equality.

1301ᵇ29 Equality is twofold. For one sort is numerical; the
30 other according to worth. By numerical equality I mean being
equal and the same in number or size. By equality according to
worth I mean being equal in ratio. For example, numerically three
exceeds two, and two one, by an equal amount; but in ratio four
exceeds two, and two one by an equal amount. For two and one are
35 equal parts of four and two; for both are halves.

1301ᵇ35 Though men agree that the just without qualification
is that which is according to worth, they differ, as has been said
before, in that some think that, if they are equal in some respect,
they are wholly equal, whereas others think that, if they are unequal in some respect, they are worthy of every unequal thing. That

is precisely why two constitutions arise most of all, democracy
and oligarchy. For good birth and virtue ⟨the basis of aristocracy⟩ 40
are found in few, whereas these things ⟨i.e. freedom and wealth⟩ are
found in a larger number. For the well-born and the good nowhere **1302ᵃ**
number a hundred, but the prosperous are numerous in many
places.

1302ᵃ2 For a constitution to be structured simply in all respects
according to either sort of equality is bad. This is evident from what
happens. For none of these sorts of constitution is enduring. The 5
reason for this is that it is impossible, starting from the first and
original mistake, not to encounter at the end something bad. That
is why one must use numerical equality in some things and equality
according to worth in others.

1302ᵃ8 Nevertheless democracy is more stable and more
faction-free than oligarchy. For in oligarchies two sorts of faction
take place, faction against one another and again faction against 10
the people, whereas in democracies there is faction against the
oligarchic party only—faction worth mentioning does not take
place among the people itself against itself. Again, the constitution
of those in the middle is closer to the constitution of the people
than the constitution of the few, and it is the most stable of these 15
kinds of constitution.

CHAPTER 2

1302ᵃ16 Since we are inquiring about the sources from which both
factions and changes with respect to constitutions come about, we
must first understand in a general way the origins and causes of
these. They are, roughly speaking, three in number, which we must
mark out each by itself in outline first. For we must understand (1) 20
the disposition of those who form factions, and (2) for the sake of
what, and thirdly (3), what are the origins of political tumults and of
factions against one another.

1302ᵃ22 (1) We must lay it down that the general cause of men
being themselves somehow disposed toward change is mainly the
one we have in fact already spoken of. For those pursuing equality
form factions if they think that they get less, though they are equal 25
to those who get more, whereas those pursuing inequality (that is
to say, superiority) form factions if they suppose that, though

3

unequal, they do not get more but equal or less. (It is possible to desire these ⟨i.e. equality and inequality⟩ justly or again unjustly.)

30 For the lesser form factions so as to be equal, and the equal so as to be greater. The disposition of those who form factions, then, has been spoken of.

1302ª31 (2) The things for which men form factions are profit and honour and their opposites. For they form factions in cities even to avoid dishonour and loss, either for themselves or their friends.

1302ª34 (3) The causes and origins of the alterations by which

35 men are themselves affected in the way spoken of and concerning the things mentioned are by one account seven in number but by another more. Two of them are the same as those that have been spoken of, though not in the same way. For it is because of profit

40 and honour that men are incited against one another—not (as we said before) in order that they may get them for themselves, but

1302ᵇ because they see others (some justly, some unjustly) getting more. Again, it is because of insolence, fear, superiority, contempt, and disproportionate growth. Or, again, in another way, it is because of electioneering, belittlement, smallness, or dissimilarity.

CHAPTER 3

5 **1302ᵇ5** Of these, what sort of power insolence and profit have and how they are a cause is pretty clear. For when those in office are insolent and take more and more, the citizens form factions both against one another and against the constitutions that gave the office-holders their authority. The more and more comes some-

10 times from private property and other times from public.

1302ᵇ10 It is also clear what honour is capable of and how it is a cause of faction. For both when men are themselves dishonoured and when they see others honoured, they form a faction. These occur unjustly when certain men are either honoured or dishonoured contrary to their worth, but justly when according to their worth.

1302ᵇ15 Men form a faction because of superiority when some-

15 one (either one person or more than one) is greater in power than accords with the city and the power of the governing class. For from such men there customarily arises a monarchy or a dynasty. That is

why people have the custom of ostracism at some places such as
Argos and Athens. And yet it is better to see to it from the beginning that no men become so pre-eminent than to apply a remedy   20
later after allowing them to arise.

1302^{b}21   Men form a faction because of fear: both those who
have committed an injustice, fearing that they will be punished, and
those who are about to suffer an injustice, wishing to act first before
they suffer it, as at Rhodes the notables banded together against
the people because of the lawsuits being brought against them.

1302^{b}25   Men also form a faction and make attacks because of   25
contempt. For example, they form a faction in oligarchies when
those who do not share in the constitution are more numerous than
those who do (for they think they are stronger), and they form a
faction in democracies when the prosperous are contemptuous of
the disorder and unruliness. Thus at Thebes, after the battle of
Oenophyta, the democracy was destroyed because they were badly
governed; and the democracy of the Megarians was destroyed   30
when they were defeated because of disorder and unruliness; and
at Syracuse before the tyranny of Gelon and at Rhodes before the
uprising the people ⟨similarly aroused contempt by its disorder and
unruliness⟩.

1302^{b}33   Changes of constitution also arise because of disproportionate growth. For just as a body is composed of parts, and   35
these must grow in proportion for its symmetry to endure (otherwise it perishes, as when a foot is four cubits long ⟨72 inches⟩, but
the rest of the body two spans ⟨15 inches⟩, or sometimes it may
change into the shape of another animal if its parts increase disproportionately not only quantitatively but also qualitatively) so too a   40
city is composed of parts, the growth of one of which often escapes   1303^a
notice, such as the mass of the needy in democracies and polities.
This sometimes happens too because of chance. For example, at
Taras when they were defeated and many of the notables were
killed by the Iapygians a short time after the Persian Wars, a   5
democracy arose from a polity. And at Argos when the men of the
seventh were killed by the Laconian Cleomenes, they were compelled to receive some of the serfs ⟨as citizens⟩. And at Athens
when they were unfortunate on land, the notables became fewer
because at the time of the Laconian War service in the army was
determined by a register ⟨of citizens⟩. This happens too in democ-   10
racies, though to a lesser extent. For when the prosperous become

numerous or their properties grow, democracies change into oligarchies and dynasties.

1303ᵃ13 Constitutions change even without faction, both on
15 account of electioneering—as at Heraea (for they caused the offices to be filled by lot instead of by election for this reason, that they were electing those who electioneered)—and on account of belittlement, when they allow those who are not friends of the constitution to enter the supreme offices. Thus, at Oreus the oligarchy was overthrown when Heracleodorus became one of the officials and established a polity, or rather a democracy, in place of an
20 oligarchy.

1303ᵃ20 Again, constitutions change because of a small difference. By a small difference I mean that often a large change of the legal system takes place unnoticed when the citizens overlook something small. Thus, at Ambracia the property qualification was small, and in the end men held office with none—the small being very near to, or no different from, none.
25

1303ᵃ25 Difference of race also tends to produce faction, until the city shares a common spirit. For just as a city does not arise from any chance multitude, so neither does it arise in any chance period of time. That is why most of those who in the past admitted joint colonists or later colonists have split into factions. For example, the Achaeans colonized Sybaris jointly with the Troezenians;
30 but after the Achaeans became more numerous, they expelled the Troezenians, which was the reason the curse fell upon the Sybarites. And at Thurii the Sybarites were factious with those who colonized jointly with them (for when the Sybarites claimed to be worthy of getting more and more on the ground that the country was theirs, they were driven out). And ⟨at Byzantium⟩ when the later colonists were detected conspiring against the Byzantines, they were driven out by force of arms. And the Antissaeans, after
35 taking in the exiles from Chios, expelled them by force of arms. The Zanclaeans, after welcoming the Samians, were themselves driven out. And the Apolloniates on the Black Sea, after bringing in later colonists, split into factions. And the Syracusans, when they made aliens and mercenaries citizens after the period of the tyrants,
1303ᵇ broke into factions and came to battle. And the Amphipolitans, after receiving later colonists from among the Chalcidians, were nearly all driven out by them.

1303ᵇ3 ⟦In oligarchies the many form a faction under the idea

6

that they are treated unjustly because, as we have said before, they
do not have equal shares, in spite of being equal, whereas in democ- 5
racies the notables form a faction because they do have equal
shares, in spite of not being equal.]]

1303ᵇ7   Cities sometimes split into factions too because of territory, when the country is not naturally suited for there being *one*
city. For example, at Clazomenae those near Chytrum make a
faction against those on the island; and the Colophonians and the 10
Notians are also riven by faction. And at Athens those who live in
the Peiraeus are not equally democratic, but more so than those of
the town. For just as in war the crossings of channels, even very
small ones, breaks up the line of battle, so every difference seems to
make a division. The greatest division perhaps is virtue and vile- 15
ness, then wealth and poverty, and so on, one being greater than
another—and one of them is that just mentioned.

CHAPTER 4

1303ᵇ17   Factions arise, then, not concerning small things, but
from small things; men form factions ⟨only⟩ concerning great
things.

1303ᵇ19   Even small factions become very powerful when they
arise among those who are supreme ⟨in a city⟩, as happened for
example at Syracuse in ancient times. For the constitution was 20
changed as a result of two young men in office engaging in faction
over a love affair. For when one of them was abroad, the other,
though being his comrade, won over the boy he loved. In retalia-
tion the first, enraged at the other, enticed the other's wife to come
to ⟨bed with⟩ him. Thereupon they gained the support of the mem- 25
bers of the governing class and split everyone into factions. That is
why one must be cautious when such things are beginning, and
break up the factions of leading and powerful men. For the mistake
arises at the beginning, and the beginning is said to be half of the
whole. Consequently, even a small mistake at the beginning is 30
proportionate to the mistakes in the other parts.

1303ᵇ31   In general the factions of the notables make the whole
city share in the suffering too. This happened, for example, in
Hestiaea after the Persian Wars when two brothers differed over
the distribution of their patrimony. For the more needy one, on the

35 ground that the other would not render an account of the property
or of the treasure that their father found, enlisted the people on his
side while the other, who had a great deal of property, enlisted the
prosperous. And at Delphi when a difference arose from a marriage alliance, the difference was the beginning of all the later
1304^a factions. For the bridegroom, interpreting as an omen some mischance as he came for his bride, went away without taking her. Her
relations, on the ground that they had been treated with insolence,
planted some sacred goods on him while he was sacrificing and then
killed him as a temple robber. And in the case of Mytilene when a
5 faction arose about heiresses, the faction was the beginning of
many bad things and in particular of the war against the Athenians,
in which Paches captured their city. For when Timophanes, one of
the prosperous, died and left two daughters, Dexander, who had
been rejected ⟨in his legal suit⟩ and did not win them for his own
sons, started a faction and incited the Athenians in his capacity as
10 their consul. And at Phocis when a faction arose over an heiress in
connection with Mnaseas the father of Mnason and Euthycrates
the father of Onomarchus, this faction was the beginning of the
Sacred War involving the Phocians. And at Epidamnus the constitution was changed due to a marriage. For a man betrothed his
daughter; and the father of the one to whom she was betrothed,
15 becoming one of the officials, fined this man, whereupon the latter
enlisted those outside the constitution as his partisans on the
ground that he had been spitefully insulted.

     1304^a17 Constitutions also change to oligarchy and to democ-
racy and to polity as a result of an official body or a part of the city
winning esteem in some way or growing in power. For example, the
20 council of the Areopagus, having won esteem in the Persian Wars,
was reputed to have made the constitution ⟨of Athens⟩ tighter; and
contrariwise the naval rabble, having been the cause of the victory
at Salamis and because of it of the hegemony ⟨of Athens⟩ because
of the power by sea, made the democracy stronger. And at Argos
25 the notables, having won esteem in the battle of Mantinea against
the Lacedaemonians, took it in hand to overthrow the people. And
at Syracuse the people, having been the cause of the victory in the
war against Athens, changed from a polity to a democracy. And at
Chalcis the people together with the notables, having destroyed the
30 tyrant Phoxus, straight away took firm hold of the constitution.
And at Ambracia again in a similar manner the people, after assist-

ing the conspirators in throwing out the tyrant Periander, brought the constitution around to themselves. And generally, then, this must not be overlooked, that those who come to be causes of power ⟨to the city⟩—private individuals and officials and tribes and gener- 35 ally any part and multitude of any kind whatsoever—stir up faction. For either those who envy them for being honoured begin the faction, or they themselves, because of their superiority, are not willing to remain on equal terms.

1304^{a}38 Constitutions are also altered when the opposites that are held to be parts of the city, such as the wealthy and the people, become equal to one another, and there is no middle class or a very **1304^b** small one. For if either of the two parts becomes much superior, the remainder is not willing to venture against the manifestly stronger part. That is precisely why those who excel in virtue do not cause faction, generally speaking; for they are few against many. 5

1304^{b}5 Universally, then, in regard to all constitutions the origins and causes of factions and changes have this character. But men alter constitutions sometimes by force, sometimes by deceit. When they do it by force, they use coercion either (1) immediately from the start or (2) later on. For deceit also is twofold. For (1) 10 sometimes after completely deceiving the others initially, they change the constitution with the others being willing, but later on keep hold of it by force with the others being unwilling. For example, ⟨in Athens⟩ at the time of the Four Hundred they completely deceived the people by saying that the king ⟨of Persia⟩ would provide money for the war against the Lacedaemonians, but after peddling this falsehood they tried to keep hold of the constitution. 15 (2) Other times they persuade them both at the start and later on again and, due to their being persuaded, rule them with them being willing.

1304^{b}17 Generally, then, in regard to all constitutions changes have happened to come about for the reasons that have been stated.

CHAPTER 5

1304^{b}19 Taking each kind of constitution separately, we must now study, in the light of the foregoing principles, and in accordance with the division of constitutions into kinds, what happens in each. 20

1304ᵇ20   Democracies change for the most part because of the licence of the demagogues. For sometimes in private suits they maliciously prosecute those who have property and fuse them together (for common fear brings even the bitterest enemies together), and sometimes in the public arena they set the mass on
25 them. And this one may see occurring in many instances in just such a way. For at Cos the democracy was changed when vicious demagogues arose (for the notables banded together), and also at Rhodes. For the demagogues provided pay for public service and prevented payment of the money owed to the trireme commanders; and these, because of the lawsuits brought against them,
30 were compelled to band together and overthrow the people. And at Heraclea the people were overthrown immediately after the foundation of the colony because of the demagogues. For the notables were driven out by the unjust treatment they received at their hands. Later those who were driven out gathered together, returned home, and overthrew the people. And the democracy at
35 Megara was overthrown in much the same way. For the demagogues, in order to be able to confiscate their goods, expelled many of the notables, until they made the exiles numerous. The exiles came back, vanquished the people in battle, and established the oligarchy. The same thing also happened with regard to Cyme in
1305ᵃ the time of the democracy that Thrasymachus overthrew. In the case of the other cities as well, a person who studies the matter would see that changes ⟨of constitution⟩ have more or less this character. For sometimes, in order to curry favour with the people, the demagogues treat the notables unjustly and drive them to-
5 gether, by causing either their property or their income to be divided up by liturgies; and sometimes they employ slander, in order that they may confiscate the possessions of the wealthy.

1305ᵃ7   In ancient times, when the same man became demagogue and general, democracies changed into tyranny. For almost the greatest number of ancient tyrants arose from demagogues. (1)
10 One reason for tyranny arising then but not now is that then the demagogues were drawn from those who were generals (for men were not yet skilled in public speaking). Now that the art of public speaking has grown, those who are able to speak in public become demagogues; but because of their inexperience in military matters, they do not attempt to establish a tyranny, though a few cases of the
15 kind may have occurred somewhere. (2) Tyrannies also arose more

frequently formerly than now because high offices were put into
the hands of certain individuals, as at Miletus a tyranny arose from
the presidency (for the president was supreme over many and great
things). (3) Again, because cities then were not large and the people lived near their fields and were busy at their work, the leaders   20
of the people, whenever they became skilled in war, attempted to
establish a tyranny. They all did this after gaining the trust of the
people. This trust was due to their hostility towards the wealthy.
For example, at Athens Peisistratus ⟨was thought worthy of the
tyranny⟩ because he made a faction against the party of the plain;
and Theagenes at Megara, because he slaughtered the herds of the
prosperous when he caught them grazing their herds on land not   25
their own along the river. And Dionysius was thought worthy of the
tyranny for denouncing Daphnaeus and the wealthy. Because of his
enmity he was trusted as a man of the people.

1305ᵃ28 Democracies also change from ancestral democracy
into the newest sort. For where the offices are elective but have no
property qualification and the people do the electing, those who   30
are zealous for office, to curry favour, bring things to this point, that
the people are supreme even over the laws. One remedy, so that
this does not occur or occurs less often, is for the tribes to elect the
officials, and not the people as a whole.

1305ᵃ34 Nearly all the changes of democracies then occur for   35
these reasons.

CHAPTER 6

1305ᵃ36 Oligarchies change principally in two ways that are most
striking. (1) The first is (*a*) when the oligarchs treat the mass
unjustly. For any leader is adequate in this situation, especially
when he happens to come from the oligarchy itself, like Lygdamis   40
at Naxos, who later even became tyrant of the Naxians. The origin
of faction initiated by others also takes different forms. (*b*) For   **1305ᵇ**
sometimes an overthrow comes from the prosperous themselves,
though not from those in office, when those enjoying such honours
are very few. This has happened, for example, in Massalia and in
Istrus and in Heraclea and in other cities. For those who did not   5
share in the offices stirred things up until first the older brothers
acquired a share, and later in turn the younger ones. (For in some

places father and son, and in others an older and younger brother,
10 do not hold office at the same time.) And there ⟨in Massalia⟩ the
oligarchy became more of a polity; in Istrus it ended in democracy;
in Heraclea it went from a smaller number to six hundred. (c) And
in Cnidus the oligarchy changed when the notables engaged in
faction among themselves due to the fact that few shared in office
15 and, as was said, if the father shared, the son could not, nor, if there
were several brothers, could any but the oldest. For when they
split into factions, the people seized the opportunity and, taking a
leader from among the notables, attacked and conquered them.
For whatever splits into factions is weak. (d) And at Erythrae
during the oligarchy of the Basilidae in ancient times, even though
20 those within the constitution managed things well, nevertheless
the people were resentful because they were ruled by a few, and
changed the constitution.

   1305^{b}22 (2) Oligarchies are also altered from within (a) when,
through rivalry, some of the oligarchs become demagogues. This
demagoguery is twofold. It may take place among the few themselves. For a demagogue can arise among them even when they are
25 very few. For example, among the Thirty at Athens those around
Charicles gained power by courting the Thirty, and among the Four
Hundred those around Phrynichus gained power in the same way.
Or it may take place when those in the oligarchy court the rabble.
For example, at Larissa the Guardians of the City courted the
30 rabble because it elected them. And it is liable to occur in all
oligarchies in which those from whom the officials are drawn are
not the ones who elect to office, but the offices are filled from
among those who satisfy a large property qualification or from
political clubs, while the hoplites or the people vote. This is what
happened at Abydos and wherever the law courts are not filled
from the governing class. For by currying favour to secure verdicts
35 the oligarchs change the constitution, which is what occurred at
Heraclea on the Pontus. Again, ⟨this second type of demagoguery
takes place⟩ when some draw the oligarchy into fewer hands.
For those who seek equality are compelled to bring the people in
as an ally.

   1305^{b}39 Changes in oligarchy also occur (b) when some of
40 the oligarchs squander their private property in loose living.
For such men also seek to make innovations, and either aim
at tyranny themselves or help to install someone else ⟨as tyrant⟩.

Thus Hipparinus helped to install Dionysius as tyrant at Syracuse; **1306ª**
and at Amphipolis a man whose name was Cleotimus introduced
colonists from among the Chalcidians and, after they arrived, split
them into a faction against the prosperous; and at Aegina the man
who conducted the transaction with Chares attempted to change 5
the constitution for a similar reason. Sometimes, then, these men
make a direct attempt to alter something; other times they steal
public property. In the latter case either they or those who fight
against them in their thievery make a faction against the oligarchs,
which is what happened at Apollonia on the Black Sea. An oligarchy that is of one mind is not easily destroyed from within. A 10
sign of this is the constitution at Pharsalus. For although the rulers
there are few, they are supreme over many because they treat each
other well.

1306ª12 (c) Oligarchies are also overthrown when the oligarchs
make another oligarchy within the original one. This takes place
when, though the whole governing class is few, not all of these few
share in the highest offices, which is what happened in Elis at one 15
time. For even though its constitution was in the hands of a few,
very few became elders because the elders, who numbered only
ninety, were permanent and because their election was dynastic in
character and similar to that of the elders at Lacedaemon.

1306ª19 (d) Change in oligarchies occurs both in time of war 20
and in time of peace. It occurs in time of war when the oligarchs are
compelled by distrust of the people to use mercenaries. (For the
individual in whose hands they place them often becomes a tyrant,
like Timophanes at Corinth. If there are several commanders, these
men win for themselves a dynasty. Sometimes, fearing these things,
the oligarchs give a share of the constitution to the mass because 25
they are compelled to make use of the people.) In time of peace the
oligarchs, out of distrust of one another, put the guarding of the city
into the hands of mercenaries and a neutral officer, who sometimes
becomes supreme over both sides, which is what happened at
Larissa in the time of the rule of the Aleuads around Simus, and at 30
Abydos in the time of the political clubs, one of which was that of
Iphiades.

1306ª31 (e) Factions also arise because some of those themselves in the oligarchy are pushed aside by others and are objects
of faction in connection with marriages or lawsuits. The factions
mentioned before arose, for example, from a marital cause; and

35 Diagoras overthrew the oligarchy of horsemen in Eretria because he was treated unjustly regarding a marriage. The faction in Heraclea, on the other hand, as well as the one in Thebes, arose from a verdict of a law court, when on a charge of adultery the citizens of Heraclea justly but factiously inflicted the punishment

1306ᵇ against Eurytion, and the citizens of Thebes did so against Archias. For out of a love of rivalry their enemies caused them to be bound in the pillory in the market-place. (*f*) Many oligarchies have also been overthrown by those within the constitution who are discontented because the oligarchies are too despotic: for example, the

5 oligarchy in Cnidus and the one in Chios.

1306ᵇ6 (3) There also occur changes by mischance—both of so-called constitution ⟨i.e. polity⟩ and of those oligarchies in which men are councillors and jurors and hold the other offices on the basis of a property qualification. For it often happens that when a property qualification is fixed at first according to present circum-

10 stances, so that in an oligarchy few, and in a polity those in the middle, share in office, good times arrive due to peace or some other good fortune and the same property comes to be worth many times the property qualification, with the result that everyone shares in every office. Sometimes this change occurs by gradual

15 increments and little by little and goes unnoticed; but other times more rapidly.

1306ᵇ16 For such reasons, then, oligarchies change and break into factions. (But, generally speaking, both democracies and oligarchies are transformed from time to time, not into opposite constitutions, but into ones of the same type. They are trans-

20 formed, for example, from democracies and oligarchies under law into the absolutist types and from the latter into the former.)

CHAPTER 7

1306ᵇ22 (1) In aristocracies factions arise in some cases because few share in the honours ⟨of office⟩, which is what has been said to stir up oligarchies as well, because an aristocracy too is an oligarchy

25 in a way (for in both the rulers are few—though not few for the same reason). Indeed, it is because of this that an aristocracy is even thought *to be* an oligarchy. (*a*) This must happen above all when there are a number of men who are swollen with pride on the

ground of being equal in virtue ⟨to the few who rule⟩—for example,
at Lacedaemon the so-called Maidens' Sons (for they were descended from the Equals), whom the Spartiates detected in a con-   30
spiracy and sent out as colonizers of Taras—or when men who are
great and inferior to no one in virtue are dishonoured by some who
are held in greater honour—for example, Lysander by the kings—
or when someone of a manly character does not share in the
honours ⟨of office⟩—for example, Cinadon, who in the time of
Agesilaus organized the attack upon the Spartiates. Again, (*b*)   35
faction breaks out when some are very needy while others are
prosperous (this occurs especially in time of war). This also happened at Lacedaemon during the Messenian War (this is clear from
the poem of Tyrtaeus entitled 'Law and Order'), for those who   **1307ᵃ**
were squeezed because of the war thought they deserved to make
a redivision of the land. Again, (*c*) if someone is great and capable
of being still greater, he may stir up faction in order to rule alone,
as Pausanias who was general during the Persian War is held to
have done at Lacedaemon, and Hanno at Carthage.   5

   1307ᵃ5   (2) Polities and aristocracies are overthrown mostly because of a deviation from the just in the constitution itself. For the
origin ⟨of overthrow⟩ in a polity is the poor mixture of democracy
and oligarchy, and in aristocracy of these two and virtue, but especially of the two. I mean by the two democracy and oligarchy; for it   10
is these that polities and most of the so-called aristocracies try to
mix. For aristocracies differ from so-called constitutions ⟨i.e.
polities⟩ in this respect, and it is due to this that some of them are
less and some are more enduring. For those constitutions that
incline more toward oligarchy they call aristocracies; those that   15
incline more toward the mass, polities. That indeed is why the latter
sort are more stable than the others; for the greater number is
stronger, and they are more content with having what is equal,
whereas those who enjoy prosperity, if the constitution gives them
superiority, try to throw their weight about and to take more and
more. In general, whichever way the constitution inclines, in that   20
direction it is transformed when either party increases its own side:
for example, polity into democracy, aristocracy into oligarchy. Or
they are transformed into their opposites: for example, aristocracy
into democracy (for the more needy, under the idea that they are
being treated unjustly, draw it round to the opposite), and polities   25
into oligarchies. For it is only equality according to worth and

having one's own that are enduring. And this is what occurred at
Thurii. Because the offices required an excessively high property
qualification, the constitution shifted to a lower one and to a larger
number of official bodies. But because the notables bought up all
30 the land contrary to law (for the constitution was too oligarchic, so
that they were able to take more and more), *** The people, who
had been trained in the war, became stronger than the guards, until
those who had too much of the land gave it up.

1307ᵃ34   Again, (3) because all aristocratic constitutions are
35 oligarchic, the notables get too much. Even at Lacedaemon, for
example, properties are coming into a few hands. Moreover, the
notables can do whatever they will too much of the time, and can
ally themselves in marriage with whomever they will. And that is
why the city of Locri was destroyed in consequence of the marriage
alliance with Dionysius, which would not have occurred in a de-
40 mocracy, nor in a well-mixed aristocracy.

1307ᵇ   **1307ᵃ40**   (4) Above all, aristocracies change imperceptibly by
being overturned little by little. This is what was said earlier of all
constitutions universally, that even a small thing may be a cause of
changes. For when men give up some constitutional point, they find
5 it easier after this to alter another slightly larger feature, until they
alter the entire system. And this happened in the case of the constitution of Thurii. For the law allowed a man to be a general after an
interval of five years. But when some of the younger men became
skilled in war and won a high reputation with the multitude of the
guards, they came to have contempt for those engaged in the affairs
10 of the city and thought they could easily gain the upper hand. So
they set to work to overturn this law first, so as to allow the same
men to be generals continuously, since they saw that the people
would vote for them with enthusiasm. Although the officials who
were charged with this matter, the so-called advisers, set out at first
15 to resist, they were persuaded to acquiesce under the idea that the
insurgents, after altering this law, would leave the rest of the constitution alone. When later the officials wished to prevent other things
from being altered, they could no longer do anything more; but the
whole structure of the constitution changed to a dynasty of those
who had set to work to make a new order.

1307ᵇ19   All constitutions are overturned sometimes from
20 within themselves and sometimes from without, when an opposite constitution is either near by or far away yet possessed of

power. This is what happened in the time of the Athenians and
Lacedaemonians. For the Athenians everywhere overthrew oligarchies, and the Laconians democracies.

1307^{b}24 Where changes of constitutions and factions come
from, then, has now been more or less dealt with.   25

CHAPTER 8

1307^{b}26 We have next to speak about preservation of constitutions both in general and of each constitution separately. First then
it is clear that if we grasp those things by which constitutions are
destroyed, we also grasp those by which they are preserved. For
opposites are productive of opposites, and destruction is opposite
to preservation.

1307^{b}30 (1) In well-mixed constitutions, then, if above anything 30
else one must take care that the citizens do nothing unlawful, one
must guard especially against small infractions. For lawlessness
creeps in unnoticed, just as a small expenditure frequently occurring consumes one's property. The expense escapes notice because
it does not occur all at once. For the mind is led by the small 35
expenditures to reason fallaciously, as in the sophistical reasoning
'If each is small, so too are all'. This is true in one way; in another
not. For the whole, that is, the all, is not small; but it is composed of
small parts. This one safeguard, then, must be taken against this
origin of destruction.

1307^{b}40 (2) Next, one must not put one's trust in things that are 40
concocted for the sake of chicanery toward the mass; for they are **1308^a**
refuted by the facts. (And what sort of constitutional chicaneries
we refer to has been explained before.)

1308^{a}3 (3) Again, one should observe that some constitutions,
not only aristocracies but even oligarchies, endure, not because
the constitutions are stable, but because those in office are on good 5
terms both with those outside the constitution and with those in the
governing class. Those who do not share ⟨in the constitution⟩ they
do not treat unjustly, and those of them who are fitted to lead they
bring into the constitution. And they are not unjust toward the
lovers of honour in respect to dishonour or toward the many in
respect to profit. As for themselves, that is, for those who share ⟨in 10
the constitution⟩—they treat one another democratically. For what

17

the democrats seek for the mass, namely, equality, is not only just
but also advantageous for those who are alike. That is why if there
are a great many in the governing class, many democratic institu-
15 tions are advantageous, such as offices being for six months, in
order that all who are alike may share in them. For those who are
alike are already like a people (which is why demagogues often
arise even among them, as has been said before). Furthermore,
when offices have short terms, oligarchies and democracies fall into
dynasties less often. For it is not as easy for officials to do wrong in
20 a short time as in a long one, since it is through this that tyrannies
arise in oligarchies and democracies. For either the greatest men in
the two constitutions aim at tyranny (the demagogues in the one
case and the dynasts in the other), or those who occupy the highest
offices, when they hold office for a long time.

25 **1308ᵃ24** (4) Constitutions are preserved not only by their distance from agents of destruction, but sometimes even by their
nearness to them. For when the citizens are afraid, they keep a
firmer grip on the constitution. Thus, those who take thought for
the constitution must contrive fears—in order that the citizens may
be on guard and, like a night watchman, not neglect the safekeep-
30 ing of the constitution—and make the distant near.

1308ᵃ31 (5) Again, they must try by the laws too to keep an eye
on the rivalries and factions of the notables, and to neutralize those
outside the rivalry before they too have inherited it, since to recognize an evil at its beginning is the work not of an ordinary man but
of a statesman.

35 **1308ᵃ35** (6) As for the change from oligarchy and polity that
occurs on account of property qualifications, when this happens
because the property qualifications remain the same while money
becomes plentiful, it is advantageous to examine the total amount
of the assessed property of the community in relation to the past
40 amount. In those cities where property is assessed annually, this
should be done on that schedule, but in larger cities every
1308ᵇ third or fifth year. And if the total amount of assessed property is
many times greater or smaller than it was before at the time when
the assessments under the constitution were established, there
should be a law to tighten or to loosen the property qualifications
too, tightening them in accordance with the multiplier if the new
5 total exceeds the old, and loosening and making the assessment
lower if it falls short. For in oligarchies and polities, when they do

not do this, what happens is the following: in the latter case an
oligarchy comes into existence in the one instance and a dynasty in
the other; in the former case a democracy arises from a polity, and
a polity or a democracy from an oligarchy.   10

1308ᵇ10   (7) It is a policy common in democracy and oligarchy
[and in monarchy] and every constitution not to magnify anyone
too much beyond due proportion, but to try to give small honours
over a long period of time rather than great ones quickly. (For
people are corrupted, and not every man can bear good fortune.)
But if they do not do this, what was given all at once they should at   15
any rate not take back again all at once, but by gradual increments.
But most of all they should try to shape things by the laws in such
a way that no one becomes greatly pre-eminent by the power of
friends or money. Failing this, they should make their banishments
banishments abroad.

1308ᵇ20   (8) Since men also seek a new order because of their   20
private lives, one should introduce an office to keep an eye on those
who live prejudicially to the constitution—prejudicially to democracy in a democracy, prejudicially to oligarchy in an oligarchy, and
similarly in each of the other constitutions.

1308ᵇ24   (9) And for the same reasons one must be on guard
against any part of the city that is flourishing at the moment. A   25
remedy for this danger is to always put actions and offices into the
hands of the opposing parts—I mean that the worthy are opposite
to the mass, and the needy to the prosperous—and to try either to
mix together the mass of the needy and the number of the prosperous or to augment the middle class (for this breaks up factions due   30
to inequality).

1308ᵇ31   (10) But the most important thing in every constitution
is for it to be so arranged by its laws and its other administration
that its offices are not a source of profit. This is something one must
watch for in oligarchies especially. For the many do not so much
resent being excluded from holding office, and are even glad if   35
someone allows them to have leisure for their private affairs; but
they do resent it if they think the officials are stealing public property. Then both things pain them, not sharing in the honours and
not sharing in the profits. The only way it is possible for democracy
and aristocracy to exist together is if someone could bring this
about ⟨i.e. could insure that offices are not a source of profit⟩. For   40
then it would be possible for the notables and the mass both to have   **1309ᵃ**

what they wish. For allowing everyone to hold office is democratic, while for the notables to actually be in the offices is aristocratic; and this will be the case when it is impossible to profit from the offices.
5 For the needy will not wish to hold office because there is no profit in it, but will want rather to attend to their private affairs, while the prosperous will be able to hold office because they need nothing from the public property. What will happen is that the needy will become prosperous through attending to their work, and the notables will not be ruled by just anybody. So that public property is not
10 stolen, then, let the handing over of the money take place when all of the citizens are present, and let copies of the accounts be deposited with the brotherhoods, companies, and tribes. So that men will hold office without seeking profit, there must be honours ordained by law for officials of good repute.

1309ᵃ14 (11) In democracies one must spare the prosperous.
15 Not only should their property not be divided up, but neither should their incomes (which occurs in some constitutions without being noticed). It is also better to prevent the prosperous, even if they wish to, from undertaking expensive but useless liturgies, such as equipping choruses, superintending torch races, and other such things.

20   **1309ᵃ20** (12) In an oligarchy, on the other hand, one must take great care of the needy, and distribute to them the offices from which gains accrue. If one of the prosperous is insolent to them, the penalties should be greater than if he is insolent to one of his own class. Inheritances should not be by bequest but by kinship, and the same person should not inherit more than one property. For in this
25 way properties would be more on a level, and more of the needy would rise to prosperity. It is advantageous both in a democracy and in an oligarchy to distribute to those who participate less in the constitution (the prosperous in a democracy, the needy in an oli-
30 garchy) either equality or precedence in all else but those offices that are supreme in the constitution. These should be put solely or mainly in the hands of those from within the constitution.

CHAPTER 9

1309ᵃ33 (13) There are three things that those who are to hold the supreme offices ought to have: first, friendliness toward the estab-

lished constitution; next, great ability in the tasks of the office; and, 35
thirdly, virtue and justice—in each constitution the kind pertaining
to that constitution. (For if what is just is not the same in relation to
all constitutions, there must also be differences ⟨in the virtue⟩ of
justice.)

1309ᵃ39 Here is a puzzle. When all these things are not found
together in the same man, how should the choice be made? For 40
example, if one man is suited to be a general but is wicked and not **1309ᵇ**
a friend of the constitution while another man is just and a friend,
how ought the choice be made? It seems that one ought to look at
two things: which of these qualities do all men share in more and
which less? That is why in the office of general one should focus on
experience more than virtue (for men share less in generalship, but 5
more in goodness), but in the office of guardian, or treasurer, the
opposite (for this office requires more virtue than the many have,
while the knowledge required is common to all).

1309ᵇ8 Someone might, however, pose this puzzle: if ability is
present and also friendliness to the constitution, what is the need of
virtue? For just the first two will furnish what is advantageous. Or 10
is it that it is possible for those who have these two to be weak-
willed, so that just as men do not ⟨always⟩ serve their own interests
in spite of knowing how and being friendly to themselves, so also
nothing prevents some men having a similar relation to the
community?

1309ᵇ14 (14) Simply put, whatever provisions in the laws we
describe as advantageous to constitutions, all these preserve consti- 15
tutions; and so does the great elementary principle so often mentioned, to take care that the group that wants the constitution shall
be stronger than the one that does not.

1309ᵇ18 (15) In addition to all these matters, one thing must not
be overlooked, which is now overlooked in the deviant constitutions, namely, the mean. For many of the measures thought demo- 20
cratic destroy democracies, and many of those thought oligarchic
destroy oligarchies. Those who think this the only virtue drag it to
excess. They are ignorant of the following point. A nose can deviate from the most beautiful straightness toward the hooked or the
snub but nevertheless still be beautiful and delight the eye. Still, if 25
someone ⟨e.g. a sculptor⟩ tightens it still further in the direction of
excess, he first throws away the due proportion of the part, and,
continuing on, will in the end make it appear not even a nose due

to the excess and deficiency of the opposites. It is the same way too
30 with the other parts of the body. Now, this also happens with
constitutions. For it is possible for an oligarchy and a democracy to
be adequate even though they have departed from the best structure. But if someone tightens either of them further, he will first
make the constitution worse, and will in the end make it not even
35 a constitution. That is why this is something the lawgiver and the
statesman should not be ignorant of—what sort of democratic
measures preserve and what sort destroy democracy, and what
sort of oligarchic measures preserve or destroy oligarchy. For
neither of these constitutions can exist and endure without the
prosperous and the mass; but when a levelling of property occurs,
40 the resulting constitution must be of another kind. Thus, by de-
1310^a stroying these classes by laws carried to excess, they destroy their
constitutions.

1310^{a}2 (16) They go wrong in both democracies and oligarchies. In democracies the demagogues go wrong where the mass is
5 supreme over the laws. For they always make the city two cities by
fighting with the prosperous, whereas they should on the contrary
always seem to be speaking on behalf of the prosperous. In oligarchies the oligarchs should seem to be speaking on behalf of the
people, and the oligarchs should swear oaths opposite to those they
now swear. For now in some oligarchies they swear 'I shall be evil-
minded toward the people and shall devise whatever evil I can
10 against them', whereas they should both hold and make a show of
holding the opposite view, signifying in their oaths that 'I shall not
treat the people unjustly'.

1310^{a}12 (17) The most important of all the things that have
been mentioned for the endurance of constitutions, which all men
now make light of, is to be educated in harmony with the constitutions. For there is no benefit in the most beneficial laws, even
15 though ratified by all who are active politically, unless people are
habituated and educated in the constitution—democratically if the
laws are democratic; oligarchically if they are oligarchic. For if
weakness of will exists in an individual, it also exists in a city. To
20 have been educated in harmony with the constitution is not to do
the things oligarchs or those who want democracy delight in, but
rather to do the things that will make it possible for the former to
rule oligarchically and the latter to rule themselves democratically.
But at present in oligarchies the sons of the rulers live in luxury

22

while those of the needy become hardened by exercise and toil, so
that they have both a stronger wish and greater power to make a 25
new order. In democracies—those that are held to be especially
democratic—the opposite of what is advantageous has come about.
The reason for this is that people define freedom badly. For there
are two things by which democracy is thought to be defined: the
supremacy of the majority, and freedom. For it is held that the just 30
is equality, that equality is the supremacy of whatever seems right
to the mass, and that freedom [[and equality]] is doing whatever one
wishes. Thus in such democracies each man lives as he wishes, and
'For what he happens to crave', as Euripides says. But this is bad.
For one should not think it slavery to live in harmony with the 35
constitution, but safety.

1310ᵃ36   Generally speaking, then, these are the causes from
which constitutions change and perish and the means by which they
are preserved and endure.

CHAPTER 10

1310ᵃ39   It remains to discuss monarchy, both the causes from
which it perishes and the means by which it is naturally preserved. 40
And the things that happen with kingships and tyrannies are much
the same as those we have described as happening with constitu- **1310ᵇ**
tions. For kingship accords with aristocracy, and tyranny is composed of ultimate oligarchy and democracy. Just for this reason
tyranny is also extremely harmful to its subjects, inasmuch as it is 5
composed of two evils and has the deviations and mistakes issuing
from both constitutions.

1310ᵇ7   The origin of each of these kinds of monarchy lies in
diametrically opposite circumstances. For kingship has arisen to
provide aid to the worthy against the ⟨depredations⟩ by the people,
and a king is selected from the worthy on the basis of superiority in 10
virtue or in actions that flow from virtue, or on the basis of superiority in a family of such a character. A tyrant, on the other hand, is
selected from the people and the mass as an aid against the notables, that the people may suffer no injustice from them. This is
evident from what has happened. For one may say that almost the
greatest number of tyrants have arisen from demagogues who came 15
to be trusted by slandering the notables. For some tyrannies were

23

established in this way when the cities had already grown large. Other tyrannies prior to these arose from kings who deviated from their hereditary privileges and desired a more despotic rule. Still
20 others arose from those elected to the supreme offices (for in ancient times democracies established civil and religious offices of long tenure). Yet others arose from oligarchies that elected some one individual supreme over the greatest offices. For in all these ways it was easy for such individuals to carry the day, should they
25 wish to, because of the power that some already possessed through the office of king, and others through an office of honour. Thus Pheidon of Argos and other tyrants established tyrannies on the basis of a pre-existing kingship; the Ionian tyrants and Phalaris established tyrannies from offices of honour; and Panaetius at
30 Leontini, Cypselus at Corinth, Peisistratus at Athens, Dionysius at Syracuse, and others established tyrannies in the same way from the position of demagogue.

1310ᵇ31 Kingship, then, as we said, is a structure that accords with aristocracy. For it accords with worth, whether this be individual virtue or that of family, or benefits, or these things together
35 with ability. For all who attained this honour conferred, or were able to confer, benefits on their cities or nations: some, like Codrus, by preventing their enslavement in war; others, like Cyrus, by setting them free, or by founding a city or acquiring territory, like the kings of the Lacedaemonians, Macedonians, and Molossians.

40 **1310ᵇ40** A king wishes to be a guardian, to ensure that
1311ᵃ those possessing property suffer no injustice and the people no insolence. Tyranny, as has often been said, has regard for no common interest, except for the sake of private benefit. The aim of a
5 tyrant is the peasant; that of a king, the noble. That is precisely why in their excesses money is characteristic of a tyrant, whereas things having to do with honour are more characteristic of a king. And the guard of a king consists of citizens; that of a tyrant is in the hands of aliens.

1311ᵃ8 That tyranny has the evils both of democracy and oli-
10 garchy is evident. From oligarchy comes its end, which is wealth (for by such means only can a tyrant maintain both his guard and his luxury), and its practice of putting no trust in the mass (that is why tyrants make a confiscation of heavy arms, and why mistreating the rabble and driving them from the town and dispersing them
15 is common both to oligarchy and tyranny). From democracy comes

its practice of making war against the notables, and of destroying them secretly and openly, and of exiling them as rivals and obstructions to its rule. For it is from the notables that conspiracies too arise, since some of them wish to hold office themselves, and others wish not to be slaves. Hence too the advice of Periander to Thrasybulus, namely, the cutting off of the outstanding stalks, 20 signifying that one must always do away with those citizens who are outstanding.

1311^{a}22   As has been more or less stated, then, the same origins of changes should be held to exist both for constitutions and for monarchies. (For it is because of injustice and fear and contempt 25 that many subjects attack monarchies—and in regard to injustice, most of all because of insolence, though sometimes too because of the deprivation of private property.) The ends ⟨of the assailants⟩ are also the same for tyrannies and kingships as for constitutions. For monarchs possess great wealth and honour, which all men 30 seek.

1311^{a}31   Some attacks are upon the person of the rulers; others are upon the office. Attacks due to insolence are upon the person. Although insolence is of many kinds, each of them is a cause of anger; and of those who are angry, almost the greatest number attack for the sake of revenge, not of superiority. For example, the 35 attack on the Peisistratids happened because they besmirched the sister of Harmodius and insulted Harmodius (for Harmodius attacked because of his sister, and Aristogeiton because of Harmodius). They also conspired against Periander, the tyrant in Ambracia, because while drinking with his boyfriend, Periander 40 asked him whether he was yet pregnant by him. The attack on 1311^b Philip by Pausanias happened because Philip allowed him to be treated with insolence by those around Attalus. And the attack against Amyntas the Little by Derdas happened because Amyntas boasted in regard to his youthfulness. And the attack of the eunuch on Evagoras of Cyprus was also for revenge. For he killed him on 5 the ground that he had been treated with insolence, because Evagoras' son had drawn away his wife.

1311^{b}6   Many attacks have also occurred because certain monarchs have brought shame upon the persons of their subjects. The attack of Crataeas on Archelaus is an example. For Crataeas was always rankled over their intercourse, so that even a smaller provocation was enough—or perhaps he attacked because Archelaus did 10

not give him one of his daughters after agreeing to do so, but gave
the elder to the king of Elimeia when he was hard pressed by a war
against Sirras and Arrabaeus, and gave the younger to his own son
Amyntas, thinking that Amyntas would then be least likely to
15 quarrel with his other son by Cleopatra. But the origin of his
estrangement at any rate was due to his being rankled over their
sexual relations. Hellanocrates of Larissa also joined the attack for
the same reason. For as Archelaus made use of his youthfulness but
did not restore him to his city after pledging to do so, he thought it
was because of insolence and not because of erotic desire that the
20 intercourse had come about. Python and Heracleides of Aenus
killed Cotys in revenge for their father, and Adamas revolted from
Cotys on the ground that he had been treated with insolence
because he had been castrated by Cotys when he was a boy.

1311ᵇ23 Many, too, who are angry because their person has
25 been violated by blows have either killed or attempted to kill, on
the ground that they were treated with insolence, even those who
hold office or are connected with kingly dynasties. For example, at
Mytilene Megacles, in company with his friends, attacked and destroyed the Penthilidae, who were going about and hitting people
with their clubs; and later Smerdes killed Penthilus after being
pummelled with blows and dragged away from his wife. And
30 Decamnichus became a leader of the attack on Archelaus, being
the first to incite the attackers. The reason for his anger was that
Archelaus had handed him over to Euripides the poet for flogging.
Euripides was upset because Decamnichus had made a remark
about his bad breath. And many others for reasons such as
35 these were either killed or conspired against.

1311ᵇ36 Similarly too because of fear; for this was one of the
causes in the case of monarchies just as in the case of constitutions.
For example, Artapanes ⟨killed⟩ Xerxes because he feared the
charge about Darius, namely, that he had hanged him without
orders from Xerxes, but thinking that Xerxes, not remembering the
40 circumstances on account of his carousing, would pardon him.

1311ᵇ40 Other attacks are due to contempt. Thus someone
1312ᵃ ⟨killed⟩ Sardanapalus after seeing him carding wool with the
women. (If what the storytellers say is true; but if it is not true of
him, it may well be of someone else.) And Dion attacked Dionysius
5 the Younger because of contempt, seeing the citizens contemptuous and Dionysius himself always drunk. Even some of the friends

of monarchs attack them because of contempt; for due to their being trusted, they feel contempt, thinking they will escape detection. And it is, in a way, because of contempt that those who think they have the power to seize the office attack. For as they have the power and are contemptuous of the danger because of their power, they readily make the attempt. Thus those who are generals attack their monarchs. For example, Cyrus attacked Astyages because he felt contempt for both his way of life and his power since his power had waned while he himself lived in luxury. And the Thracian Seuthes attacked Amadocus when he was his general.

1312ᵃ15 Some men, too, attack for several of these reasons, for example, out of contempt and after profit, as Mithridates attacked Ariobarzanes. For this reason especially, those men make the attempt who are bold by nature and possess military honour under monarchs. For boldness is bravery that possesses power, and on account of both of these ⟨i.e. bravery and power⟩ men make their attacks, thinking they will easily prevail.

1312ᵃ21 With those who attack for love of honour there is a different sort of cause beside those mentioned before. For it is not the case that because some people raise their hand against tyrants with an eye to the great profits and the great honours they possess, this is also why each person who attacks for love of honour chooses to take the risk. It is rather that, while the former attack for the reason mentioned, the latter, just as they would be part of any other uncommon action by which men become renowned and notable to others, in the same spirit too raise their hand against monarchs, wishing to gain not a monarchy but glory. None the less those who are impelled by this reason are very few in number. For it presupposes disregard of their safety should they fail to carry the action through. The opinion of Dion must guide them, but it is not easy for it to be engendered in many men. For with a small force he campaigned against Dionysius, saying that he was of such a mind that, however far he might be able to proceed, it would be enough for him to share to that extent in the action—if, for example, it should happen that, having set foot on land for a short time, he should straight away meet his end, this death would be fine for him.

1312ᵃ39 One way tyranny is destroyed, like each of the other constitutions, is from outside, if some opposite constitution is stronger. For the wish to destroy it will clearly be present due to the opposition of policy, and all men do what they wish when they have

the power. The constitutions opposite to tyranny are, on the one
5 hand, democracy—as Hesiod says 'potter rages at potter' (for the
ultimate democracy is tyranny)—and, on the other, kingship and
aristocracy, because of the opposition of the constitution. That is
why the Lacedaemonians overthrew a great many tyrannies, and so
did the Syracusans during the time when they were well governed.

1312ᵇ9 Another way tyranny is destroyed is from within itself,
when those who share in it form factions, as in the tyranny of those
10 around Gelon and, in our own day, in the tyranny of those around
Dionysius. The tyranny of Gelon was destroyed when Thrasybulus,
the brother of Hieron, curried favour with Gelon's son and impelled him toward pleasures in order that he himself might rule. In
reaction the family banded together in order that the tyranny might
not be overthrown completely but only Thrasybulus. But those
15 who banded together with them, once they had the opportunity,
expelled them all. Dion campaigned against Dionysius, an in-law,
and after gaining the support of the people expelled him, but was
then himself destroyed.

1312ᵇ17 There are two causes that chiefly move men to attack
tyrannies, hatred and contempt. Though the first of these, hatred,
20 always attaches to tyrants, it is in consequence of the contempt they
incur that many of the overthrows come about. The proof is that
most of those who acquired the offices themselves also carefully
guarded them, whereas all who inherited them (generally speaking) lose them straight away. For living lives of enjoyment, they
25 readily become contemptible and offer many opportunities to attackers. Anger too must be regarded as a part of hatred. For in a
way it is a cause of the same actions. Often it is even more conducive to action than hatred; for those who are angry attack more
vehemently, because their passion does not employ calculation.
(It comes about that men give way to violent feelings most of
30 all because of insolence, for which reason the tyranny of the
Peisistratids was overthrown, and many others.) But hatred is more
calculative. For anger is associated with pain, so that it is not easy
to calculate; but enmity is without pain.

1312ᵇ34 To speak summarily, the causes we have mentioned of
35 the destruction of unmixed and ultimate oligarchy and of extreme
democracy must all be regarded as causes of destruction of tyrannies as well. For these constitutions are actually parcelled-out
tyrannies.

1312^{b}38 Kingship is destroyed least by outside forces. That is why it is long-lasting. In most cases its destruction arises from within itself. It is destroyed in two ways. The first is when those who share in the kingship form factions. The other way is when kings 1313^a attempt to govern more tyrannically, claiming supremacy over more and more things and contrary to law. Kingships do not spring up any longer now, but if they do, they are rather monarchies, or tyrannies. This is because kingship is rule that is willingly accepted, 5 though supreme over greater matters. But men of similar quality are numerous, and no one is outstanding enough to fit the greatness and the dignity of the office. So because of this, men do not willingly endure such rule; and if someone rules by deceit or force, this is already held to be tyranny. In kingships based on family one 10 should set down as a cause of destruction, in addition to those mentioned, that many kings readily become contemptible and, though not possessing the power of a tyrant but only the honour due a king, behave insolently. For their overthrow was easily effected. For when his subjects do not wish it, a king will straight away not be a king. But the tyrant is a tyrant even when his subjects 15 do not wish it.

1313^{a}16 Monarchies are destroyed, then, due to these and other such causes.

CHAPTER 11

1313^{a}18 And clearly they are preserved, generally speaking, by the opposite causes, though kingships, in particular, are preserved by guiding them to greater moderation. For the fewer things over 20 which kings are supreme, the longer time must their rule remain whole. For they themselves become less despotic and in their character more an equal, and are less envied by their subjects. For this is why the kingship among the Molossians endured such a long time, and that of the Lacedaemonians as well. The latter endured because from the beginning the office was divided into two parts, 25 and again because Theopompus moderated it in other ways and in addition established the office of the ephors. For by diminishing the power of the kingship he increased its duration, so that in a way he made it not lesser but greater. This is precisely what they say he 30 replied to his wife when she wondered if he felt no shame in

handing down to his sons a lesser kingship than he had inherited
from his father. 'Not at all', he said, 'for I am handing down a more
permanent one.'

    1313ᵃ34 Tyrannies are preserved in two ways that are polar
35 opposites. One of them is the way that has been handed down and
in which most tyrants conduct their rule. The majority of these
tyrannical measures they say Periander the Corinthian instituted,
but many similar ones may also be gleaned from the rule of the
Persians. They are the measures for the preservation (so far as
this is possible) of tyranny mentioned some time ago—cutting
40 off those who are outstanding and doing away with the proud-
hearted—and also such things as permitting neither public meals
1313ᵇ nor political clubs nor education nor anything else of that sort, but
keeping an eye on everything that customarily generates two
things, pride and trust, and allowing neither schools nor other
scholarly gatherings to spring up, and doing everything to insure
5 that people shall be as unknown to one another as possible (for
knowledge increases trust towards one another).

    1313ᵇ6 And another measure is to require those residing in
town to always be in sight and to spend their time hanging around
the palace doors (for in this way what they are doing would be least
likely to escape notice, and they would be habituated to think small
by always living like slaves). And the other Persian and barbarian
10 measures of a similar sort are characteristic of tyranny (for they all
accomplish the same thing). And a tyrant should try not to let what
any of his subjects say or do escape his notice, but to have spies, like
the so-called gossipmongers at Syracuse, and the listeners Hieron
sent out wherever there was a meeting or a gathering. For men
15 speak less freely when they fear such persons; and if they do speak
freely, they are less likely to escape notice. And another measure is
to get men to squabble with one another and to cause friends to
clash with friends, the people with the notables, and the wealthy
with themselves.

    1313ᵇ18 And it is characteristic of a tyrant to make his subjects
20 poor, so that no guard may be maintained ⟨by them⟩ and so that
they may be too busy to conspire, being caught up in their daily
affairs. Examples of this are the pyramids of Egypt, the offerings
of the Cypselids, the building of the temple of the Olympian Zeus
by the Peisistratids, and among the works at Samos those of

Polycrates. For all of these accomplish the same thing: lack of
leisure and poverty among those who are ruled.   25

1313ᵇ25   Another measure is the levying of property taxes, as at
Syracuse. For in five years during the reign of Dionysius it came
about that a person's entire property was paid in taxes. And the
tyrant is also a war-maker, so that his subjects may be busy and
continually in need of a leader.

1313ᵇ29   And whereas a kingship is preserved by its friends, it is 30
characteristic of a tyrant to distrust his friends most of all, on the
ground that, though all men have the wish ⟨to overthrow him⟩,
these most of all have the power.

1313ᵇ32   And the things that occur in ultimate democracy are all
characteristic of tyranny: the reign of women in the household in
order that they may tell tales on the men, and the indulgence
towards slaves for the same reason. For slaves and women not only 35
do not conspire against tyrants, but, by flourishing under them,
must also feel goodwill both to tyrannies and to democracies (for
the people too wish to be a monarch). That is why the flatterer too
is honoured in both: in democracies the demagogue (for the dema- 40
gogue is a flatterer of the people), and among tyrants those who
fawn over them, which is a work of flattery. For it is because of **1314**^a
this that tyranny is also a friend to the vicious. For tyrants delight
in being flattered; and this is not something one who has a free
mind would do, but the worthy are true friends, or at least do not
flatter.

1314ᵃ4   The vicious are also useful for vicious things. For nail is
driven out by nail, according to the proverb. And it is characteristic 5
of a tyrant to delight in no man who is dignified or free. For the
tyrant thinks he alone is worthy to be a person of that sort; and the
man who matches his dignity, or acts like a free man, takes away
the superiority and the mastery of his tyranny. Consequently,
tyrants hate such men as undermining their rule.

1314ᵃ10   And it is characteristic of a tyrant to have as messmates 10
and cronies aliens rather than citizens, thinking the latter to be
hostile, but the former to offer no opposition.

1314ᵃ12   These and similar measures are characteristic of tyranny and preserve its rule, but they lack no part of vileness.
Broadly speaking, all of these measures are included in one or
another of three kinds. For tyranny aims at three things. The first is 15

for its subjects to think small; for a small-minded man would not conspire against anyone. The second is for its subjects to thoroughly distrust one another; for a tyranny is never overthrown until some men trust each other. That is precisely why tyrants make war on the worthy. To their mind the worthy are harmful to their rule
20 not only because they think they do not deserve to be ruled despotically, but also because they are trusted among themselves and by others and do not inform against themselves or others. The third aim of tyranny is powerlessness for action in its subjects; for as no one attempts impossibilities, so no one attempts to overthrow even
25 a tyranny when he does not have power. The marks of tyranny, then, to which the wishes of tyrants can be referred, are in fact these three. For a person might refer all the measures characteristic of tyranny to these fundamental principles: that its subjects not trust one another, that they have no power, and that they think small.

30   **1314ᵃ29**   This, then, is one way by which the preservation of tyrannies comes about. The other requires diligence of a sort almost opposite to what has been described. One may grasp the latter by considering the destruction of kingships. For just as one way of destroying kingship is by making its rule more
35 tyrannical, so one way of preserving tyranny is to make it more like a kingship. The tyrant must guard one thing only, his power, so that he may rule not only when his subjects wish it but also when they do not. For when he gives this up, he also gives up being a tyrant. But while this preservation of power must remain as a fundamental principle, he should, with respect to other things, do some of them and seem to do others, beautifully playing the part of
40 a king.

      1314ᵃ40   First of all, he must seem to take thought for the public
1314ᵇ funds. He must not spend them upon the sort of presents that the masses get angry about when tyrants take greedily from those who work and toil, and give freely to courtesans and aliens and crafts-
5 men; and he must also render an account of what he receives and what he spends (which some tyrants have done already). For one who conducts his affairs like this would seem to be a head of a household rather than a tyrant. He need not fear that he may at some time be in want of money, since he is supreme over the city. But, in any event, for those tyrants who go off from their own
10 country ⟨on campaigns⟩, this policy is also more advantageous than

collecting a hoard and leaving it behind. For it makes it less likely that those standing guard over the city would make an attempt on power, and those standing guard are more to be feared by tyrants who go abroad than are the citizens. For the latter go abroad with them ⟨on their campaigns⟩ while the former remain behind. Next, the tyrant should be seen to levy taxes and liturgies for the sake 15 of administration and, should the need ever arise, for use in times of war; and in general he should make himself appear a guardian and treasurer as it were of public funds rather than of a private hoard.

1314ᵇ18   And the tyrant should appear not bad-tempered but dignified, and also such that those who meet with him feel not fear but awe. This, however, is not easily achieved if he is contemptible. 20 That is why, even if he pays no attention to any other virtue, he should pay attention to military virtue, and make a reputation of this sort for himself.

1314ᵇ23   Again, not only should the tyrant himself not be seen behaving insolently toward any of his subjects, whether boy or girl, but neither should any of the men around him. The women of his 25 household should be similarly respectful toward other women, inasmuch as many tyrannies have also been destroyed because of the insolence of women.

1314ᵇ28   And as to bodily enjoyments, the tyrant should do the opposite of what some tyrants do now. For not only do they revel from early dawn, and continuously for many days, but they also 30 wish to be seen doing so by others, in order that people may admire them as happy and blessed. But the best course for the tyrant is to be moderate in such things; failing that, he should at least avoid being seen by others in his revels. For the man who is easily attacked or easily held in contempt is not the man who is sober, but the one who is drunk—not the man who is awake, but the one who 35 is asleep.

1314ᵇ36   The tyrant must do the opposite of almost everything that was mentioned before. For he must build and adorn his city as if he were an overseer, not a tyrant.

1314ᵇ38   Again, in matters relating to the gods the tyrant should always be seen to be extremely zealous. For people have less fear of suffering something illegal from such men if they think their ruler 40 is fearful of the divine and takes thought of the gods, and they also **1315ª** conspire against him less under the impression that he has even the gods as allies. But the tyrant must appear to be like this without lapsing into foolishness.

1315ᵃ4 The tyrant should so honour those who become good at
5 something that they would never expect to be honoured more by citizens who live under their own laws. And such honours he should distribute himself, whereas punishments should be meted out by others—officials and law courts.

1315ᵃ8 A common safeguard of every monarchy is to make no one individual great—but if one, then several (for they will keep
10 watch on one another). If the ruler must after all make someone great, it should at least not be a bold character (for such a character is highly enterprising in all his actions). And if it seems best to remove someone from power, the ruler should do this by gradual increments and not take back all the authority at once.

1315ᵃ14 Again, the tyrant should abstain from every sort of
15 insolence, and from two above all others: corporal punishment and insolence toward youth. This caution he should exercise especially in connection with honour-lovers. For whereas it is a slight affecting their money that money-lovers find hard to bear, it is a slight involving dishonour that honour-lovers and worthy people find hard to bear. That is why the tyrant should either have no dealings
20 with such men, or should be seen to administer his punishments paternally and not because of belittlement, and to have intercourse with youth for erotic reasons and not because of his authority. In general he should buy off what are taken to be dishonours with greater honours.

1315ᵃ24 Of those who make an attempt at his physical destruc-
25 tion, the ones most to be feared and most in need of watching are those who do not plan to save their own lives while destroying his. That is why the tyrant must be extremely cautious of those who think that they themselves, or those they happen to care about, have been treated with insolence. For men who attack out of spir-
30 itedness are unsparing of themselves, just as Heraclitus said when he asserted that it is hard to fight against spirit, for ⟨whatever it wills⟩ it buys with ⟨a man's⟩ soul.

1315ᵃ31 Since cities are composed of two parts, the needy people and the prosperous, the prime necessity is for them both to hold that they are preserved because of the tyrant's rule and that neither of them is treated unjustly in any way by the other on account of it.
35 But failing this, whichever of the two parts is stronger, these indi-

viduals especially should be made part of his rule, because if this support is given to his interests, there will be no necessity for the tyrant to effect a freeing of slaves or a confiscation of heavy arms. For one of the two parts added to his power will be enough to make them stronger than the attackers.

1315^a40 It is superfluous to discuss such matters individually. 40 For the aim is clear. The tyrant should appear to his subjects not as a tyrant but as a head of a household or a king, and not as an **1315^b** appropriator but as an overseer. He should pursue the moderate things of life, not the excesses. And, again, the notables he should win by daily companionship, and the many by courting popularity. For from these measures it necessarily follows not only that his rule 5 will be nobler and more enviable (by being rule over better men and over men who have not been humbled, and by his not being continually hated and feared), but also that his rule will be of longer duration, and further that he himself in his character will be either nobly disposed toward virtue or at least half-good, and not vicious but half-vicious.   10

CHAPTER 12

1315^b11 And yet of all constitutions oligarchy and tyranny are the shortest-lived. For the tyranny that existed for the longest time was the one at Sicyon, that of Orthagoras' sons and of Orthagoras himself, which lasted for a hundred years. The reason for this was that they dealt moderately with their subjects and in many things 15 were subservient to the laws; and because he was skilled in war, Cleisthenes was not easily held in contempt, and in many ways they curried favour by acts of concern. At any rate it is said that Cleisthenes crowned the man who judged the victory against him. Some say the seated figure in the market-place is a statue of the man who rendered the judgement. They say that Peisistratus 20 too submitted once to being summoned in a lawsuit before the Areopagus.

1315^b22 The second longest tyranny was that of the Cypselids at Corinth. For this too lasted long—seventy-three years and six months. For Cypselus was tyrant for thirty years, Periander for 25 forty and a half, and Psammitichus, the son of Gorgus, for three years. The reasons for the durability of this tyranny are also the

same. For Cypselus was a demagogue and during his rule lived
without a bodyguard; and Periander, though he was tyrannical, was
skilled in war.

1315ᵇ29   The third longest was that of the Peisistratids at
30 Athens. But it was not continuous. For twice Peisistratus was banished from his tyrannies, so that in thirty-three years he was tyrant
for only seventeen of them. His sons ruled for eighteen years, so
that the tyranny existed for thirty-five years in all.

1315ᵇ34   Of the remaining tyrannies the one around Hieron and
35 Gelon at Syracuse was the longest. Even this did not endure for
many years, but only eighteen altogether. For Gelon, after being
tyrant for seven years, met his end in the eighth; Hieron was tyrant
for ten; and Thrasybulus was driven out in his eleventh month. The
majority of tyrannies have all been very short-lived.

40 **1315ᵇ40**   With respect, then, to constitutions and monarchies,
the reasons they perish and again are preserved have pretty well all
been stated.

1316ᵃ   **1316ᵃ1**   In the *Republic* the changes of constitution are discussed by Socrates, but not discussed well. For in the case of the
best and first constitution, he does not discuss the change distinctive of it. For he says that the cause is that nothing endures but
5 everything changes in a certain cycle, and that the origin is in those
things 'whose ratio of four to three reduced to its lowest terms,
yoked to five, gives two harmonies' when, as he says, the number of
this diagram becomes cubed—his idea being that nature sometimes
produces men who are bad and beyond education. In advancing
10 this idea itself he does not perhaps go wrong (for there may be
some people who cannot be educated and become good men), but
why should this change be distinctive of the constitution he calls
best rather than of all the others and of everything that comes into
existence? Yes, and is it because of time, through whose agency he
15 says that everything changes, that even things which did not begin
to exist together change together? For example, if a thing came into
existence the day before the turnabout, does it then change together with everything else?

1316ᵃ17   Furthermore, for what reason does the constitution
change from this one to the Laconian? For all constitutions change
more often to their opposite than to the one close by. The same
20 remark also applies to the other changes. For, he says, from the
Laconian the constitution changes to oligarchy, from this to democ-

36

racy, and from democracy to tyranny. And yet constitutions also change in the opposite direction. For example, from democracy they change to oligarchy even more often than to monarchy.

1316ᵃ25   Again, as to tyranny, Socrates does not say whether it 25 will or will not change, what will cause it to change, and what sort of constitution it will change into. The reason for this is that he could not easily have said. For it is indeterminable, since according to him tyranny must change into the first and best constitution. For only in this way would the change be continuous and in a circle. But tyranny changes also into tyranny, as the tyranny of Sicyon 30 changed from that of Myron into that of Cleisthenes; into oligarchy, like the tyranny of Antileon at Chalcis; into democracy, like the tyranny of Gelon's house at Syracuse; and into aristocracy, like the tyranny of Charilaus at Lacedaemon, and at Carthage.

1316ᵃ34   Constitutions also change from oligarchy to tyranny, 35 as did almost the greatest number of ancient oligarchies in Sicily: at Leontini to the tyranny of Panaetius, at Gela to that of Cleander, at Rhegium to that of Anaxilaus, and at many other cities similarly.

1316ᵃ39   And it is absurd for Socrates to think that a constitution changes into oligarchy because those in office become money- 40 lovers and money-makers, and not because those who are greatly **1316ᵇ** superior in property think it is not just for those possessing nothing to have an equal share in the city with those having possessions. And in many oligarchies office-holders are not allowed to make money, and there are laws preventing it. Furthermore, in Carthage, which has a democratic constitution, office-holders engage in 5 money-making and have not yet changed its constitution.

1316ᵇ6   It is also absurd for him to say that the oligarchic city is two cities, one of the wealthy and one of the poor. For why is this more true of this city than of the Laconian, or of any other in which they don't all have equal possessions or aren't all equally good men? And even though no one has become poorer than before, 10 constitutions none the less change to democracy from oligarchy if the needy become more numerous, and from democracy to oligarchy if the prosperous element is stronger than the mass, and the latter are negligent while the others set their mind to bringing a change about.

1316ᵇ14   Although there are many causes by which the changes come about, Socrates mentions but one: that by living lavishly, 15

borrowing at usurious rates of interest, they become poor, as if
from the beginning all or most were wealthy. This is false. On the
contrary, when some of the leaders lose their property, they make
innovations; but when some of the others lose theirs, nothing terri-
20 ble occurs. And constitutions do not even then change to democracy more than to any other constitution.

1316ᵇ21   Again, if men do not share in offices of honour, and if
they are treated unjustly or with insolence, they form factions and
change their constitutions. They do so even if they have not squandered their property, because it is open to them to do whatever
they wish—the cause of which Socrates says is too much freedom.

25 **1316ᵇ25**   Although there are many forms of oligarchies and
democracies, Socrates discusses their changes as though there
were only one form of either.

BOOK SIX

CHAPTER I

1316ᵇ31 (1) How many varieties and what varieties there are (*a*) of the deliberative and supreme element of the constitution, (*b*) of the system of offices, and (*c*) of courts, and (2) which variety has been organized with a view to which sort of constitution, and also (3) regarding the destruction and preservation of constitutions, from which sorts of thing they come about and through what 35 causes—these subjects have already been discussed.

1316ᵇ36 Since there are actually many kinds of democracy and similarly of the other constitutions, it will be well to examine any points left over about them, and at the same time to determine the mode of organization that is appropriate and advantageous to each. Furthermore, we must also examine the combinations of all the ways of organizing the forementioned elements. For these ways, when 40 coupled, make the constitutions overlap, so as to produce oligarchic **1317ª** aristocracies and somewhat democratic polities. I mean those couplings that ought to be examined, but at present have not been: for example, where the deliberative element and the method of electing 5 officials are organized oligarchically but the regulations as to the courts aristocratically, or where these regulations and the deliberative element are organized oligarchically but the method of electing officials aristocratically, or where in some other way not all the institutions appropriate to a particular constitution are combined.

1317ª10 Which sort of democracy is suited to which sort of city, 10 and similarly which sort of oligarchy is suited to which sort of population, and which of the remaining constitutions is advantageous to whom—these subjects have already been discussed. Still, it must be made clear not only which variety of these constitutions is best for cities, but also how to establish both these and the others. 15 Let us pursue this matter briefly. And first let us speak about democracy. For at the same time the facts about the opposite constitution will also be manifest, that is, the one which some call oligarchy.

1317ª18 For the purpose of this inquiry we must take account of all the things that are democratic and are held to go with democra-

20 cies. For in consequence of these things being combined, the kinds
of democracy come into being, and more than one democracy and
different ones exist. For there are two reasons that democracies are
of many kinds. The first is the one mentioned earlier, that peoples
25 are different. For there is the mass of farmers and that of artisans
and labourers; and when the first of these is added to the second,
and the third again to both of them, not only does it differ in respect
of the democracy's becoming better or worse, but also in respect of
its becoming not the same. The second reason is the one we speak
30 about now. For the things that go with democracies and are held to
be appropriate to this constitution, when they are combined, cause
democracies to be different. For a smaller number of these things
will go with one kind of democracy, a larger number with a second,
and all of them with a third. It will be useful to gain knowledge
of each of them both for the purpose of establishing whichever kind
of democracy one happens to wish and for the purpose of the
35 rectification ⟨of existing democracies⟩. For those who institute constitutions seek to bring together everything appropriate to the
fundamental principle; but in doing this they go wrong, as we said
earlier in our discussion concerning the destruction and the preservation of constitutions.

1317ª39 Now let us speak of the axioms and the ethical character ⟨of democratic constitutions⟩ and the things such constitutions
aim at.

CHAPTER 2

40 **1317ª40** A fundamental principle of the democratic constitution
is freedom. (For this is what people are accustomed to say, on
the ground that only in this constitution do they have a share of
1317ᵇ freedom—which is what they declare every democracy aims at.)
One component of freedom is ruling and being ruled in turn. For
democratic justice is having an equal share on the basis of number,
5 not worth. When this is what is just, the mass is necessarily supreme; and whatever seems right to the majority—this is the end,
and this is what is just. For they say that each of the citizens ought
to have an equal share, so that in democracies it comes about that
the needy are more sovereign than the prosperous. For they are a

majority, and the opinion of the majority is supreme. This, then, is 10
one sign of freedom, which all democrats take as a mark of the
constitution. Another is to live as one wishes. For this they say is
the function of freedom, if indeed it is a feature of one who is
enslaved not to live as he wishes. This, then, is the second mark of
democracy; and from it has come the call not to be ruled, preferably 15
not by anyone, or failing that, ⟨to rule and be ruled⟩ in turn. And in
this way the second mark contributes to the freedom based on
equality.

1317^{b}17 When these things are laid down, and when the starting point is of this sort, the following institutions are democratic:
(1) for all to elect to the offices from all; (2) for all to rule each, and
for each in turn to rule all; (3) for either all offices or as many as do 20
not need experience or skill to be filled by lot; (4) for the offices to
require no property qualification or as low a one as possible; (5) for
the same person to hold no office twice, or more than a few times,
or only in a few cases apart from those relating to war; (6) for either
all offices, or as many as possible, to be of short duration; (7) for all 25
to adjudicate (that is, ⟨for those who adjudicate to be selected⟩ from
all) and on all matters, or on most and the greatest and most
sovereign, such as audits, the constitution, and private contracts;
and (8) for the assembly to be supreme over all or the greatest
matters, but for no office to be supreme over any or only over as
small a number as possible. (Of the offices the most democratic is 30
the council, except where there is plenty of pay for everybody; for
where there is, they deprive even this office of its power. For the
people draw all decisions to themselves when they receive plenty of
pay, as was said before in the inquiry before this one.) Also it is
democratic (9) for the parts of the constitution to receive pay,
preferably all parts—the assembly, the courts, and the offices—or 35
failing that, the offices, the courts, the council, and the supreme
meetings of the assembly, or those offices that necessitate eating
with each other. ⟦Further, since oligarchy is defined by birth,
wealth, and education, what is democratic is held to be their oppo- 40
sites, low birth, poverty, and vulgarity.⟧ Next, (10) in respect to the
offices it is democratic for none to be perpetual; and if such an
office survives after an ancient change of constitution, it is demo- **1318^a**
cratic for its power to be taken away and for it to be filled by lot and
no longer by election.

1318ᵃ3   The things common to democracies, then, are these.
And from the justice that is agreed to be democratic (which is for
5   all to have an equal share on the basis of number) what is held to
be most of all a democracy and a people comes about. For to be
equal is for the needy to rule no more than the prosperous, nor to
be alone supreme, but for all to rule equally on the basis of number.
For in this way men would recognize that equality and freedom
10   belong to the constitution.

CHAPTER 3

1318ᵃ11   The next issue is the puzzle how they are to have equality. Should they divide the assessed property so that that of the five
hundred is equal to that of the thousand, and give the thousand
power equal to the five hundred? Or is this not the way to institute
the equality that accords with this principle ⟨of balance⟩? Should
they instead divide in the foregoing manner but then take equal
15   numbers from the five hundred and from the thousand and make
these men supreme over the elections and the courts? Is this, then,
the justest constitution according to democratic justice, or is it
rather the one based on the quantity ⟨of free men⟩? For the democrats say that justice is whatever seems right to the majority,
20   whereas the oligarchs say it is whatever seems right to the owners
of the most property. For the latter say that it is on the basis of
quantity of property that it ought to be judged. But both views
involve inequality and injustice. For if justice is whatever the few
decide, there will be tyranny (for if one man has more property
than the other prosperous men, on the basis of oligarchic justice it
is just for him to rule alone); if, on the other hand, justice is
25   whatever the majority decide on the basis of number, they will act
unjustly by confiscating the property of the rich, who are fewer—as
we said before.
   1318ᵃ27   What, then, would be an equality that both parties will
agree on? We must examine this question in the light of the definitions of justice they both offer. For they say that whatever seems
right to the majority of the citizens ought to be supreme. Let this
30   stand, though not completely. But since it happens that there are
two parts of which the city is composed, rich and poor, let whatever
seems right to both or to the majority of both be supreme, and if

opposing views are held, let whatever seems right to the majority
(that is, to those whose assessed property is greater) be supreme.
For example, if the rich are ten in number and the poor twenty, and
opposing views are held by six of the rich on one side and fifteen of
the needier on the other, four of the rich have been added to the 35
poor, and five of the poor to the rich. The side, then, whose property assessment is greater when both parts are added together
should be supreme. If the totals happen to be equal, one should
recognize this as a common problem, as one does now when the
assembly or the court is split. For one should settle the matter by lot 40
or devise some similar expedient.   1318ᵇ

   1318ᵇ1   But as for equality and justice, even if it is very difficult
to discover the truth about them, still this is easier than to persuade
men of it who have the power to get more and more. For it is the
weaker who always seek equality and justice; the strong give them 5
no thought.

<h3 align="center">CHAPTER 4</h3>

   1318ᵇ6   Of the four types of democracy, the first in order is the
best, as was said in our previous discussions. It is also the most
ancient of all. But I call it first in the sense in which one might
distinguish peoples. For the agricultural people is best, and so it is
also possible to fashion a democracy where the mass lives by agri- 10
culture or grazing. For because it does not have much property, it
lacks leisure, so it does not attend the assembly frequently. And
because they do not have the necessities of life, they are busy with
their work and do not desire the possessions of others. Indeed,
working is more pleasant to them than engaging in politics and 15
holding office, where large gains are not to be gotten from the
offices. For the many desire profit more than honour. Here is proof.
They endured the ancient tyrannies and continue to endure oligarchies, if no one prevents them from working or takes anything
from them. For in no time some of them become wealthy while the 20
others escape poverty. Further, their being supreme over elections
and audits fills the need, if they have any love of honour. In fact,
among some peoples, even if it is not they who share in the election
of the offices but only certain persons who are elected in rotation
from all, as in Mantinea, still if they are supreme over deliberation, 25

this is sufficient for the many. And one must consider even this a form of democracy, as it was once in Mantinea. Just for this reason it is both advantageous and customary in the forementioned democracy for all the citizens to elect to the offices and to conduct

30 audits and to judge, but for men elected on a property qualification to hold the highest offices (the higher the office, the higher the property qualification), or else for no office to be based on a property qualification, but rather to be held by men who are able ⟨to rule⟩. Men governed this way are necessarily governed well (for the offices will always be in the hands of the best men with the people

35 being willing and not envious toward the worthy), and this arrangement is certain to be satisfactory to the worthy and the notables. For they will not be ruled by others who are their inferiors, and they will rule justly because others are supreme over the audits. For to be constrained and not to be able to do everything that strikes one's fancy is advantageous. For the licence to do whatever one

40 wants has no power to keep guard over the evil in each man.

1319ᵃ So what is most beneficial in constitutions necessarily comes about: the worthy, being kept from error, rule, while the mass in no way loses.

1319ᵃ4 That this, then, is the best type of democracy is evident,

5 and also the reason why—because the people are of a certain quality. For the purpose of making a people agricultural, certain of the laws laid down by many in ancient times are extremely useful, such as prohibiting the possession of more land than a certain measure, either completely or situated between a certain place and

10 the town or city. There was, in ancient times at least, in many cities legislation forbidding even the sale of the first allotments; and there is also a law which they attribute to Oxylus that has a similar sort of power, forbidding lending against a certain part of the land belonging to each person. But nowadays one should also rectify things by the law of the Aphytaeans, for it is useful for the purpose of which

15 we speak. For the Aphytaeans, though numerous and possessing little land, are nevertheless all engaged in agriculture. For they assess the value of properties not as wholes, but by dividing them up in parts so small that even the poor can exceed in the valuations of their property ⟨the value required for citizenship⟩.

1319ᵃ19 After the agricultural mass, the best people is where

20 they are herdsmen and live off livestock. For in many respects their work is similar to agriculture; and in regard to military actions they

are very well trained in their dispositions, serviceable in body, and able to live in the open. The other masses, from which the remaining democracies are composed, are almost all much worse than 25 these. For their life is bad, and there is no connection with virtue in the work to which the mass of artisans and that of men of trade and the labouring class put their hand. Furthermore, because they roam around the market-place and the town, this entire class (roughly speaking) can easily attend the assembly, while those who farm, 30 because they are scattered about the country, neither attend so readily nor have a similar need of this meeting. And where it also happens that the country is so situated that it is far removed from the city, it is even easier for a good democracy or polity to be constructed. For the mass is compelled to make their settlements in 35 the fields, so that even if there is a rabble of traders, one should simply not hold meetings of the assembly in democracies without the mass of citizens scattered over the country.

1319ᵃ38   How, then, one ought to go about establishing the best and first democracy has been described. It is also evident how one ought to establish the others. For they should deviate in order, and 40 always exclude the worse mass of people.

1319ᵇ1   The ultimate democracy, because everyone participates in the constitution, is one that not every city can bear; nor is it easy for it to endure, if it is not well constituted in its laws and habits. (The things that serve to destroy both this and the other constitutions have for the most part been spoken of before.) With a view to 5 establishing this sort of democracy and making the people strong, the leaders are accustomed to add as many as possible to the citizen body and to make citizens, not only of those who are legitimate, but also of those who are illegitimate or descended from a citizen on only one side—I mean the side of the father or the mother. For all 10 this element is congenial to this sort of democracy particularly. Popular leaders are accustomed, then, to establish such a constitution in this way; but they should add citizens only until the mass outnumbers the notables and those in the middle, and not go beyond this. For when they overshoot, they make the constitution more disorderly and incite the notables even more toward reluctant 15 endurance of the democracy, which was in fact a cause of the faction at Cyrene. For a small base element is overlooked; but when it becomes numerous, it is more before one's eyes.

1319ᵇ19   Again, the sorts of devices useful to a democracy of 20

45

this kind also include the sort that Cleisthenes used at Athens when he wished to augment the democracy, and the sort used at Cyrene by those who established the democracy. For different and more numerous tribes and brotherhoods should be formed, and one should unite private religious rites into a few public ones, and one 25 should devise everything so that all citizens mix as much as possible with one another and the former intimacies are broken up.

1319^{b}27 Again, the devices characteristic of tyranny are also all held to be democratic. I mean, for example, the unruliness of slaves (which may be advantageous up to a point) and of women and 30 children, and indulgence to live as one wishes. For numerous will be the element supporting this sort of constitution. For it is more pleasant for the many to live orderlessly than temperately.

CHAPTER 5

1319^{b}33 For the lawgiver and those wishing to frame a constitution of this sort, it is not the work of establishing the constitution 35 that is their greatest or only work, but rather of seeing that it is preserved; for it is not difficult for those who govern themselves in any way whatsoever to hold their ground for one or two or three days. That is why the lawgivers must draw upon our earlier studies about what preserves and destroys constitutions and from these try to establish stability, avoiding what destroys constitutions while 40 enacting the sort of laws, both unwritten and written, that will best **1320^a** encompass what preserves constitutions. And they must not consider that measure to be democratic or oligarchic which will make the city to be governed in the highest degree democratically or oligarchically, but which will make it to be so governed for the longest time.

1320^{a}4 The demagogues nowadays, to curry favour with the 5 people, confiscate a large amount of property through the courts. That is why those who care about the constitution must act in opposition to these confiscations by passing a law that nothing belonging to those who are condemned is to be public property and go to the community, but is to be sacred property. For those who act unjustly will be no less cautious (for they will be fined in the 10 same way); but the rabble will vote less often to condemn those who are brought to trial, when they themselves are going to get nothing. Again, those who care about the constitution must always make the public lawsuits that occur as few as possible by deterring with large penalties those who indict at random. For they are accustomed to prosecute, not the people, but the notables; but all of the citizens ought, if possible, to be well-disposed toward the 15 constitution, or failing that, they should at least not regard those who are supreme as enemies.

1320ᵃ17 Since ultimate democracies are populous and since it is difficult for the citizens to attend the assembly without pay, this situation, unless there happen to be ⟨special⟩ revenues, is hostile to the notables. For the pay for the assembly must come from property taxes and confiscation and bad courts, things which have 20 before now overturned many democracies. Where, then, there do not happen to be ⟨special⟩ revenues, one should hold few assemblies and have courts with many jurors, but sitting only on a few days. (For this leads to the wealthy not fearing the expense, if the prosper- 25 ous do not take jury pay but only the needy. And it leads also to lawsuits being judged much better; for the prosperous are not willing to be absent from their private affairs for many days, though for a short time they are willing.) On the other hand, where there are ⟨special⟩ revenues, one should not do what nowadays de- magogues do. (For they distribute the surplus; but as soon as the 30 poor receive it, they need the same again; for this sort of aid to the needy is like the jar that has been punctured.) But the truly demo- cratic man should see that the mass is not too needy; for this is a cause of the democracy being bad. Measures must, therefore, be devised so that prosperity may be long-lasting. Since this is also 35 advantageous to the prosperous, they should pool the proceeds from the ⟨special⟩ revenues and distribute it in lump sums to the needy, especially if someone is able to amass enough for acquiring a small plot of land, or, failing that, for a start in trade or agriculture. And if this is not possible for all, they should distribute the funds in **1320ᵇ** rotation according to tribes or some other section. In the meantime the prosperous should contribute the pay for the necessary meet- ings, while being excused themselves from senseless liturgies.

1320ᵇ4 By governing in such a way the Carthaginians have 5 made the people a friend. For by constantly sending out some of the people to the outlying hamlets, they make them prosperous. It is possible, too, for notables who are refined and sensible to divide up the needy and to give them a start in pursuing some line of work.

It is also proper to imitate the policies of the Tarantines. For by
10 making their possessions communal for use by the needy, they
make the mass well-disposed. Again, they made all the offices of
two kinds, some elective and others filled by lot: some filled by lot,
so that the people may share in them; others elective, in order that
they may be governed better. But it is possible to do this also by
15 dividing the holders of the same office between those selected by
lot and those who are elected.

1320^{b}16 We have said, then, how democracies should be
established.

CHAPTER 6

1320^{b}18 With regard to oligarchies also it is fairly evident
from these considerations how they ought to be established.
For it is from their opposites that one must put together each
20 oligarchy, calculating its structure in comparison with the opposite
democracy.

1320^{b}21 The most well-tempered of the oligarchies and first in
order is the one near to so-called constitution ⟨i.e. polity⟩. In it the
lawgivers should divide the property qualifications, making some
smaller and some larger, the smaller providing the basis upon
which men will share in the necessary offices, and the larger that
25 upon which they will share in the more supreme. They should allow
anyone who acquires the qualifying property to share in the constitution, bringing in through the property qualification so large a
number of the people that with this number those who share in the
constitution will be stronger than those who do not; and they
should always take the participants in the constitution from the
better section of the people.

1320^{b}29 In a similar way the lawgivers should also establish
30 the oligarchy that comes next by tightening the qualifications a
little.

1320^{b}30 As for the constitution opposite to ultimate democracy, the most dynastic and tyrannical of the oligarchies, to the
extent that it is worst, it requires proportionately more safeguarding. For just as bodies that are in a good condition with respect to
health, and ships that are well constituted for sailing and in respect
35 of their crews, admit of more mistakes without being destroyed by

48

them, whereas bodies that are diseased and ships whose joints are unstrung and that are manned with bad sailors are unable to bear even the smallest mistakes, so too the worst constitutions are in need of the most safeguarding.

1321ᵃ1 In democracies, then, it is populousness that generally   **1321ᵃ** preserves them (for this is opposed to justice according to worth), but oligarchy on the contrary must clearly secure its safety by good structure.

CHAPTER 7

1321ᵃ5 Since there are four principal parts of the mass—farmers, 5 artisans, traders, and labourers—and four forces useful for war— mounted, hoplite, light-armed, and naval—where the country happens to be suited to horsemen, there it is natural to establish an oligarchy that is strong (for the safety of the inhabitants is through 10 this sort of force, and the keeping of horses is the privilege of those possessing large properties), and where it is suited to hoplites, there it is natural to establish the next kind of oligarchy (for the hoplite force is made up of the prosperous rather than the needy), and the light-armed force and the naval force are entirely democratic.

1321ᵃ14 As things are, then, where such a mass is numerous, when they quarrel, the rich often get the worst of it; but one should 15 adopt a remedy for this from the generals who are skilled in war, who conjoin to their mounted and hoplite forces an appropriate force of the light-armed. It is in this way that in party quarrels the people prevail over the prosperous; for though they are light- armed, they contend easily against mounted and hoplite forces. 20 For the rich, then, to institute this force from these elements of the people is to institute it against themselves. Rather, since age is divided into periods, and some people are older and some young, they should have their sons, while young, taught light-armed and unarmed exercises so that when they have been taken out of 25 the ranks of the boys, they will themselves be masters of these tasks.

1321ᵃ26 There should be an awarding of a share in the governing class to the mass either, as we said before, to those who acquire the property qualification, or, as with the Thebans, to those who refrain for a certain time from vulgar occupations, or, as at

30 Massalia, by making a judgement about who is worthy of
inclusion among those already in the governing class and those
outside it.

1321ᵃ31   Again, the most supreme offices also, which those
within the constitution must hold, should have liturgies attached to
them, in order that the people may be willing not to participate in
them and may have sympathy for those who rule, on the ground
that they pay a high price for office. It is fitting that upon entering
35 office they should offer magnificent sacrifices and should build
something public, so that the people, sharing in the feasting and
seeing the city being adorned with votive offerings and with buildings, are glad to see the constitution enduring; and it will also
transpire that the notables have memorials of their expenditure.
40 But nowadays those connected with oligarchies do not do this,
but the opposite; for they seek the profits no less than the honour
of office. That is why it is well to call these constitutions small
1321ᵇ democracies.

1321ᵇ1   Let us, then, take the matter of how democracies and
oligarchies should be instituted as settled in this way.

CHAPTER 8

1321ᵇ4   Following what has been said there is the matter of
properly dividing what relates to the offices, how many offices
5 there are, and what they are, and what they deal with—as has
already been said. For without the necessary offices a city cannot
exist; and without those relating to good structure and order, it
cannot be well managed. Again, in small cities the offices are
necessarily fewer, whereas in large cities they are more numerous
10 (as has already been said). For this reason what sorts of office it
is fitting to combine and what sorts to separate must not be
overlooked.

1321ᵇ12   First, then, among the necessary offices is supervision
of the market-place, over which there must be an office to keep an
eye on contracts and good order. For it is necessary in nearly all
15 cities for the inhabitants to buy some things and to sell others in
order to supply each other's necessary needs; and this is the readi-
est means of securing self-sufficiency, on account of which men are
thought to come together into one constitution.

1321ᵇ18   Another kind of supervision, which comes next to this
and is close to it, is the supervision of the public and private
properties in town, so that there may be good order; and the
preservation and rectification of crumbling buildings and roads;   20
and the supervision of the boundaries between each other's property, so that they are not a source of dispute; and any other sorts of
supervision similar to these. Most people call this sort of office
town-management, though its parts are more than one in number;
and they appoint different men to these different parts in the more   25
populous cities: for example, wall-builders, superintendents of the
fountains, and guardians of the harbours.

1321ᵇ27   Another office is necessary and very similar to the last
one; for it deals with the same things, though it concerns the country and matters outside town. Some people call these officials country managers; others call them forest wardens.   30

1321ᵇ30   These, then, are three sorts of supervision of these
things; but another office is that through which the public revenues
are received, guarded, and disbursed to each department. People
call these officials receivers or treasurers.

1321ᵇ34   Another office is that through which private contracts
and the verdicts from the law courts must be registered. With these   35
same officials, too, indictments and initiations of lawsuits must take
place. In some places they divide this office also into several,
though there are places where one office is supreme over all these
things. The officials are called sacred recorders, supervisors,
recorders, and other names close to these.

1321ᵇ40   Coming next after this—perhaps the most necessary   40
and most trying of all offices—is the one that is concerned with
exacting the penalties from those who have been condemned and
from those who have been posted according to the lists ⟨as debtors
to the city⟩, and with the custody of their persons. The office is   **1322ᵃ**
trying because it evokes a great deal of hostility, so that where it is
not possible to make great profits from it, people either do not
consent to hold it or, when they do consent, are unwilling to act in
accordance with the laws. The office is necessary in that lawsuits   5
about matters of justice are of no benefit when they do not attain
their end, so that if when lawsuits do not take place, it is impossible
for men to associate with each other, it is also impossible when
exaction of penalties does not take place. That is why it is better for
this office not to be a single office, but to consist of different

persons from different law courts, and why in regard to the posting
10 of the names of those registered as debtors, one should try to divide
the task in the same way. Furthermore, the officials too should
exact some penalties, and especially the new officials the penalties
imposed by last year's officials; and in the case of penalties imposed
by officials currently in office, when one office has condemned, a
different office should be the one that exacts the penalty. For
example, the town managers should exact the penalties imposed by
the market managers, and other officials those imposed by the
15 former. For the less hostility in it for those who exact the penalty,
the more will such exactions attain their end. Where the same
persons both condemn and exact the penalty, there is double hostility; but where they are the same in all cases, there is total enmity.
In many places the office of keeping custody is combined with the
20 one that exacts penalties, as, for example, at Athens with the so-
called Eleven. This is why it is better to separate off this office too
and to seek the appropriate stratagem with regard to it as well. For
it is no less necessary than the one that has been spoken about; but
what happens is that while the worthy shun this office most of all,
it is not safe to make bad men supreme. For they are more in need
25 of custody themselves than capable of exercising custody over
others. That is why there should not be one office specially assigned
to attend to them ⟨i.e. those in custody⟩, nor the same office continuously, but different persons—successive sections both of the
young (where an organization of cadets or guards exists) and of the
officials—should take charge of the matter.

1322^a29 These offices, then, must be placed first as most
30 necessary, and after these must be set those that are no less necessary, but ranked higher in dignity; for they require much experience and trustworthiness. Such would be the offices concerned with
guarding the city, and any that are appointed for military needs. In
35 peace just as in war there must be officials who supervise the
guarding of gates and walls and the inspecting and marshalling of
the citizens. In some places the offices for all these things are
greater in number, in others fewer—in small cities, for instance,
there is one office for all of them. People call these sorts of officials
1322^b generals and warlords. Again, if there are also mounted or light-
armed troops or archers or a navy, an office is sometimes instituted
over each of these as well. These offices are called naval commands, cavalry commands, and corps commands; and those under

them in turn trireme commands, company commands, and squadron commands; and similarly for any parts of these. The totality of   5
these things is a single kind, supervision of military affairs.

1322^{b}6   In regard to this office, then, this is the way things are.
But since some offices, if not all, manage large amounts of public
property, it is necessary for there to be a different office that
receives an account and also does an audit, an office that manages
nothing else itself. Some people call these officials auditors; others   10
call them accountants, inspectors, or advocates.

1322^{b}12   Besides all these offices there is the one that is most
supreme in all things; for the same office often has in its hands the
implementation as well as the introduction of a measure, or presides over the mass, where the people are supreme. For there must
be a body that convenes the supreme element in the constitution.   15
In some places these officials are called pre-councillors because
they conduct preliminary deliberations; but where the mass rules,
they are called a council instead.

1322^{b}17   The offices that are political are about this many. But
another kind of supervision is that concerning the gods: for example, priests and superintendents of matters concerning the temples
(such as the preservation of existing buildings and the restoration   20
of those that are crumbling) and of all other things that have been
set aside for the gods. It happens that this supervision in some
places is unified, for instance, in small cities; but in other places it
involves many officials who are separate from the priesthood: for
example, masters of the sacrifices, guardians of the shrines, and
treasurers of the sacred funds. Next to this is the office set aside for   25
all the public sacrifices that the law does not assign to the priests
but which have the honour ⟨of being celebrated⟩ from the public
hearth. Some people call these officials archons; others call them
kings or presidents.

1322^{b}29   The necessary sorts of supervision, then, are con-   30
cerned with the following, to speak summarily: with religious and
military matters; with revenues and expenditures; with the market-
place; with the town, harbours, and country; and further with the
courts, registration of contracts, exacting of penalties, custody of
prisoners, accounts, and inspection and auditing of officials—and   35
finally they are concerned with the element that deliberates about
public affairs.

1322^{b}37   On the other hand, peculiar to the cities that have

more leisure and are more flourishing and that also pay attention to
good order are the offices of superintendent of women, guardian of
the laws, superintendent of children, director of gymnastics, and
1323ᵃ in addition to these the supervision of gymnastic and Dionysiac
contests and of any other such spectacles there may happen to be.
Some of these offices, such as those of superintendent of women
and superintendent of children, are clearly not democratic; for the
5 needy must use their wives and children as attendants due to their
lack of slaves.

   1323ᵇ6 There are three offices under whose supervision various
people elect the highest officials: the guardians of the law, the pre-
councillors, and the council. Of these the guardians of the law
are aristocratic, the pre-councillors oligarchic, and the council
democratic.

   1323ᵃ9 Regarding the offices, then, we have spoken in outline
10 about nearly all of them.

COMMENTARY

BOOK FIVE

This book is a study of political pathology. Aristotle regards faction as a disease of the body politic and change from one sort of constitution to another as its death. He wishes to understand the causes of faction and constitutional change so that he can suggest remedies to the physicians of the body politic—the lawgiver and the statesman (9. 1309^{b}35–6).

CHAPTER I

In the brief opening section Aristotle lists the questions he intends to discuss in Book V. The first of these occupies the first four chapters. As he begins to address the first question in the present chapter, he introduces the main concepts he will deploy throughout the rest of this book. This makes the chapter the philosophically richest part of Book V.

1301^{a}19–25

The five questions listed in this section fall under four heads: the change, destruction, transformation, and preservation of constitutions. The fourth and fifth questions are both about the preservation of constitutions; and some scholars have thought that they are not distinct, the fifth being either Aristotle's alternative formulation of the fourth or the marginal note of a later reader that has crept into the text. But Newman notes that the same two questions are posed elsewhere in much the same terms (IV. 2. 1289^{b}23–6 and VI. 1. 1316^{b}34–5), and he finds other passages where Aristotle similarly distinguishes a *way* in which something comes about from *the means by which* it comes about (III. 18. 1288^{a}39–40, VII. 8. 1328^{a}41–^{b}1, VII. 15. 1334^{b}5). There is a good illustration of this distinction in Aristotle's discussion of tyranny where he distinguishes two ways of preserving tyranny, repression and moderation, from the many means along each path (11. 1313^{a}34, 1314^{a}29–32).

The five questions are almost, but not quite, the programme of Book V, as the following Table of Contents shows:

A. Introduction (1. 1301ᵃ19–25).
B. The general causes of factions and constitutional change (1. 1301ᵃ25 to the end of Ch. 4).
C. The causes of factions and constitutional change that are specific to particular constitutions:
    i. Democracy (Ch. 5);
    ii. Oligarchy (Ch. 6);
    iii. Aristocracy and polity (Ch. 7).
D. The means by which constitutions are preserved (Chs. 8–9).
E. Monarchies:
    i. The causes of their destruction (Ch. 10);
    ii. The means by which they are preserved (Ch. 11);
    iii. The short lives of tyrannies (12. 1315ᵇ11–39).
F. Plato's discussion of constitutional change in the *Republic* (12. 1316ᵃ1–end).

The first, second, and fourth questions correspond to items B, C, and D respectively in this Table of Contents while the third question is dealt with in passing in Chapters 5 through 7 and elsewhere in the book.

Nothing in the introductory section prepares us for the distinction between monarchy, the one-man rule of tyrants and kings, and constitutions proper, which is such a prominent feature of Aristotle's discussion of monarchy (10. 1311ᵃ22–5, ᵇ37; 12. 1315ᵇ40–1; see also III. 15. 1286ᵇ11–13) and a major organizing principle of the whole book. The book in effect splits into two major parts (see 10. 1310ᵃ39–ᵇ3), the first on constitutions proper and the second on monarchy. The elaborate treatment afforded the destruction and preservation of monarchies occupies fully one-third of the whole book and almost balances the attention afforded the four constitutions proper.

1301ᵃ25–ᵇ4

Aristotle begins with a reference to the summary of his theory of distributive justice in Book III (9. 1280ᵃ7–25 and 12. 1282ᵇ14–23), which in its turn refers back to the more elaborate development of the theory in *Nicomachean Ethics* V. 3. Distributive justice, according to this theory, is a kind of geometric proportion (*EN* V. 3. 1131ᵇ12–13) involving at least two persons, *A* and *B*, and two things, *C* and *D* (1131ᵃ18–20). In a just distribution the ratio of *C* to *D* is the same as that of *A* to *B*:

$$\frac{C}{D} = \frac{A}{B}.$$

In the passage before us Aristotle calls this equality of ratios 'the proportionately equal'. When he says that 'all agree about the just and the proportionately equal', the 'and' is explanatory. What he means is that all agree about the just *in the sense of* the proportionately equal: they all agree, in other words, about the principle of distributive justice (III. 12. 1282ᵇ18–21, *EN* V. 3. 1131ᵃ10–14).

This principle is both simpler and more complex than the formula above suggests. It is simpler in that its formula requires only two dummy names rather than four. The letters '*C*' and '*D*' disappear when one reflects that *C* is the thing allotted to *A*, and *D* the thing allotted to *B*. The first ratio can thus be replaced by the following one:

$$\frac{\text{the thing allotted to } A}{\text{the thing allotted to } B}.$$

The principle is more complex in that, as Aristotle implicitly acknowledges, persons do not stand in ratios to each other *per se* but only in certain respects such as height, age, wealth, and so forth; nor do things. The ratios in the formula imply a basis of comparison both of the persons and of the things. The basis of comparison of the things is their positive or negative value (*EN* V. 3. 1131ᵇ19–23), and that of the persons is their worth, or *axia* (*EN* V. 3. 1131ᵃ24, 26). So the formula becomes:

$$\frac{\text{the value of the thing allotted to } A}{\text{the value of the thing allotted to } B} = \frac{\text{the worth of person } A}{\text{the worth of person } B}.$$

According to Aristotle's theory of distributive justice a distribution is just if it follows this formula—if the value of the thing it allots to one person stands to the value of the thing it allots to another as the worth of the one person stands to the worth of the other.

The things being distributed are identified simply as shares in the constitution (1301ᵃ38). The expression 'to share in the constitution' (*metechein tēs politeias*) occurs frequently in the *Politics* (II. 8.

1268ᵃ27–8, 10. 1272ᵃ15; III. 2. 1275ᵇ31; IV. 5. 1292ᵃ41, 6. 1292ᵇ39, 1293ᵃ3–4, 8. 1294ᵃ14, 13. 1297ᵇ5–6, 23–4; V. 3. 1302ᵇ26–7; VI. 6. 1320ᵇ26; VII. 10. 1329ᵇ37, 13. 1332ᵃ33–5), and is apparently short for 'to share in *the offices under* the constitution'. The most basic offices in a Greek city were those of assemblyman (*ekklēsiastēs*) and juror (*dikastēs*). Aristotle defines a full citizen (*politēs haplōs*) as one who has the right to sit in the assembly or to serve on a jury (III. 1. 1275ᵃ22–3, ᵇ13–21). Thus, to share in a constitution is at a minimum to be a full citizen under it (III. 2. 1275ᵇ31–2). There are many other offices in a city besides those of assemblyman and juror. A citizen will have a larger or smaller share of the constitution depending upon how these other offices are distributed.

The broadest possible distribution of full citizenship considered in the *Politics*, though it reflects the general consensus of the classical period, stops far short of the total population of a city. Except for a quick glance at the scheme of Plato's *Republic* at II. 5. 1264ᵇ5–6, Aristotle never questions the exclusion of women, children, aliens, and slaves from among the claimants to a share of the constitution. The only ones with a reasonable claim to full citizenship in his eyes are free men, where a free man is taken to be an adult male who is neither foreign-born (see III. 2. 1275ᵇ22–4) nor a slave. A man who is free in this sense and does not share in the constitution—a poor man in an oligarchy, for example—is at most a second-class citizen.

In his earlier summary of his theory of justice Aristotle says that men 'agree about the equality of the thing but disagree about the equality for persons' (III. 9. 1280ᵃ18–19). They agree, in other words, about the value or disvalue of things but disagree about worth, or *axia*. Their disagreement is not in the first instance a disagreement about the worth of particular individuals but rather a more fundamental disagreement about the standard to be used in judging the worth of individuals. Is the standard freedom, wealth, good birth, virtue, or something else entirely? 'All agree', Aristotle says, 'that the just in distribution must be according to worth of some sort, though all do not recognize the same sort of worth; but democrats say it is freedom, oligarchs wealth or good birth, and aristocrats virtue' (*EN* V. 3. 1131ᵃ25–8).

It may be useful at this point to borrow the distinction drawn by John Rawls (pp. 5–6, 9–10) between the *concept* of distributive justice, the formal principle of distribution to which everyone assents, and the various *conceptions* of distributive justice, about which there is controversy. A *conception* of distributive justice is the *concept* with a particular standard of worth embedded. The democratic conception of distributive justice, for example, evaluates a person's worth according to the standard of freedom; and the oligarchic conception according to the standard of wealth. Everyone shares the same concept of distributive justice, but not the same conception.

We can now understand the arguments that Aristotle attributes to the champions of democracy and oligarchy. The basic premiss of the democratic argument is the democratic conception of justice, that shares of the constitution should be distributed on the basis of freedom:

$$\frac{\text{the value of the office allotted to } A}{\text{the value of the office allotted to } B} = \frac{\text{the freedom of } A}{\text{the freedom of } B}.$$

Its other premiss is that freedom does not come in degrees—that if A and B are free men, the freedom of A is equal to the freedom of B. From these two premisses it follows that all free men should have an equal share of the constitution. The oligarchic argument is similar. Its basic premiss, the oligarchic conception of justice, asserts that political office should be distributed on the basis of wealth:

$$\frac{\text{the value of the office allotted to } A}{\text{the value of the office allotted to } B} = \frac{\text{the wealth of } A}{\text{the wealth of } B}.$$

Its other premiss is that wealth is not evenly distributed among free men. It follows that not all free men should have an equal share of the constitution. A free man, A, who is richer than another free man, B, should have a larger share of the constitution than B; and B should have no share at all if he has no property at all. Aristotle thinks that these arguments explain the institutions that are characteristic of democracy and oligarchy.

He also thinks that the basic premiss of each argument is an expression of a mistaken standard of worth. The champions of democracy are wrong in thinking that free men are equal without qualification, and the champions of oligarchy are wrong in thinking that those who are unequal in wealth are unequal without qualification. To understand his point we must first of all understand what he means by 'without qualification', or *haplōs*. He explains the notion in the *Topics*: 'That thing is ⟨noble or the contrary⟩ without qualification (*haplōs*) which, without anything being added, you will say is noble or the contrary. For example, you will not say that sacrificing one's father is noble, but that it is noble for certain people. It is not therefore noble without qualification. But you will say that honouring the gods is noble, without adding anything; for it is noble without qualification. So whatever seems to be noble or shameful or anything else of the sort, without anything being added, will be called so without qualification' (II. 11. 115ᵇ29–35). The champions of democracy think they are equal without qualification because they are equal in respect of freedom; the champions of oligarchy think they are unequal without qualification because they are unequal in wealth (III. 9. 1280ᵃ22–5). Aristotle thinks they are both mistaken because neither democratic equality nor oligarchic inequality is unqualified. Democratic equality bears the qualification 'in respect of freedom' and oligarchic inequality the qualification 'in wealth'.

Aristotle himself thinks that the only persons who are unequal without qualification are those who are unequal in virtue (1301ᵃ40–ᵇ1). It is difficult, however, to understand why he is not making precisely the same mistake he attributes to the champions of democracy and oligarchy. According to his explanation of 'without qualification', two people are unequal without qualification if, and only if, we can say truly, without adding anything, that they are unequal. But when we say that two people are unequal in virtue, we do not, without adding anything, say they are unequal. We add the qualification 'in virtue'.

What, then, does 'without qualification' mean in the section before us? Perhaps we should try a different tack. Aristotle sometimes uses 'wholly' (*holōs*) as a synonym for 'without qualification' (*haplōs*) and opposes being equal or unequal in a certain respect to being wholly equal or wholly unequal (1301ᵃ31, ᵇ37; see also III. 9. 1280ᵃ22–5). Perhaps in the section before us 'without qualification' means simply 'in all relevant respects (not just one)'. But this does not seem to work either. The champions of democracy do not think that men who are equal in freedom are equal in wealth. Nor do the champions of oligarchy think that men who are unequal in wealth are unequal in freedom. The former think rather that men who are equal in freedom are equal in the only respect that counts, and the latter that men who are unequal in wealth are unequal in the only respect that counts. Aristotle's own idea is more subtle. He thinks that wealth and freedom count when shares of the constitution are being distributed—that is why he says that democracy and oligarchy have a bit of justice (1301^{a}35–6, III. 9. 1280^{a}9)—but that they do not count as much as virtue. When he says that those who are unequal in virtue are unequal without qualification, he means neither that they are unequal in the only respect that counts (for other respects do count) nor that they are unequal in every relevant respect (for those who are unequal in virtue may be equal in wealth and freedom and good birth). It seems, then, that in the section before us 'without qualification' cannot mean 'in all relevant respects'.

It is better to return to the definition of *haplōs*, or 'without qualification', in the *Topics* and to ask the following question: How, according to this definition, can those who are unequal in virtue be unequal without qualification? The answer seems to be that Aristotle regarded certain additions, such as 'by nature' (*kata phusin*) and 'in truth' (*kat' alētheian*), as redundant (for 'by nature' see *An. Post.* I. 2. 71^{b}33–72^{a}4, *Phys.* I. 1. 184^{a}16–18, *Met. Δ.* 11. 1018^{b}11, *EN* VII. 12. 1153^{a}5–6; for 'in truth' see *EN* III. 4. 1113^{a}23–4). To say that something has a given property by nature or in truth is not to say that it has the property in a particular respect but rather to say that it has the property without qualification. Thus, Aristotle will be able to say, consonant with his definition of 'without qualification', that those who are unequal in virtue are unequal without qualification if he can somehow equate inequality in virtue with inequality by nature or inequality in truth (i.e. true inequality). And that is precisely what he tries to do. He attempts to ground the aristocratic standard of worth in nature by demonstrating that it is the standard that would be used in a city that is in a natural condition (for details see Keyt 1991, pp. 238–78). In Books V and VI he tacitly assumes the success of this venture.

Aristotle must hold that there is a correct standard of worth. Otherwise, one conception of justice will be as good as any other, and he will end up with Protagorean relativism by which 'whatever things appear just and noble to each city are so for it as long as it holds by them' (Plato, *Theaet.* 167c4–5). If Aristotle is to avoid his old enemy (see *Met. Γ.* 3–6), he cannot rest content with the merely analytical view that there are different conceptions of justice corresponding to different standards of worth, such as wealth, freedom, and virtue. If he is to hold that there is truth and falsity among conceptions of distributive justice, he must hold that one of these standards or some combination of them is the true or correct standard and that the others are false. The standard that he defends is sometimes virtue alone (III. 9. 1281ᵃ4–8) and sometimes virtue backed by wealth (*aretē kechorēgēmenē*) (IV. 2. 1289ᵃ31–3, VII. 1. 1323ᵇ41–1324ᵃ1).

1301ᵃ28–35 Democracy and oligarchy

The Greek word for democracy, *dēmokratia*, means literally 'rule of the people (*ho dēmos*)'; and the Greek word for oligarchy, *oligarchia*, means literally 'rule of the few'. Who are the people and who are the few in a Greek city? The people are its farmers, herdsmen, traders (merchants and shopkeepers), craftsmen, artisans, labourers, and seamen (IV. 3. 1289ᵇ32–3, 4. 1291ᵇ18–28; VI. 1. 1317ᵃ24–6, 4. 1318ᵇ9–11, 1319ᵃ19–28, 7. 1321ᵃ5–6). Roughly speaking, they are all the male inhabitants, not counting slaves and aliens, who must work for a living. Over against the people stand the few, the men of wealth and privilege called 'the notables' (*hoi gnōrimoi*) (IV. 14. 1298ᵇ20–1; V. 4. 1304ᵃ25–7, 30, 6. 1305ᵇ16–17, 7. 1307ᵃ29–33, 10. 1310ᵇ12–14, 11. 1313ᵇ18). Notability, in the most expansive sense of the term, requires wealth, good birth, virtue, and education (IV. 3. 1289ᵇ33–1290ᵃ2, 4. 1291ᵇ28–30).

Both oligarchy and democracy are mistaken and deviant constitutions in which the rulers seek their own, rather than the common, advantage (III. 1. 1275ᵇ1–3, 6. 1279ᵃ17–21, 7. 1279ᵇ4–6). They are differentiated from each other in four different ways in the *Politics*, corresponding to four different ways of taking the opposition between the notables and the people. (1) Oligarchy is the rule of the few; democracy, of the many (III. 6. 1278ᵇ12–13, 8. 1279ᵇ21–2, 24–5; III. 7; VII. 9. 1328ᵇ32–3). (2) Oligarchy is the rule of the rich; democracy, of the poor (III. 7. 1279ᵇ7–9, 8. 1279ᵇ39–1280ᵃ5; IV. 4. 1291ᵇ7–13). (3) Oligarchy is the rule of those who own property; democracy, of those who are free (1301ᵃ28–33; see also III. 8. 1279ᵇ17–19; IV. 4. 1290ᵇ1–3, 8. 1294ᵃ11; VI. 2. 1317ᵃ40–1). (4) Oligarchy is defined by birth, wealth, and education; democracy by low birth, poverty, and vulgarity (VI. 2. 1317ᵇ38–41).

These different definitions of the two constitutions are not extensionally equivalent. A city that is a democracy by one definition can be an oligarchy by another—for example, if its rulers are a rich majority or a poor minority (III. 8 and IV. 4. 1290^a30–^b7). Though Aristotle emphasizes this point himself, he makes no attempt to stick with one definition of each constitution throughout the *Politics* but uses whichever definition suits his purpose for the matter at hand.

1301^a35–6 Aristotle says that democracy and oligarchy have a bit of justice because their standards of worth, unlike (say) height or athletic ability, are at least things that enter into the composition of a city (III. 12. 1283^a9–19). A city must have both wealth and free men: 'A city could not consist entirely of the needy, any more than of slaves' (1283^a18–19). A correct theory of distributive justice, Aristotle thinks, will need to distinguish three sorts of personal attribute: (1) those that are irrelevant to political office (e.g. athletic ability, height), (2) those that are relevant but not central (e.g. freedom, wealth), and (3) those that are central (e.g. virtue).

1301^a37–9 When their share of political power does not fit their mistaken conception of justice, the champions of democracy and oligarchy engage in faction, or *stasis*. *Stasis* is the Greek word for civil war as opposed to foreign war, or *polemos*. As Plato says in the *Republic*, 'It seems to me that just as these two names are used, *polemos* and *stasis*, so there are also two things, set off by two differentiae. The two ⟨differentiae⟩ I mean are the domestic and akin, and the foreign and alien. *Stasis* is used for hostility in the domestic sphere and *polemos* for hostility in the foreign' (V. 470b4–9). In the *Laws* Plato uses *polemos* as a generic term for war and defines *stasis* as one of its species, namely, the kind distinct from *polemos* against outsiders and foreigners (I. 629d1–5). But this generic use of *polemos* is unusual in Greek. *Polemos* and *stasis* are usually related as co-ordinate species rather than as genus to species.

Stasis was the curse of Greek political life and was justifiably regarded as worse than foreign war. After distinguishing the two kinds of war in the *Laws*, Plato calls civil war, or *stasis*, 'the cruellest of all wars' (I. 629d2), echoing an earlier evaluation of Herodotus, who remarks that '*stasis* among one's own people is worse than war by common consent in the same proportion as war is worse than peace' (8. 3. 1). Thucydides' famous account of the *stasis* that broke out in Corcyra during the Peloponnesian War vividly depicts its savagery (3. 69–85).

Within a political community *stasis* is opposed to *homonoia*, like-mindedness or concord, which Aristotle identifies with political friendship (*EN* IX. 6. 1167ᵇ2–3). 'We say that cities are of one mind,' Aristotle says, 'when they ⟨i.e. the citizens of each city⟩ agree about what is advantageous, choose the same things, and do that which is decided upon in common' (*EN* IX. 6. 1167ᵃ26–8), whereas 'when each of two persons wishes himself ⟨to rule⟩ . . . they engage in *stasis*' (*EN* IX. 6. 1167ᵃ32–4). Plato draws the same distinction between *stasis* and *homonoia* in the *Republic* (I. 351d4–6).

Greek has a variety of words from a single root to speak about *stasis*. To engage in *stasis* is signified by the infinitive *stasiazein*; a person who engages in *stasis* is called a *stasiōtēs*; and a band of *stasiōtai*, as well as the activity in which they are engaged, is referred to as a *stasis* (Her. 1. 59). There are other words from the same root, but these are the most important.

Stasis, *stasiōtēs*, and *stasiazein* present a special problem for the translator since there are no English words from a single root that capture their meaning. Three that come close are 'conspire', 'conspiracy', and 'conspirator'; but they lack the political implications of *stasis*. 'Rebellion' and 'rebel' (as both a noun and a verb) are closer in meaning, but English lacks a word from the same root for the party of rebels. 'Faction' has the appropriate political implications and is used both for partisan conflict and for the party of partisans. James Madison's definition of 'faction' in the famous paper *Number 10* of *The Federalist* captures the second sense of the word and could stand as the corresponding part of the definition of *stasis*: 'By a faction I understand a number of citizens, whether amounting to a majority or a minority of the whole, who are united and actuated by some common impulse of passion, or of interest, adverse to the rights of other citizens, or to the permanent and aggregate interests of the community' (Hamilton, p. 43). The main problem with 'faction' is the lack of a verb from the same root, though this obstacle can be surmounted at the price of a bit of wordiness. The best, though far from ideal, solution seems to be to translate *stasis* by 'faction' and to translate *stasiazein* by a variety of expressions that contain the word 'faction' such as 'to form a faction', 'to make a faction', 'to engage in faction', 'to fall into faction', 'to split into factions', and so forth. We do not need to find a translation for *stasiōtēs* since it does not occur in the *Politics*.

1301ᵃ39–40   The statement here that 'those who excel in virtue would form a faction with the most justice of anyone' is as close as Aristotle ever comes to acknowledging that faction might sometimes be justified.

1301ᵇ1–4   In the *Rhetoric* Aristotle distinguishes being well-bred (*gennaios*) from being well-born (*eugenēs*): 'Being well-born refers to the virtue of one's family; being well-bred refers to ⟨being from a good family and⟩ not departing from its ⟨virtuous⟩ nature, which is not usually the case among the well-born, many of whom are worthless' (II. 15. 1390ᵇ22–4). And he draws the same distinction in the *History of Animals*: 'Being well-born is being from a good family; being well-bred is ⟨being from a good family and⟩ not departing from its ⟨virtuous⟩ nature' (I. 1. 488ᵇ18–20). In the *Politics*, on the other hand, *eugenēs* and *gennaios* are used interchangeably. The latter occurs only twice (III. 13. 1283ᵃ35, IV. 12. 1296ᵇ22), and in both places it seems to be no more than a stylistic variant of *eugenēs*.

Aristotle defines *eugeneia* three times in the *Politics*. One definition—'Good birth is virtue of family' (III. 13. 1283ᵃ37)—repeats the definition of *eugenēs* in the *Rhetoric*. The definition in the passage before us—'those are reputed to be well-born who *have* the virtue and wealth of their forebears'—in spite of the fudging of most translators, corresponds to the definition of *gennaios* in the *Rhetoric*. Call this the strong sense of *eugenēs*. The third—'Good birth is ancient wealth and virtue' (IV. 8. 1294ᵃ21–2)—can be taken to define either the weak or the strong sense of *eugeneia*.

The argument of the passage before us, that the well-born are more worthy of office than the ill-bred, also seems to demand the strong sense of the term; for the worthless progeny of wealth and virtue would seem to have no special claim on political office. The passage is ambiguous none the less. For it is those who are superior *in family* who are said to claim a larger share of political office, which suggests that they differ from other claimants in descent from, rather than possession of, wealth and virtue. Perhaps the ambiguity here between a strong and a weak sense of 'well-born' is one that those who base their claim on family wish to cultivate.

1301ᵇ4–26

Aristotle distinguishes two sorts of constitutional change (*metabolē*): replacement and modification. These two sorts of constitutional change seem to be instances of the two sorts of change that he distinguishes in the *Physics*: (1) coming-to-be and ceasing-to-be (*genesis* and *phthora*) and (2) alteration (*kinēsis*) (*Phys.* V. 1. 224ᵇ35–225ᵃ20). The first is change *of* substance, such as Socrates coming to exist at conception and ceasing to exist at death; the second is change *of a* substance, such as Socrates walking to the market-place, growing bald, or getting fat. The difference between the two kinds of change is that the one destroys identity, the other does not.

The analysis of the *Physics* applies to cities as well as to plants and animals, the ordinary Aristotelian substances. It is Aristotle's view that a city is at least a quasi-substance. It exists by nature (I. 2. 1252ᵇ30, 1253ᵃ2, 25; VII. 8. 1328ᵃ21–2) and is a compound of form and matter. Its matter (*hulē*) is its population, especially its citizen population, and its territory (VII. 4. 1325ᵇ37–1326ᵃ8); its form is its constitution (III. 3. 1276ᵇ1–4). Since the identity of a composite, and of a natural composite in particular, is constituted by its form rather than its matter, it follows that one city ceases to be and a different one comes to be when one constitution is replaced by another (III. 3. 1276ᵃ17–ᵇ13; Irwin, pp. 254–5). A city retains its identity when its constitution is merely modified. (See Polansky, pp. 324–5.)

In some translations of the *Politics metabolē* is rendered as 'revolution'. But this is misleading for at least two reasons. First of all, the word 'revolution' usually refers to the complete overthrow of a system of government and not simply to the modification of an existing system; but Aristotle explicitly counts the modification of a constitution, as well as the replacement of one constitution by another, as a *metabolē*. Secondly, translations of the *Physics* universally render *metabolē* as 'change'; hence to translate it as 'revolution' in the *Politics* conceals a connection between two parts of Aristotle's philosophy and makes the *Politics* seem more self-contained than it actually is.

Aristotle distinguishes three sorts of constitutional modification. A faction that seeks something less than the complete overthrow of an established constitution might wish (*a*) to replace those currently in office with its own members, or (*b*) to moderate or radicalize the existing constitution, or (*c*) to change a part of the constitution.

1301ᵇ4–5 Factions originate in disputes over equality and inequality, not exclusively, but 'generally speaking'. Other origins and springs of faction are listed in Chapter 2.

1301ᵇ9 Polity, in which the rulers are many, and aristocracy, in which they are few, are the correct constitutions from which democracy and oligarchy respectively deviate (III. 7). A correct constitution is one under which the rulers of a city seek the common advantage rather than their own (III. 6. 1279ᵃ17–21). They won't do this unless they have at least some of the moral virtues. For this reason a correct constitution must have an ethical standard of worth rather than an economic or juristic one like wealth or freedom. Aristocracy, however, has a higher standard than polity. Complete virtue is its standard whereas military virtue, which is but one part of complete virtue, is the standard of polity (III. 7. 1279ᵃ37–ᵇ4). The reason for the weaker requirement in a polity is the paucity of men of complete virtue (III. 7. 1279ᵃ39–ᵇ2). Military virtue seems to be the same thing as bravery (see II. 9. 1271ᵇ2–3 together with Plato, *Laws* II. 666e1–667a5; *EN* III. 6).

Although the account just given is Aristotle's basic account of polity and aristocracy, it does not explain the reference to polity and aristocracy in the passage before us. Consider aristocracy. Aristotle speaks of an established oligarchy being replaced by an aristocracy and of an established aristocracy being replaced by an oligarchy. But by Aristotle's strict standard there were no aristocracies in classical Greece (or anywhere else for that matter). Men of complete virtue are rare indeed. What sort of aristocracy, then, is he referring to?

The Greek word for aristocracy, *aristokratia*, means 'rule of the best men (*hoi aristoi*)'. (Aristotle suggests rather fancifully that it might also mean that the rulers under such a constitution aim at the best (*to ariston*) (III. 7. 1279ᵃ35–7).) Who are the best men in a city? For Aristotle they are the men of full virtue; for the ordinary Greek, as Aristotle tells us himself, they would be the men who possess wealth, good birth, and education (IV. 8. 1293ᵇ37–42, 1294ᵃ17–19; see also II. 6. 1266ᵃ20–1 and V. 1. 1301ᵇ40). But if these latter are the best men in actual cities, we will need to distinguish the aristocracies of wealth and birth of Greek history from the idealized aristocracies of virtue of Aristotle's definition. It can only be to an aristocracy in the vernacular sense that Aristotle refers when he speaks of an established aristocracy becoming an oligarchy.

A similar distinction must be drawn within the concept of a polity. Aristotle in effect draws the distinction himself. For after characterizing polity as a constitution based on military virtue (III. 7. 1279ª37–ᵇ2), he immediately adds: 'That is why the element that defends the city in war is most supreme in this constitution and why those possessing heavy arms share in it' (1279ᵇ2–4; see also II. 6. 1265ᵇ28–9 and IV. 13. 1297ᵇ1–2). But having military virtue—being brave—and possessing heavy arms do not mark out the same set of individuals. In the *Nicomachean Ethics* Aristotle mentions some of the devices used by commanders to make up for a lack of true bravery in their troops (III. 8. 1116ª29–ᵇ3). Consequently, we have distinct definitions of polity, one of which defines a polity of the brave and the other, a polity of hoplites. When Aristotle says that men make a faction in order to introduce a polity in place of a democracy, it is to a polity of hoplites that he presumably refers.

Aristotle uses the same word, *politeia*, both for a constitution in general and for a polity—for the genus and for a species of the genus (III. 7. 1279ª37–9). This presents the translator with a problem. Should *politeia* be consistently rendered by the same word or not? Most, but not all, translators favour a compromise between accuracy and clarity, and use the transliteration 'polity' when *politeia* standing alone signifies the species and use the translation 'constitution' otherwise. The drawback to this compromise is that Aristotle has his own way of signifying the species: he uses the phrase 'so-called constitution' (*hē kaloumenē politeia*), whose meaning will be lost unless *politeia* is consistently rendered as 'constitution'. I follow the compromise in my translation nevertheless, and signal the meaning of 'so-called constitution' by adjoining '⟨i.e. polity⟩'. (For the expression *hē kaloumenē politeia* see IV. 3. 1290ª17–18, 7. 1293ᵇ9, 20; 9. 1294ª31; 11. 1295ª33–4; V. 6. 1306ᵇ6–7; VI. 6. 1320ᵇ22.)

1301ᵇ19–21 The kingship and the ephorate were two of the four parts of the Spartan constitution. The other two were the council of elders (*gerousia*) and the assembly (*ekklēsia*). (Aristotle discusses the Spartan constitution at length in II. 9 and returns to the subject at IV. 7. 1293ᵇ14–19, 9. 1294ᵇ13–40, and VII. 14. 1333ᵇ5–1334ᵃ10.) The Spartans were graced (or cursed) by the presence of two kings from two royal houses, the Agiad and the Eurypontid. The chief function of the two kings was to command the army (III. 14. 1285ᵇ26–8), though to preserve a unified command only one king could take the field at a time. The ephorate, the dominate part of the Spartan constitution, was composed of five ephors, who were elected annually by the assembly. Aristotle regarded the ephorate as a democratic element of the constitution because the office of ephor was open to any member of the assembly. The council of elders, so-called because only citizens over 60 could be elected, consisted of twenty-eight elders and, as ex officio members, the two kings. Once elected by the assembly, the elders held office for life. The principal function of the council of elders was to prepare measures for submission to the assembly. The assembly consisted of all Spartan males over 30 in good standing. In addition to electing the elders and the ephors, it voted on proposed laws and decided questions of war and peace.

On Lysander see the note to 7. 1306ᵇ31–3.

There were two famous men named 'Pausanias' in Spartan history, one of whom (following the Greek custom of naming) was the grandson of the other. The elder Pausanias, a member of the royal house of the Agiads, led the combined Greek army to its great victory over the Persians at Plataea in 479 BC. The younger Pausanias, an Agiad king, led the Spartan blockade of Athens in 405 BC. Aristotle refers to a Pausanias in two other places in the *Politics*. At VII. 14. 1333ᵇ34 (as in the passage before us) he is identified as 'the king'; at V. 7. 1307ᵃ4–5 he is identified as the man 'who was general during the Persian War'. It is a matter of controversy whether all three references are to the same man (see Newman's note to 1333ᵇ34). But since the elder Pausanias was not really a king, it would require a good deal of looseness on Aristotle's part to refer to him as one.

1301ᵇ21–6 Epidamnus (the later Roman Dyrrhachium and modern Durrës) was a colony of a colony. It was established around 627 BC by Corcyra, which in its turn was a colony of Corinth. By the middle of the fifth century BC Epidamnus was torn by faction, which eventually drew in Corcyra and Corinth and set them against each other (Thuc. 1. 24–30). This conflict between Corcyra and Corinth in its turn was one of the proximate causes of the Peloponnesian War.

As Aristotle describes it, the constitution of Epidamnus before it was modified had three main elements: an assembly of full citizens, a board of tribal leaders, and a single supreme official. The single supreme official is mentioned earlier in a chapter on kingship: 'and many make one man supreme over the administration ⟨of the city⟩; for there is an office of this sort in Epidamnus' (III. 16. 1287ᵃ6–7). The point of this remark is to contrast the internal administration of a city by a single individual with a permanent generalship. The constitution was changed in part by replacing the board of tribal leaders with a council. Compared to a board of tribal leaders, a council, being larger, is a democratic institution (IV. 15. 1299ᵇ32–6; see also VI. 2. 1317ᵇ30–1 and 8. 1323ᵃ9). (Oligarchy is rule of the few; democracy, of the many. See the note to 1301ᵃ28–35 above.) We can infer then that Aristotle is offering an example of an oligarchy being modified in a democratic direction.

It is an example of a modification rather than a change of constitution since the constitution retained two oligarchic features. First, office-holders alone are required to attend the assembly when officials are being elected. This is an oligarchic feature since attendance is likely to be slack among those for whom it is not required, thus giving the current office-holders a disproportionately large voice in the selection of their successors (compare IV. 9. 1294ᵃ37–9, 13. 1297ᵃ17–19, 21–4, 14. 1298ᵇ16–18). The single supreme official is the second oligarchic feature since it concentrates power in the smallest number of hands possible—one pair.

When did this modification take place? Aristotle does not say, though his use of the present tense—'it is still compulsory' (1301ᵇ23–4)—indicates that something resembling the modified constitution was still in existence in Epidamnus in Aristotle's own day. The constitution may have undergone further modification beyond the replacement of the board of tribal leaders while Aristotle was writing the *Politics*, for he switches from the present to the past tense in describing the second oligarchic feature. At 1287ᵃ7 he says that there *is* a single supreme official at Epidamnus whereas at 1301ᵇ26 he says there *was* such an official. (See Newman's note to 1301ᵇ25.)

1301ᵇ26–1302ᵃ8

This section on equality and inequality closely follows Plato's *Laws* VI. 756e8–758a2. But see also Isocrates, *Areopagiticus* 21.

1301ᵇ26–9 It is difficult to make sense of this sentence as it stands. Given that distributive justice is an equality of two ratios, its opening clause about faction being due to inequality and its final clause about men engaging in faction in pursuit of equality mean simply that injustice drives men to form factions in pursuit of justice (see also III. 9. 1280ᵃ11, III. 12. 1282ᵇ18, and *EN* V. 1. 1129ᵃ34–ᵇ1). So much is clear. But why is the inequality that gives rise to faction restricted to unequals not receiving the unequal shares that their conception of justice dictates? There is also inequality when equals receive unequal shares (*EN* V. 3. 1131ᵃ22–4; see also *Pol.* VII. 3. 1325ᵇ8–9). Indeed, as Aristotle parenthetically remarks, a permanent kingship among equals is just such an inequality. This leads one to suspect that some words have been lost. The sentence would make better sense if the phrase 'or equals receive unequal things' were inserted immediately preceding the parenthetical remark.

A permanent king is distinguished from a temporary one such as the official at Athens called 'king' (*basileus*), who had certain religious and judicial functions and was appointed by lot for one year only (see VI. 8. 1322ᵇ26–9). Aristotle's parenthetical remark implies that permanent kingship is just among unequals. To understand why, we need to see how his theory of distributive justice applies to kingship.

Kingship is one-man rule (*monarchia*) that looks to the common advantage (III. 7. 1279ᵃ33–4); it is the correct constitution from which tyranny deviates (III. 7. 1279ᵇ4–5). As a correct constitution it has an ethical standard of worth, but a higher standard than either aristocracy or polity. One might wonder how there could be a higher standard than the complete virtue of true aristocracy. But Aristotle maintains that just as there is a state of character worse than vice, so there is another that is better than virtue (*EN* VII. 1. 1145ᵃ15–27). Bestiality is worse than vice; heroic virtue is better than virtue. Thus, the three correct constitutions represent successively higher steps in an ethical hierarchy:

71

Heroic virtue   kingship
Complete virtue   aristocracy
Military virtue   polity.

If a man who is 'like a god among men' (III. 13. 1284ᵃ10–11) should
appear, Aristotle thinks that it is just for him to be king and to rule
as the gods are reputed to rule men, namely, without sharing power
(I. 12. 1259ᵇ10–17, III. 13. 1284ᵃ3–17, ᵇ25–34, III. 17. 1288ᵃ15–29,
VII. 14. 1332ᵇ16–23; *EN* VIII. 10. 1160ᵇ3–7). By the true, or aristocratic, conception of distributive justice:

$$\frac{\text{the value of the office allotted to } A}{\text{the value of the office allotted to } B} = \frac{\text{the virtue of } A}{\text{the virtue of } B}.$$

Suppose now that the virtue of A is to the virtue of everyone else as
the virtue of a god is to the virtue of a human being—incommensurably superior. It follows that the value of the office allotted to A
should be incommensurably superior to the value of the office
allotted to anyone else. A should have all the power, and every
other person B none.

The argument that a kingship among equals is unequal is the
reverse of this. Suppose that the virtue of a king A is equal to the
virtue of every other free man B. Since A is a king, the value of
the office allotted to A is greater than the value of the office
allotted to anyone else. Hence:

$$\frac{\text{the value of the office allotted to } A}{\text{the value of the office allotted to } B} > \frac{\text{the virtue of } A}{\text{the virtue of } B}.$$

Thus, A's kingship is unequal.

There is a basic unclarity, it should be noted, in the notion that
one person's virtue is some given fraction (or multiple) of a second
person's. One person can be more virtuous than a second person; it
is sometimes even possible to rank a number of persons according
to their virtue or lack thereof—there can be little doubt how Plato
would rank Socrates, Pericles, and Critias—but it has no clear sense
to say that one person is x times as virtuous as a second. Virtue
differs from wealth in this respect: one person can be twice as
wealthy as another, but not twice as virtuous.

1301ᵇ29–35 Equality according to worth, or proportionate equality (1301ᵃ27), is an identity of ratios. For example, $^4/_2 = {}^2/_1$. Numerical equality is identity in size or number. For example,

$3 - 2 = 2 - 1$. Aristotle could have given a simpler example of numerical equality: for instance, $1 = 1$. But he wants his two examples to be as similar as possible. And, furthermore, identity statements are usually used to assert the identity of a thing under one description with the same thing under a different description. For both reasons $3 - 2 = 2 - 1$ is a better example to use than $1 = 1$.

$1301^b35-1302^a2$ Aristotle returns to the dispute related earlier in the chapter (1301^a25-35) between the free and the wealthy over personal worth, and explains the fact that democracy and oligarchy are more common than aristocracy in Greece on the grounds that the free and the wealthy vastly outnumber the well-born and the good in individual cities. The unstated premiss of his argument is that men tend to favour a conception of justice that favours them in the distribution of political office.

1302^a2-8 When Aristotle says that it is bad for a constitution to be structured entirely according to either sort of equality, he implies that oligarchy is structured according to proportionate equality and democracy according to numerical equality. In Book VI democratic justice and numerical equality are explicitly connected (2. 1317^b3-4, 1318^a3-6). This connection is both puzzling in itself and contrary to what Aristotle said earlier (1301^a25-35, 1301^b35-40). It is puzzling because the democratic conception of justice is one specification of the concept of distributive justice, which in turn is an instance of proportionate equality. So why does Aristotle associate democratic justice with numerical equality?

The answer seems to be that Aristotle is conflating the democratic *conception* of justice and the democratic *argument* for the equal distribution of political office. The democratic argument, it will be recalled, has two premisses: the democratic conception of justice and the notion that the freedom of one man is equal to the freedom of any other. These two premisses entail that the value of the office allotted to one free man should equal the value of the office allotted to any other free man—they entail a numerical equality. Thus, given the premiss that the freedom of one man is equal to the freedom of any other, the democratic conception of justice reduces to a numerical equality. By the same token in any city in which all wealthy men are equally wealthy, the oligarchic conception of justice reduces to a numerical equality. Even so, there is an important difference between the two cases. For it is *necessary* for all the free men in a city to be equally free, but not for the wealthy to be equally wealthy. And premisses that express necessary truths are normally suppressed as redundant, since their deletion does not destroy an argument's validity.

1302ᵃ4–8　No constitution based on one of the two kinds of equality to the exclusion of the other is enduring. As the surrounding context makes plain, Aristotle is referring here to democracy and oligarchy. The point is elaborated in Chapter 9 (1309ᵇ18–ᵇ35). The bad thing that lies in store for a city whose constitution is based on one kind of equality only is of course faction. The remedy, Aristotle suggests, is to use numerical equality in some things and proportionate equality in others. One way to do this might be to use numerical equality (i.e. freedom) in determining who is to sit in the assembly but proportionate equality (i.e. wealth) in determining who is eligible to stand for an executive or administrative office.

1302ᵃ8–15

The reason there is less faction in a democracy than in an oligarchy, Aristotle says, is that in a oligarchy faction breaks out both among the oligarchs themselves and between the oligarchs and the people whereas in a democracy it breaks out only between the people and the partisans of oligarchy. This argument seems to assume that factional conflict is easily sparked and increases with an increase in the potential sources of friction.

Aristotle's statement that 'faction worth mentioning' does not arise within the populace itself might seem to imply that the interests of the people were monolithic. But this was not so. As Newman points out (ad loc.), there were numerous potential sources of friction and hence of faction within the populace itself arising from differences in occupation, wealth, extraction, race, and so forth. Artisans and farmers did not always see eye to eye (Aristoph. *Eccles.* 431–3); the needy were sometimes a drain on the revenue of a city to the detriment of farmers and artisans (see VI. 5. 1320ᵃ29–32); those of pure extraction would disenfranchise those of tainted blood when the opportunity arose (III. 5. 1278ᵃ27–34; see the note to 3. 1303ᵃ38–ᵇ2); and colonists of different stock often came to blows (3. 1303ᵃ25–ᵇ3).

Aristotle says that the constitution of those in the middle is 'the most stable of these kinds of constitution'. Those in the middle (*hoi mesoi*) are those who are neither rich nor poor (IV. 3. 1289ᵇ29–31, 11. 1295ᵇ1–3). The constitution in which they predominate is the middle constitution (*hē mesē politeia*), the constitution between oligarchy and democracy, which is sometimes identified with polity (II. 6. 1265ᵇ26–9; IV. 11. 1296ᵃ7, 37–8; see also the note to 9. 1309ᵇ18–1310ᵃ2 and the introductory note to VI. 6). It is the most stable, not of all constitutions, but of all those that deviate from true aristocracy (IV. 8. 1293ᵇ22–7, 11. 1296ᵃ13–18; Jowett, ad loc.).

CHAPTER 2

The prime interpretative question of this chapter is the relation of its threefold classification of the causes of faction and constitutional change to the analysis of causation of Aristotle's general philosophy.

In his general philosophy Aristotle distinguishes four kinds of cause, traditionally referred to as final, formal, efficient, and material (*An. Post.* II. 11; *Phys.* II. 3, 7; *Met.* A. 3. 983ᵃ26–32, Δ. 2). Not everything possesses all four causes (*Met.* H. 4. 1044ᵇ6–12); but the complete explanation of those that do must mention all four (*Met.* H. 4. 1044ᵃ32–4). Such an explanation tells what the thing is, what it is made of, what its purpose is, and what brought it into existence: it describes its form (formal cause), matter (material cause), end (final cause), and origin (efficient cause). A house, for example, is 'a shelter to prevent destruction by wind and rain and heat' made of 'stones and bricks and timber' (*Anim.* I. 1. 403ᵇ3–6; see also *Met.* H. 2. 1043ᵃ14–18); its purpose is the preservation of one's goods (*An. Post.* II. 11. 94ᵇ8–11); and it owes its existence to 'the art of building and the builder' (*Met.* B. 2. 996ᵇ6–7, Δ. 4. 1070ᵇ29). The production of artefacts provides the best illustration of the four causes, but Aristotle intended the doctrine to be of broad application and to apply in particular to the generation of plants and animals (*GA* I. 20–3; *Met.* H. 4. 1044ᵃ34–ᵇ1).

Though the explanatory framework of the four causes is scarcely visible in the *Politics*, the subject matter of the treatise clearly falls within its scope. For the ultimate focus of the treatise is upon the city, and a city has all four causes. The material cause of a city is its population, especially its citizen population, and its territory (VII. 4. 1325ᵇ37–1326ᵃ8). Its formal cause is its constitution (III. 3. 1276ᵃ17–ᵇ13), which 'is a certain structure of those who inhabit the city' (III. 1. 1274ᵇ38; see also III. 6. 1278ᵇ8–10; IV. 1. 1289ᵃ15–18, 3. 1290ᵃ7–13). Its final cause is the end, or goal, of its constitution (IV. 1. 1289ᵃ15–18)—for example, conquest and war in the case of the Spartan constitution (II. 9. 1271ᵇ2–3, VII. 2. 1324ᵇ2–9, and VII. 14. 1333ᵇ12–14). And its efficient cause is the lawgiver or lawgivers who designed its constitution (VII. 4. 1325ᵇ40–1326ᵃ5)—the crafts-man or craftsmen (*dēmiourgoi*) of its constitution (II. 12. 1273ᵇ32–4, 1274ᵇ18–19)—such men as Lycurgus at Sparta and Solon at Athens.

Two of the three causes of faction and constitutional change fit easily into the fourfold framework. The second of the three is clearly the final cause of faction and constitutional change. In refer-ring to it at 1302ᵃ21 Aristotle uses one of his expressions for a final cause, 'for the sake of' (*heneken*); and in a later chapter the two things for the sake of which men are said to form factions, profit and honour (1302ᵃ31–2), are explicitly called ends (*telē*) (10. 1311ᵃ28–31). The third of the three, the origin, or *archē*, of political tumult and faction (1302ᵃ21), is just as clearly an efficient cause. In the *Metaphysics* Aristotle distinguishes six senses of 'origin'. From his examples of the various senses it is clear that the sense of the word in the passage before us is the fourth: 'That non-constituent from which a thing first comes to be, and from which its alteration and change naturally originate: for example, a child comes from the father and the mother, and a fight from abuse' (*Met. Δ*. 1. 1013ᵃ7–10). A fight arising from abuse is similar to faction arising from one of the seven causes and origins mentioned at 1302ᵃ34–ᵇ3. But the definition of this sense of 'origin' in *Metaphysics Δ*. 1 is virtually identical with the definition of an efficient cause in *Metaphysics Δ*. 2 (1013ᵃ29–32). It seems clear, then, that the third of the three causes must be an efficient cause.

This interpretation of the second and third of the three causes of faction and constitutional change is reinforced by Aristotle's dis-cussion of the four causes in the *Physics* and the *Posterior Analytics*. In the former treatise (*Phys.* II. 7. 198ᵃ14–21), he illustrates the difference between a final and an efficient cause by a political example not far removed from those in the present chapter. He says that the number of causes corresponds to the number of answers to the question 'On account of what?' One kind of answer yields an efficient cause. For example, 'On account of what did they go to war?' 'Because they made a raid.' Another kind yields a final cause. For example, 'For the sake of what did they go to war?' 'In order that they may rule.' From the passage in the *Posterior Analytics* (II. 11. 94ᵃ36–ᵇ8) we can see that Aristotle had a concrete example in mind, namely, the Persian expedition against Eretria and Athens in 490 BC, which culminated in the Persian defeat at Marathon. The Persians made war on Athens because the Athenians, together with the Eretrians, attacked Sardis. (The story is told in Herodotus 5. 96–6. 117.) By Aristotle's account, the attack on Sardis was the occasion, or efficient cause, of the war; but the goal, or final cause, of the Persians in making war was dominion over the Athenians. But this distinction between the occasion and the goal of the Persian expedition corresponds to the distinction drawn in the present chapter between the origin and the goal of faction and constitutional change.

The first of the three causes—'the disposition of those who form factions'—is the most problematic. Benjamin Jowett, without argument or explanation, takes it to be a material cause (vol. ii, p. 188); but it seems more like an efficient or a formal cause. The distinction that Aristotle draws in the present chapter between the end, or goal, of an action and the disposition from which the action proceeds crops up elsewhere in other treatises (*EN* VII. 3. 1146ᵇ14–18; *Rhet.* I. 10. 1368ᵇ27, 12. 1372ᵃ4–5). Though he never connects the distinction with the four causes, such a connection can perhaps be forged. For what Aristotle discusses in these other passages, as well as in the one before us, is the disposition which, when sparked, leads to action; and this disposition seems analogous to the art, or *technē*, of a craftsman, which, when sparked, leads to the production of an artefact—a house, for example. The suggestion, then, is that the disposition of those who form factions is the same sort of cause as the technical or artistic capacity of a craftsman. But what sort of cause is that? Aristotle calls it both an efficient cause (*Phys.* II. 3. 195ᵃ5–8; *Met.* Λ. 4. 1070ᵇ26–9) and a formal cause (*Met.* Z. 7. 1032ᵇ13–14, 9. 1034ᵃ24). He thinks of it as a formal cause because an artefact gets its form from the craftsman's knowledge of the form (*Phys.* II. 2. 194ᵃ21–7; *Met. Z.* 7. 1032ᵃ32–ᵇ14). He thinks of it as an efficient cause because it is the form of the artefact in the craftsman's mind that makes him the efficient cause of the form in the artefact itself (*Phys.* II. 7. 198ᵃ24–7; *GA* II. 1. 734ᵇ36–735ᵃ3; *Met.* Λ. 4. 1070ᵇ30–4). The suggestion, then, is that as a craftsman acts from his art, the members of a faction act from their conception of justice, and that as a craftsman seeks to impose a form upon his materials, the members of a faction seek to impose their conception of justice on the population of their city. By this idea the disposition of the members of a faction is the formal and efficient cause of faction and constitutional change in exactly the same way that the artistic capacity of a craftsman is the formal and efficient cause of a work of art.

1302ᵃ34–ᵇ5

The seven causes and origins that Aristotle refers to in the first sentence of this section are profit and honour plus the five causes listed in the penultimate sentence. There are more than seven causes when the four listed in the last sentence are added. These four are discussed in the next chapter (1303ᵃ13–ᵇ17). The reason the four are distinguished from the seven is that they do not fit easily into the third pigeon-hole, that of an origin and (efficient) cause. In the cases of belittlement and smallness, constitutional change takes place because those in power belittle a threat to the existing constitution or overlook a small but important distinction (1303ᵃ16–25). Belittlement and smallness are thus instances of poor judgement and carelessness, which are only partial or contributory causes. This may be the way Aristotle thought of electioneering too. For in his example electioneering is the cause of its own demise (1303ᵃ13–16). The last item on the list is dissimilarity. The sort of dissimilarity that Aristotle has in mind is dissimilarity of population and territory (1303ᵃ25–ᵇ17). Such dissimilarity provides, not an efficient cause of faction, but the fertile soil in which such a cause can take root. Just as population and territory are the material cause of a city (VII. 4. 1325ᵇ37–1326ᵃ8), a dissimilar population or territory would seem to be a material cause of faction. Thus, in the end Aristotle's analysis of the origins and causes of faction reflects the whole fourfold scheme of causes.

1302ᵃ37–ᵇ2   Profit and honour operate as both final and efficient causes of faction, but in different ways. The sight of profit or honour in the hands of others spurs men to form a faction; but the goal, or final cause, of the faction is profit or honour for its members or their friends. Attacks on tyrants are a good example. Men attack tyrants, Aristotle says, 'because they see the great profits and the great honours they possess' (1312ᵃ22–4); but the end (*telos*) they seek is the enjoyment of such profits and honours themselves (see 10. 1311ᵃ28–31).

CHAPTER 3

This chapter follows on the last without a break. It begins with a demonstrative pronoun referring to the eleven causes and origins of faction and constitutional change listed in the preceding section, which are now discussed in turn.

1302ᵇ5–1303ᵃ13

Aristotle starts with his list of seven: insolence and profit (1302ᵇ5–10), honour (1302ᵇ10–14), superiority (1302ᵇ15–21), fear (1302ᵇ21–4), contempt (1302ᵇ25–33), and disproportionate growth (1302ᵇ33–1303ᵃ13).

1302ᵇ5–10   In this section Aristotle writes as if insolence and profit were links in a single causal chain, insolence leading to depredations of public and private property. But they are not always so linked. For profit operating independently of insolence see 10. 1312ᵃ16, 22–4; for insolence as an independent cause see 4. 1303ᵇ37–1304ᵃ4 and note, and 10. 1311ᵃ32–ᵇ34.

   'Insolence' is an imperfect translation of *hubris*. Aristotle explains the concept in the *Rhetoric*: 'And the man who is insolent belittles his victim. For insolence (*hubris*) is doing and saying things which bring shame to the victim, not in order that something may come out of it for the doer other than the mere fact that it happened, but so that he may get pleasure. . . . The cause of the pleasure enjoyed by those who are insolent is that they think that in doing ill they are themselves much superior. That is why the young and the wealthy are insolent. For they think that in being insolent they are superior' (*Rhet.* II. 2. 1378ᵇ23–9). Suppose, for example,

79

that one man strikes another. The blow is an act of *hubris* if its purpose is to dishonour the person struck and to give the striker the pleasurable feeling of superiority (*Rhet.* I. 13. 1374ᵃ13–15), but it is not an act of *hubris* if it is in response to something that happened in the past or for the sake of some future reward (*Rhet.* II. 2. 1379ᵃ30–2, 24. 1402ᵃ1–2) or a part of some erotic game (10. 1311ᵇ19–20). Not all acts of *hubris* are physical, like striking. Other pleasurable ways of humiliating a person are by laughing, mocking, or jeering at him (*Rhet.* II. 2. 1379ᵃ29–30). Those particularly prone to such activity are the beautiful, the strong, the well-born, the wealthy, the fortunate, the young, and the powerful (IV. 11. 1295ᵇ5–11; VII. 15. 1334ᵃ26–8; *Rhet.* II. 12. 1389ᵇ7–12, 16. 1390ᵇ32–4, 1391ᵃ18–19). The Greeks, with their acute sense of personal honour, particularly abhorred *hubris*. In Athens there was a law against *hubris*, which protected even slaves from its sting. The Athenians, moreover, regarded *hubris* as an offence against the community, not just the victim; and, consequently, any free adult male, not just the victim, was entitled to prosecute an alleged offender (MacDowell, pp. 129–32).

The distinction in this section between factions against one another and factions against the constitution harks back to Aristotle's distinction in Chapter 1 between factions that are and factions that are not against the established constitution. Among the latter are factions whose members 'intend ... for the established constitution ... to remain the same, but wish it to be in their hands' (1301ᵇ11–13).

1302ᵇ10–14 Honour is the greatest of external goods (*EN* IV. 3. 1123ᵇ20–1), and thus a natural cause of faction when distributed unjustly. Honour includes not only respect and tokens of esteem (*Rhet.* I. 5. 1361ᵃ27–ᵇ2) but also political office. 'We say', Aristotle observes, 'that the offices are honours' (III. 10. 1281ᵃ31). Since honour is the prize of virtue (*EN* IV. 3. 1123ᵇ35) and virtue the basis of aristocracy, honour is a cause of faction particularly in aristocracies (for examples see 7. 1306ᵇ22–36).

1302ᵇ17–18 As a monarchy is the rule of one man, dynasty (*dunasteia*) is the rule of a handful. Since there is a correct form of monarchy, namely kingship, and a deviant form, namely tyranny (III. 7. 1279ᵃ32–4, ᵇ4–5; V. 10. 1310ᵇ7–14, 1311ᵃ28–31), we expect there to be both a correct and a deviant form of dynasty.

But Aristotle, though he does speak of 'kingly dynasties' (*basilikai dunasteiai*) in one passage (10. 1311^{b}26), usually associates dynasty with tyranny (IV. 14. 1298^{a}32–3, V. 6. 1306^{a}22–5, VI. 6. 1320^{b}31–2).

1302^{b}18–19   Ostracism was an institution adopted by a number of democratic cities (III. 13. 1284^{a}17–18) for sending into exile for a set period of time—ten years at Athens—a citizen who had violated no law. In the passage before us Aristotle says that it was instituted to prevent the overthrow of the constitution of a city by one or more powerful citizens and the establishment of a monarchy or a dynasty, though he reports elsewhere that it was invariably twisted into an instrument of faction—a tool for eliminating political rivals (III. 13. 1284^{b}20–2; *AP* 22. 6).

Aristotle clearly thought that ostracism was justified, for he endorses it under a correct constitution (III. 13. 1284^{a}17–^{b}22) and even under the best constitution. 'But in case of the best constitution', he writes, 'there is a big puzzle ⟨about ostracism⟩, not (1) about superiority in the other goods such as strength and wealth and abundance of friends, but (2) when someone becomes preeminent in virtue—what should be done?' (III. 13. 1284^{b}25–8.) In the passage just quoted Aristotle distinguishes two cases, and finds a puzzle only in the second. The answer to the puzzle, Aristotle thinks, is not to ostracize the man who is pre-eminent in virtue but to accept him as an absolute king (III. 13. 1284^{b}28–34). Since he sees no puzzle in the first case, the passage implies that he regards ostracism as a perfectly acceptable method of removing individuals who threaten the stability of the city, not by their pre-eminent virtue, but by their political strength, wealth, or influence. He never examines ostracism from the standpoint of its prey: he never questions the justice of laying the heavy burden of exile on a law-abiding citizen in anticipation of an overt act on his part.

1302^{b}23–4   There are two other references to Rhodes in Book V. Aristotle refers to an uprising against the people immediately below (1302^{b}32–3), and in a later chapter he uses language virtually identical with that of the passage before us to describe the formation of a faction of trierarchs (5. 1304^{b}27–31). The three passages almost certainly refer to the same event, an uprising of oligarchs in a democracy.

The island of Rhodes is distinct from the city of Rhodes. The city was formed in 408/7 BC by the union of the three cities on the island, Ialysus, Lindus, and Camirus (Diod. 13. 75. 1). Since cities rather than bodies of land have constitutions, the reference in the passage before us must be to the city, not the island. For a reference to the island see II. 10. 1271ᵇ37.

During the fifth and fourth centuries Rhodes oscillated three times between democracy and oligarchy as the power of Athens or Sparta waxed or waned in the south-eastern Aegean Sea. After the Persian War the three cities on the island joined the Athenian Alliance. Their constitutions were democratic and remained democratic as long as Athens maintained its power in the region. But in 412 BC, as the fortunes of Athens ebbed in the Peloponnesian War, the Rhodians were persuaded by a Spartan force that had landed on the island to revolt from Athens (Thuc. 8. 44). This led to the establishment of oligarchies in the three cities. But Spartan influence was broken in 395 BC by a Persian fleet under the command of a Greek admiral; and the pro-Spartan oligarchs were overthrown (Diod. 14. 79. 4–8). The democracy that followed did not remain long in power; for in 390 BC the oligarchs, again with Spartan support, rose against it (Xen. *Hell.* 4. 8. 20–4; Diod. 14. 97). When Athens eventually regained its power in the Aegean, Rhodes became a member of the Second Athenian Alliance and a democracy for the third time. But in 357 BC, at the beginning of the War of the Athenian Allies, Rhodes severed her connection with Athens and for the third time set up an oligarchy (Dem. *For the Liberty of the Rhodians* 14, 19).

In the three passages about Rhodes, Aristotle cannot be referring to the events of 412 BC since in that year the city of Rhodes did not yet exist. So he must be referring to the oligarchic revolution of 390 or 357 BC. Newman points out that Diodorus' use of the verb *epanistanai* in describing the revolution of 390 echoes Aristotle's use of the noun *epanastasis* ('uprising') at 1302ᵇ33, and on this slender basis opts for the revolution of 390 (note to 1302ᵇ23).

1302ᵇ29–30   The location of the Boeotian village of Oenophyta is unknown. In 457 BC, during the period of Athenian supremacy following the Persian Wars, the Athenian general Myronides won a victory at Oenophyta over an army of Thebans and other Boeotians, which led to the Athenian domination of Boeotia for the next ten years. The Theban democracy mentioned in this passage, presumably established as a result of the Athenian victory (though our sources do not make this clear), was a short-lived break from the city's customary oligarchy. (For the battle of Oenophyta see Thuc. 1. 108, Diod. 11. 81–3.)

1302ᵇ31 There are two other passages in the *Politics*, in addition to the one before us, that refer to an overthrow of a democracy in Megara (IV. 15. 1300ᵃ17–19, V. 5. 1304ᵇ35–9); and it seems likely that all three refer to the same event. The two other passages indicate that the democracy was overthrown by a body of returning exiles. Thus, when Aristotle says that 'the democracy of the Megarians was destroyed when they were defeated because of disorder and unruliness', the defeat he is referring to is not a defeat of the city by a foreign enemy, but a defeat of the people by the notables. Aristotle does not tell us when the change from democracy to oligarchy took place, but his description of the overthrow meshes with Thucydides' account of a revolution in Megara in 424 BC (Thuc. 4. 66–74).

We hear of the disorder and unruliness in Megara from another writer. Plutarch tells a story, whose source may be Aristotle's lost *Constitution of the Megarians* (Halliday, pp. 99–100), about a sacred embassy passing through the Megarid on its way to Delphi during the time of 'the intemperate democracy' in Megara. When the envoys camped for the night beside a lake in their wagons with their wives and children, a band of drunken Megarians, out of insolence and savagery, pushed the wagons into the lake, and many of the envoys drowned. The citizens of Megara, however, 'because of the disorder of their constitution, took no notice of the wrong'; and it was left to the Amphictyonic Council, an international body charged with the protection of the temple of Apollo at Delphi, to proceed against and to punish the wrongdoers (Plut. *Gr. Q.* q. 59 (304 E–F)).

1302ᵇ31–3 The reference is to the first democracy in Syracuse, which was overthrown in 485 BC. It was preceded by an aristocracy of landowners (*gamoroi*). The landowners were driven out of Syracuse by the people with the aid of the landowners' own slaves, the Killyrioi, and took refuge in the town of Kasmenē. According to the passage before us, the democracy earned the contempt of the exiled landowners by its disorder and unruliness. Sensing the weakness of the democracy, the landowners appealed to Gelon, the tyrant of Gela, for support. Gelon marched on the city, and the people surrendered without a fight. Gelon brought back the land-owners but remained himself as tyrant of Syracuse. (Her. 7. 155; Dunbabin, pp. 410–15.)

For the uprising against the people at Rhodes see the note to 1302ᵇ23–4 above.

1302ᵇ33–1303ᵃ13 Aristotle's discussion of constitutional change due to disproportionate growth presupposes an account of the parts of a city and an understanding of the concept of chance.

The Parts of a City
In the *Politics* (see I. 1. 1252ᵃ18–20), as in his biological works (*HA* I. 1. 486ᵃ5–8), Aristotle distinguishes two types of part: simple and composite. The simple parts (*elachista moria, asuntheta*) of a city are individual human beings; the composite parts (*suntheta*) are groups or classes of individuals.

Though Aristotle takes the simple parts of a city to be individual human beings, he does not always subscribe to the converse—that every individual human being living in a city is a simple part of the city. Sometimes he does, as when he refers to 'each of us' as a part without any further specification (I. 2. 1253ᵃ18–20). Since he goes on to say that anyone who is not a part of a city is either a beast or a god (1253ᵃ27–9), he evidently means to count every inhabitant of a city—free or slave, citizen or alien—as a part. In other passages, however, he adopts a narrower view and explicitly counts only citizens as parts (III. 1. 1274ᵇ38–41; see also VII. 4. 1326ᵃ16–21).

Aristotle analyses the city into composite parts in at least five different ways. In one passage or another, all of the following are said to be parts of a city:

1. households (I. 3. 1253ᵇ1–3, 13. 1260ᵇ13; IV. 3. 1289ᵇ28–9), composed in turn of the relations of master and slave, husband and wife, father and child (I. 3. 1253ᵇ3–12);
2. social classes as defined by degree of wealth, good birth, education, and virtue (III. 12. 1283ᵃ14–13. 1283ᵃ26; IV. 3. 1289ᵇ40–1290ᵃ5, 4. 1291ᵇ28–30, 12. 1296ᵇ15–24; VI. 2. 1317ᵇ38–41; see also IV. 8. 1293ᵇ37–8);
3. economic classes, especially the rich and the poor (IV. 4. 1291ᵇ7–8, V. 11. 1315ᵃ31–3, VI. 3. 1318ᵃ30–1), though the middle class is sometimes included (IV. 11. 1295ᵇ1–3);

4. functional groups such as farmers, artisans, traders, warriors, office-holders, and so forth (IV. 4. 1290^{b}38–1291^{a}40, VII. 8. 1328^{b}2–23);

5. the political stations of ruler and subject (VII. 14. 1332^{b}12–13; compare I. 5. 1254^{a}28–33).

The strict and loose senses of 'simple part' carry over to 'composite part'. Certain groups such as farmers, artisans, or traders are sometimes counted as composite parts and sometimes not, depending upon whether every inhabitant, or only every citizen, of the city is counted as one of its simple parts (see IV. 4. 1291^{a}24–8, VII. 8. 1328^{a}21–5, and VII. 9. 1329^{a}34–8).

Chance

In the *Rhetoric* Aristotle defines chance (*tuchē*) as follows: 'The things that come to be by chance are those whose cause is undefined and do not come to be for the sake of something and not always nor for the most part nor in an orderly manner' (I. 10. 1369^{a}32–4; see also *Phys.* II. 4–6). Chance is distinguished from both nature (*phusis*) and reason (*nous*) (*Phys.* II. 6. 198^{a}9–10; see also *Met.* Z. 7. 1032^{a}12–13, Λ. 3. 1070^{b}6–7; *Pol.* II. 9. 1270^{b}19–20, VII. 13. 1331^{b}41). An object that comes to be by nature or the use of reason, in contrast to one that comes to be by chance, always gets its form from a possessor of the form. A human being comes to be from a human being, and a house comes to be from a thought of a house in the mind of a builder (*Met. Z.* 7. 1032^{a}25, ^{b}11–12; for a restriction on the principle see *Met.* Z. 9. 1034^{b}16–19).

In the *Nicomachean Ethics* and the *Politics* Aristotle relativizes chance to the agent, where the agent may be either an individual or a city (*EN* I. 9. 1100^{a}5–9, 32–^{b}11; VII. 13. 1153^{b}17–21). Something happens to an agent by chance if, and only if, it is neither something the agent himself controls nor something that flows from the agent's own nature. A man who dies in battle dies by chance (even though his opponent killed him intentionally), but a man who dies of old age or by his own hand does not (see VII. 13. 1331^{b}39–41; *EN* III. 3. 1112^{a}30–3; *Rhet.* I. 4. 1359^{a}35–9, 5. 1361^{b}26–1362^{a}12). Sometimes Aristotle takes an even broader view of chance and counts everything 'external to the soul' as due to chance (VII. 1. 1323^{b}27–8; *EN* I. 8. 1099^{a}31–^{b}8). By this reckoning everything bodily, even death in old age, is due to chance.

The chance events mentioned in this section are all military defeats. In each of the examples the number of the poor in a city becomes disproportionately large due to a heavy loss of notables. Such cases are presumably meant to stand in contrast to cases where the disproportionate increase of the poor comes about by nature (because of their greater fertility) or by design (because, say, of the intentional impoverishment of the middle class).

Aristotle claims that the growth of the parts of a city obeys the same general principle as the growth of the parts of an animal. The general principle asserts that the parts of a whole must preserve their mutual proportionality for the whole to retain its symmetry (and identity). Two features of Aristotle's use of this principle should be noted. First, he does not stick with one conception of the composite parts of a city—the parts of a city that grow or shrink—but shifts from one conception to another: sometimes the parts that grow (or shrink) disproportionately are social classes (1303^{a}4, 9); sometimes they are economic classes (1303^{a}2, 12). And, secondly, the increase may be qualitative as well as quantitative (1302^{b}39–40).

Aristotle says that if the parts of a body do not grow in proportion, the body will either perish or change into the shape of another animal. An example of the latter would be a person's face coming to be like that of a satyr (*GA* IV. 3. 768^{b}27–36). Constitutional change is the political analogue of perishing; constitutional modification the analogue of a change of shape (see the note to 1. 1301^{b}4–26). Aristotle even considers a case that might be regarded as a political analogue of a satyr's face on a human being—or rather of a human face on a satyr. In Chapter 11 he envisages a tyrant who by an increase in virtue—by becoming only half-vicious—takes on the appearance of a king (1314^{a}29–1315^{b}10).

1303^{a}3–6 Iapygia (the Roman Calabria and the southern portion of modern Apulia) is the heel of the Italian peninsula. The city of Taras (the Roman Tarentum and modern Taranto), in the instep of the peninsula, was a colony of Sparta (7. 1306^{b}29–31). Herodotus describes this defeat of the Tarentines, which occurred around 473 BC, as 'the greatest slaughter of Greeks of all those we know about' (7. 170. 3). (Diod. 11. 52.)

1303^{a}6–8 The Spartans and the Argives, though both of Dorian stock, were perennial adversaries in the Peloponnese. The battle referred to here, which was fought at Sepeia (near Tiryns) around

495 BC, was the climactic battle in a series stretching back for generations. The Argives were decisively defeated with a loss of 6,000 men, and Argos itself barely escaped capture. The serfs who were granted citizenship to redress the scarcity of men gained, along with their citizenship, the right to marry Argive women. But when the Argive boys grew to manhood, they drove the former serfs out of Argos.

It is unclear why the Argive dead are referred to as 'the men of the seventh'. Newman thinks it was probably because the battle was fought on the seventh day of the month. There are other possibilities such as that the number of dead was 7,777, that the battle was fought during (and in violation of) a truce of seven days, and so forth. (For the battle and its aftermath see Her. 6. 76–83, 7. 148; Paus. 3. 4. 1; Plut. *Bravery of Women*, ch. 4 (245 C–F), *Sayings of Spartans* 223 A–C.)

1303^{a}8–10 The Laconian War is the Peloponnesian War (431–404 BC). The register of citizens referred to is the register of all male citizens of the hoplite class from 18 to 60 years of age. The members of this class had to possess sufficient wealth to equip themselves as hoplites. Since notability is dependent on wealth, the loss of many men from this class would deplete the number of notables.

Aristotle implies that there is another system of obtaining hoplites besides the one based on a register of citizens. What is it? Perhaps Aristotle wishes to contrast the service of citizens as hoplites with the employment of mercenaries.

1303^{a}13–^{b}17

Aristotle turns now to the four causes of constitutional change that operate in a different manner from the original seven: electioneering (1303^{a}13–16), belittlement (1303^{a}16–20), smallness (1303^{a}20–5), and dissimilarity (1303^{a}25–^{b}17). The first three of these produce constitutional change without faction.

1303^{a}13–16 The word translated as 'electioneering' (*eritheia*) seems to refer to intriguing or campaigning for election to office. In determining its meaning there is little to go by beyond the present context.

Aristotle reports that at Heraea, a city on the Alpheus river in western Arcadia in the Peloponnese, the citizens put an end to electioneering by replacing election with sortition. Since the filling of offices by lot, rather than by election, is characteristic of democracy (VI. 2. 1317ᵇ17–21; *Rhet.* I. 8. 1365ᵇ31–2; Plato, *Rep.* VIII. 557a2–5), this amounted to a change of constitution in a democratic direction.

1303ᵃ16–20   Oreus is a few miles west of Artemisium on the north end of the island of Euboea. It is mentioned under its original name of Hestiaea in the next chapter (4. 1303ᵇ33). Hestiaea was sacked by the Persians in 480 BC following the naval battle off Artemisium and the retreat of the Greek fleet. After the Persians were repulsed, Hestiaea joined the Athenian Alliance. But when the Athenian Alliance was gradually transformed into an Athenian Empire, the allies became restive; and in 446 BC all the cities in Euboea revolted. The Athenians regained the island; expelled the Hestiaeans for their part in the revolt; and, with 1,000 Athenian settlers, converted the city into the Athenian colony of Oreus. After the defeat of Athens in the Peloponnesian War, the exiled Hestiaeans returned, allied themselves with Sparta, and established an oligarchy. The alliance lasted until 377 BC when Hestiaea-Oreus expelled a Spartan garrison and joined the Second Athenian Alliance. This would have been an opportune occasion for the overthrow of the oligarchy that Aristotle refers to. According to Aristotle, the oligarchy was overthrown because the citizens of Oreus made light of—belittled—the danger of allowing Heracleodorus, no friend of the established constitution, to hold a high office. (See Her. 8. 23; Thuc. 1. 144. 3; Xen. *Hell.* 5. 4. 56–7; and Diod. 12. 22.)

1303ᵃ23   Ambracia, on the Arachthus river north of the Gulf of Ambracia in north-west Greece, was a colony of Corinth, founded around 625 BC by Gorgus, the illegitimate son of Cypselus, the tyrant of Corinth (Strabo 10. 2. 8; 7. 7. 6). Gorgus, like his father, reigned as a tyrant and was succeeded by his son Periander, whose overthrow is mentioned twice by Aristotle (4. 1304ᵃ31–3, 10. 1311ᵃ39–ᵇ1). In the first of these notes on Periander Aristotle tells us that the tyranny at Ambracia was replaced by a democracy.

A constitution under which admissibility to office is based on a low property qualification is one form of democracy (IV. 4. 1291ᵇ39–41). Thus the change of constitution at Ambracia referred to in the passage before us was from a less to a more radical form of the same constitution. The relation of the less radical form of democracy to the democracy that replaced the tyranny of Periander is obscure.

1303ᵃ25–ᵇ17 The eleventh and final origin of faction and constitutional change is dissimilarity of population (1303ᵃ25–ᵇ3) and territory (1303ᵇ7–17).

1303ᵃ28–33 The Achaeans were from the little cities of Achaea on the north coast of the Peloponnese, and the Troezenians from Troezen on the peninsula of Argolis, which faces Attica across the Saronic Gulf. Sybaris, the city founded by the Achaeans and Troezenians around 720 BC in the instep of the Italian peninsula, became the richest city in the West with a population that may have reached 500,000 (Hammond 1986, p. 200) and was renowned for its luxury and softness (hence the word 'sybarite'). It was said that the sight of work was enough to give a Sybarite a hernia, and the mere mention of it, a pain in the side.

We know nothing about the curse that fell on Sybaris because the Achaeans expelled the Troezenians except that it seemed to work. Around 510 BC, after a relatively brief two centuries of existence, the city was totally destroyed by neighbouring Croton. Strabo's one sentence is both an epitaph and a judgement: 'By reason of luxury and insolence ⟨the Sybarites⟩ had all their happiness taken from them by the Crotoniates in seventy days' (Strabo 6. 1. 13). (See Her. 5. 44–5, 6. 127, and Diod. 12. 9.)

The city was destined to be reborn several times. The Sybarites who escaped the destruction of their city took refuge in neighbouring cities in southern Italy. Fifty-eight years later their descendants and the survivors among the original refugees refounded Sybaris. But within five years the city was again destroyed by Croton. The Sybarites who survived invited Athens and Sparta to help them refound the city a second time. Although Sparta declined, Athens sent colonists from Athens and the Peloponnese; and Sybaris was reborn once more—the third Sybaris. But the Sybarites soon quarrelled with their joint colonists and were either killed or expelled by them. The remaining colonists appealed to Athens for more settlers. Athens responded by inviting the cities of old Greece to send colonists to found a Panhellenic colony, named Thurii, at a new site close to the original Sybaris. The physical layout of the city was planned by Hippodamus of Miletus, some of whose ideas

Aristotle discusses in *Politics* II. 8; and its laws and constitution, which were democratic, were drawn up by Protagoras. (Diod. 12. 10–21; Strabo 6. 1. 13; Plut. *Prec. Stat.*, ch. 15 (812 D); D.L. 9. 50; Ehrenberg.)

In the passage before us Aristotle says that the Sybarites were driven out of Thurii, not Sybaris. This can be reconciled with our other sources if we suppose that Aristotle counted the foundation of the third Sybaris as the initial phase of the foundation of Thurii.

1303[a]33–4 Nothing further is known about this conspiracy at Byzantium.

1303[a]34–5 Antissa, a city on the north coast of the island of Lesbos, was Aeolian, whereas the island of Chios, directly south of Lesbos, was Ionian. Since Aristotle is discussing factions produced by difference of race, it is probably safe to infer that it was the admission of Ionians into an Aeolian city that caused trouble.

1303[a]35–6 Zanclē (the modern Messina) is on the Sicilian side of the Straits of Messina. The island of Samos is at the opposite end of the Greek world off the coast of Asia Minor midway between Ephesus and Miletus. The episode that Aristotle mentions took place soon after the Ionian defeat in the sea battle off Miletus near the island of Lade in 495 BC, which doomed the Ionian revolt. Fleeing the consequences of the Ionian defeat, the wealthy citizens of Samos, accompanied by a few Milesians, sailed west at the invitation of Zanclē to found an Ionian colony on the north coast of Sicily in territory currently occupied by the native Sicels. When they reached the toe of Italy, the Zanclaeans were besieging a Sicel town (presumably to pave the way for the new colony). Anaxilaus, the tyrant of Rhegium, the city facing Zanclē across the Straits of Messina, suggested to the Samians that they might avoid the labour of founding a new city by occupying Zanclē instead. The Samians responded with enthusiasm and seized the undefended city. They were not destined to remain in possession of it for long. Although the attempt of the Zanclaeans to reclaim their city ended in disaster due to yet further treachery, the Samians were soon driven out of Zanclē by Anaxilaus, the very man who had suggested they seize it. (The whole sorry story of betrayal on top of betrayal is found in Her. 6. 22–4 and Thuc. 6. 4. 5–6. See also Dunbabin, pp. 380–99.)

1303ᵃ36–8   Apollonia Pontica, on the western shore of the Black
Sea, one of several cities in Greece bearing the name of the most
Greek of all of the Greek gods, is referred to one other time in the
Politics (6. 1306ᵃ7–9). The second passage also mentions the formation of a faction but attributes it, not to difference of race, but to the
theft of public property. This suggests, though it does not entail,
that the two passages are about different events. We know of
neither event from any other source.

1303ᵃ38–ᵇ2   The period of the tyrants at Syracuse to which
Aristotle refers is the eighteen-year period beginning around 485
BC when the three brothers Gelon, Hieron, and Thrasybulus each
ruled in turn as tyrant (12. 1315ᵇ34–8). After Thrasybulus was
overthrown in 466 BC, Syracuse was first a polity and then in 413 BC
a democracy (see note to 4. 1304ᵃ27–9 below). With the rise of
Dionysius I at the end of the fifth century, Syracuse reverted a
second time to tyranny—a stronger and longer lasting one.
    The incident that Aristotle mentions is explained by Diodorus.
The tyrants had hired aliens as mercenaries and had made them
citizens. The restored democracy allowed them to remain citizens
but not to hold office. Since the right to hold office is the mark of a
full citizen (III. 1. 1275ᵃ22–3, ᵇ17–20), the native Syracusans effectively took away with the one hand what they had given with the
other. Not satisfied with such second-class citizenship, the new
citizens rebelled, and were only driven out of Syracuse after a long
and hard struggle. (Diod. 11. 72–3, 76.)
    Newman thinks that Aristotle is mistaken in attributing the
faction in Syracuse to difference of race. The new citizens, he says,
'rebelled, in fact, not because they were citizens of a different stock
from the rest, which is the cause assigned by Aristotle for their
rebellion, but because the citizenship conferred on them was of an
inferior kind [the cause assigned by Diodorus]' (Newman, ad loc.).
But this is to take too narrow a view of the causal chain leading to
the rebellion. For the reason the old citizens conferred an inferior
kind of citizenship on the new was that the new citizens were not
native Syracusans. We need to distinguish the proximate, or immediate, cause of the rebellion from its ultimate, or first, cause. The
immediate cause was the conferral of second-class citizenship on
the new citizens; the originating cause was the difference of
race between the new and the old. This analysis is borne out by

Aristotle's more detailed account a few lines earlier of the faction at Thurii, which mentions both its proximate and its ultimate cause. The faction was sparked by the Sybarites' claim of deserving more than the later colonists, but this claim itself originated in the Sybarites' belief that there was a significant difference between natives and non-natives.

1303ᵇ2–3 Amphipolis got its name, which means 'city encompassed ⟨by a river⟩', from the fact that it was surrounded on three sides by the river Strymon. The river is east of Chalcidice, the three-pronged peninsula projecting from Macedonia. Amphipolis was founded in 436 BC as an Athenian colony. Twelve years later during the Peloponnesian War it became the focus of a Spartan campaign in northern Greece. When the Spartan Brasidas appeared before its gates and offered its inhabitants favourable terms, it surrendered without a battle. Thucydides, the historian, happened to be commanding a small Athenian fleet at the island of Thasos, a half-day's sail from the city, and for his share in the debacle was expelled from Athens for the remainder of the war. Athens tried to regain her colony in 422 BC. The army that was sent to retake the city was led by the demagogue Cleon and numbered among its troops the 47-year-old hoplite Socrates (Plato, *Apol.* 28e). Brasidas' army routed the Athenians and killed Cleon, but Brasidas himself was mortally wounded. Amphipolis remained an independent city until 357 BC, when it was conquered by Philip II of Macedon and became a Macedonian city. (Thuc. I. 100. 3, 4. 102–8, 5. 6–11, 5. 26; Diod. 16. 8. 2.)

The event to which Aristotle refers, the introduction of Chalcidian colonists, is described in a bit more detail later in Book V (6. 1306ª2–4); but otherwise we know nothing about it.

1303ᵇ3–7 This passage is clearly out of place. Newman believes it belongs at I. 1301ª39 after the sentence that ends with 'faction'.

1303ᵇ9–12 Clazomenae, the birthplace of Anaxagoras, is on a small island in the Gulf of Smyrna in Asia Minor. The city was originally built on the mainland at Chytrum, the site of which is unknown, but was moved to the island out of fear of the Persians, probably at the time of the Ionian revolt. Alexander the Great had a causeway constructed between the mainland and the island. (Paus. 7. 3. 8–9; Strabo I. 3. 17, 14. I. 36; Gomme *et al.*, note to 8. 14. 3.)

Colophon, the birthplace of Xenophanes, is a few miles south of Clazomenae on the coast of Asia Minor. Notium and Peiraeus are the seaports of Colophon and Athens respectively.

Those who live on an island or in a seaport naturally have different interests from those who live ashore or inland since the livelihood of the one depends upon the sea whereas that of the other depends upon the land. Seafarers will need, for example, to be on good terms with those who control the sea whereas those who own land will not want to provoke a land power that could ravage their estates. When faction breaks out between seafarers and townsmen, the two sides will seek assistance from opposite sources. This is what happened at Colophon in an incident that Thucydides describes (3. 34). When the Colophonians split into faction early in the Peloponnesian War, it was the townsmen who called in the Persians and their opponents who looked to Athens for help.

Aristotle says only that those who live in the Peiraeus are more democratic than those who live in town, not that the two sections of the population form factions against each other. But they did do so after the end of the Peloponnesian War during the reign of the Thirty Tyrants (Xen. *Hell.* 2. 4; *AP* 38). The Peiraeus was more democratic than the town because of its seafaring population, especially its trireme oarsmen (see IV. 4. 1291ᵇ23–4, V. 4. 1304ª22–4, VI. 7. 1321ª13–14). Democracy is rule of the poor (see note to 1. 1301ª28–35 above), and only a poor man would serve as an oarsman (see VII. 6. 1327ᵇ7–14).

1303ᵇ12–14 'Every difference seems to make a division': by a division Aristotle means a source of friction. Thus, his laconic observation is an expression of one of the iron laws of history: no difference among people is too small to be a basis of conflict.

1303ᵇ15–17 Aristotle offers a list of differences ranked according to the distance, measured by some philosophical yardstick, between their opposite poles. The first two differences are difference in character, whose opposite poles are virtue and vileness, and difference in material goods, whose poles are wealth and poverty. The gulf between virtue and vileness is wider than that between wealth and poverty because goods of the soul outrank external goods: it is better to be poor than vile (VII. 1. 1323ª24–ᵇ21). The last item on the list—the difference 'just mentioned'—would be difference of territory, preceding which would be difference of race.

93

This chapter concludes Aristotle's discussion of the general causes of faction and constitutional change.

1303ᵇ17–1304ᵃ17

What does Aristotle mean when he says that factions arise not 'concerning' (*peri*) small things, but 'from' (*ek*) small things? The most obvious suggestion is that the two prepositions signal final and efficient causes respectively. Aristotle wrote earlier in Book V about a final cause using the word *peri*—'The things for (*peri*) which men form factions are profit and honour and their opposites' (2. 1302ᵃ31–2)—and since he is speaking of factions originating 'from' small things, 'from' (*ek*) evidently signals an efficient cause. But this cannot be right. For he goes on to contrast the small things from which factions arise with the great things with which they are concerned, and he does not think that the final causes of faction are always great things. Otherwise he would think that profit is a great thing. Jowett suggests a second interpretation. He thinks Aristotle is contrasting small personal and private reasons with large public and political causes: 'Some spark sets fire to materials previously prepared' (ad loc.). (The metaphor calls to mind Gavrilo Princip igniting World War I by assassinating Archduke Francis Ferdinand and his wife in Sarajevo in the summer of 1914. Though Princip precipitated the war, its causes were much deeper.) But Jowett's interpretation seems wrong too. For nowhere in this chapter does Aristotle contrast small personal and private *reasons* with large public and political *causes*. Jowett is right in taking the 'great' things to be things that are public and political, but he is wrong to identify them as a cause. What happens in all of Aristotle's examples is that a few disputants in a private quarrel draw in enough outsiders to turn their private dispute into a public one (just as the Allies and the Central Powers drew in enough other countries to turn a European War into World War I). Aristotle never mentions smouldering public conflicts that private disputes ignite. His point rather is that large consequences may flow from small beginnings: what starts as a dispute between two men may wind up as a civil war involving the whole city. Aristotle does not believe that factions always have deep underlying public and political causes, that they always spring from festering sores in the body politic. On the contrary he believes that they often spring from nothing more than small personal and private disputes. The proper metaphor for his idea is not a pile of dry leaves ignited by a spark but a broad river originating in a mountain spring.

1303ᵇ20–6 This story is a miniature portrait of Greek bisexuality. The rift between the two young men is over both a male and a female. The boy is referred to only as the beloved (*erōmenos*, the masculine passive participle of *erān*, to love), but it was customary for the beloved in these relationships between two males to be a youth who was younger than his lover (*erastēs*) (Dover, pp. 85–7). The story is also found in Plutarch, who supplies the detail that the second young man had undertaken to protect the boy while his comrade was abroad (*Prec. Stat.*, ch. 32 (825 c)).

1303ᵇ28–9 'For the mistake arises at the beginning (*en archēi*)': Aristotle has just spoken of 'two young men in office (*en tais archais*)', so we seem to have a pun on the word *archē*, which means both beginning and office. In his chapter in the *Metaphysics* on the different senses of *archē* Aristotle attempts to connect the two meanings: 'That by whose choice that which is altered is altered and that which is changed is changed ⟨is called an *archē*⟩, as the offices (*archai*) in cities, and dynasties and kingships and tyrannies, are called *archai* ⟨i.e. types of rule and beginnings⟩' (*Δ*. 1. 1013ᵃ10–13). The idea is that offices, dynasties, and kingships are called *archai* because both officials and rulers are initiators of action.

1303ᵇ29–31 From the premiss that the beginning is half the whole Aristotle infers that a mistake at the beginning is proportionate to the mistakes in the other parts. Aristotle is tacitly assuming that mistakes are made all along the way and that the mistakes in any given part are proportionate to the mistakes in any other part that is the same proportion of the whole as the given part. Thus, the mistakes in the two halves of a whole—the beginning and all the rest—are proportionate. ('Well begun is half done.')

1303ᵇ32–7 On Hestiaea see note to 3. 1303ᵃ16–20 above. Aristotle mentions the finding of treasure several times (*EN* III. 3. 1112ᵃ27, *Rhet.* I. 5. 1362ᵃ9); and Herodotus tells a tale, which is close in time and space to the incident Aristotle relates, of a man who picked up treasure washed ashore from some of the 400 Persian ships lost off the coast of Magnesia in the violent storm that delayed the battle of Artemisium for several days (7. 190).

1303ᵇ37–1304ᵃ4 Plutarch gives us more details (*Prec. Stat.*, ch. 32 (825 B)). When libations were being made at the wedding-feast in the house of the bride's father, the bowl in which the wine and water were mixed broke down the middle spontaneously. This might seem an ill omen even in a modern wedding. A little later, while the jilter, Orsilaus, and his brother were sacrificing in a temple, the bride's father, Crates, planted on them a sacred object of gold and then, as summary punishment for robbing a temple, had them thrown from a cliff. Not stopping with this, Crates also killed some of Orsilaus' friends and relations. Eventually the Delphians had their fill of Crates and his faction, and put them to death and confiscated their property.

1304ᵃ4–10 Mytilene together with the four other cities on the island of Lesbos (Methymna, Eresus, Antissa, and Pyrrha) was a free ally of Athens in the period between the Persian and the Peloponnesian Wars, though it remained an oligarchy. In 428 BC, in the fourth year of the Peloponnesian War, the entire island except for Methymna revolted from the alliance. Paches, the Athenian general sent to put down the revolt, invested Mytilene by land and sea. In response, the oligarchs distributed heavy armour to the people for an attack against the besiegers. But once armed as hoplites the people turned on their rulers and threatened to come to terms with the Athenians. Their hand being forced, the oligarchs surrendered to Paches. As retribution for the revolt, the Athenian assembly voted to execute the entire adult male population of Mytilene and to enslave the women and children, but changed its mind the following day. The ship dispatched to Mytilene to countermand the previous day's decree of execution arrived just as it was about to be carried out. But a thousand of the oligarchs who had been sent to Athens were executed. The story of the revolt is one of the great dramatic episodes in Thucydides (3. 2–6, 3. 8–18, 3. 25–50).

Although Thucydides does not mention Dexander by name, he does say that among those who tipped off the Athenians about the preparations for the revolt were 'men in private station among the Mytileneans themselves, consuls of the Athenians, ⟨who acted⟩

because of faction' (3. 2. 3). A consul (*proxenos*) was a citizen of the city where he served, not of the city he represented. In return for honours and privileges in the city he represented, a *proxenos* looked after its interests in his native city.

An heiress (*epiklēros*) was the daughter of a man who died leaving no legitimate male issue such as a son or grandson or great-grandson. The family property was attached to the *epiklēros* and remained with her until it could be inherited by her son. To furnish her with a son she would be married to a man whose duty it was to sire a legitimate son and to look after the family property until that son came of age. The *epiklēros* herself had no voice in whom she married, though the fact that it was through her that her husband had control of the family property sometimes gave her the upper hand in the marriage (*EN* VIII. 10. 1161^{a}1–2). If there were two daughters, the property was divided equally. Since Timophanes was wealthy, the control of half of his estate would still be a valuable prize. Aristotle does not tell us the basis of Dexander's legal suit. One possibility is that Dexander's sons were named in Timophanes' will, but that the will was rejected by the court.

1304^{a}10–13 Phocis is a district of central Greece north-west of Boeotia. The Sacred War, so-called because its ostensible ground was sacrilege against Apollo, kept the Greek world in turmoil for a decade and drew Philip II of Macedon into the heart of Greece. The war was declared against Phocis in 356 BC by the Amphictyonic League, an association of tribes organized around the temple of Apollo at Delphi. Onomarchus was an outstanding Phocian leader in the war. Under his leadership Phocis became for a few years one of the leading powers in Greece. As a general he was skilful enough to defeat Philip twice before meeting defeat and death himself in a third battle in 352 BC. Mnaseas, who was also a Phocian general, fell a year later. The war was brought to an end in 346 BC by Philip's intervention. (Diod. 16. 23–5, 16. 27–33, 16. 35–8, 16. 56–61.)

Mnason is reported to have been a comrade of Aristotle (Athen. VI, 264d).

1304^{a}13–14 Whether the change of constitution at Epidamnus referred to here is the same as the constitutional modification described earlier at 1. 1301^{b}21–6 is uncertain.

1304ᵃ17–38

This section is filled with examples illustrating the general principle that any individual, office, or section of the city that becomes a source of military power or wins esteem in some other way is a potential cause of faction and constitutional change.

1304ᵃ20–4 By the time of the Persian Wars the council of the Areopagus, so-called because it met on the hill of Ares, was composed entirely of ex-archons, who entered the council automatically when their one-year tenure of the archonship was over. Since there were nine new ex-archons each year and since membership on the council was for life, the Areopagus was a large body. The oligarchic bent of the Areopagus (II. 12. 1273ᵇ39–40) was due to the fact that the archonship, and consequently the membership of the Areopagus, was restricted (until the middle of the fifth century BC) to citizens of the two wealthiest classes (*AP* 26. 2).

The sea battle off the island of Salamis in 480 BC crushed the Persian fleet and propelled Athens to greatness. The Areopagus won esteem in the Persian Wars by providing the money required to get the poorer citizens to man the triremes and to fight at Salamis—eight drachmas for each man who would go on board (*AP* 23. 1–2). The naval rabble gained power by winning the battle.

Aristotle says that the council of the Areopagus tightened the constitution, that is, made it more oligarchical, whereas the naval rabble made the democracy stronger. So the very same event had opposite effects: it made Athens both more and less oligarchical. But the father of logic has not been caught in a contradiction. The law of non-contradiction is not violated as long as the opposite effects are at different times, or in different places, or in different respects. In this case the same event had opposite effects at different times. For the seventeen years following the battle of Salamis Athens became more oligarchical under the influence of the Areopagus (*AP* 25); but then, as the naval rabble gained power, Athens became more democratic (II. 12. 1274ᵃ7–15).

The connection of the growth of Athenian democracy with the increasing importance of the naval rabble is an instance of an empirical principle, which Aristotle reiterates several times, that the constitution of a city tends to reflect the relative importance to

that city of the various kinds of armed force: oligarchy is a reflec-
tion of the preponderance of cavalry; polity, of hoplites; and democracy, of light infantry and the navy (IV. 3. 1289ᵇ33–40, 13.
1297ᵇ16–24; VI. 7. 1321ª6–14). It is difficult to deny a share of the
constitution to those upon whose prowess the military fortunes of
a city depend.

1304ª25–7 At the battle of Mantinea in 418 BC Sparta and her
allies won a decisive victory over a coalition of Argos, Mantinea,
and Athens. (Mantinea is about twenty miles directly west of
Argos.) The Argive notables who won esteem in the battle were a
thousand specially trained warriors recruited from the strongest
and wealthiest of the younger citizens (Diod. 12. 75. 7, 12. 79. 2).
Soon after distinguishing themselves in the battle, these picked
warriors overthrew the democracy in Argos with help from Sparta
and set up a short-lived oligarchy favourable to their recent foe.
(Thuc. 5. 63–84; Diod. 12. 79, 12. 80. 1–3.)

1304ª27–9 The tide turned against Athens in the Peloponnesian
War when the expedition she sent to Sicily in 415 BC was annihi-
lated by Syracuse two years later. The fate of the expeditionary
force was sealed when its siege of Syracuse was broken and the
Athenian navy was decisively defeated in a series of battles in the
Great Harbour of Syracuse. (The story of the expedition, related in
Books VI and VII, is the climax of Thucydides' history.)

Who were the people (*ho dēmos*) that were the cause of the
victory? Aristotle is apparently referring to the poorer citizens
of Syracuse, who served as light infantry and trireme oarsmen. For
he distinguishes hoplites from the people (see 6. 1305ᵇ33 together
with IV. 3. 1289ᵇ29–32) and describes the constitutional change
the people brought about as a change from polity—a constitution
under which those who possess heavy arms are supreme (III. 7.
1279ª37–ᵇ4)—to democracy—one under which the people are supreme (III. 6. 1278ᵇ11–12). Thus, in Aristotle's view it was the sea
battles in the Great Harbour that won the war.

Newman notes that the constitutional history of Syracuse from
the overthrow of the tyranny in 466 BC until the Syracusan victory
in 413 BC is inconsistently described in Book V (ad loc.). Aristotle
seems to hold that Syracuse was a polity or an aristocracy (10.
1312ᵇ6–9) during this period, yet in one passage (12. 1316ª32–3) he
says that the tyranny was followed by a democracy. This apparent

contradiction can perhaps be resolved by recalling that Aristotle remarks elsewhere that 'what we now call polities the men of earlier times called democracies' (IV. 13. 1297ᵇ24–5).

1304ᵃ29–31 We know nothing about the tyrant Phoxus.

1304ᵃ31–3 The incident that led to Periander's overthrow is related at 10. 1311ᵃ39–ᵇ1 below. The constitution the people established was a democracy. See 3. 1303ᵃ23 above and note.

1304ᵃ38–ᵇ18

Aristotle now claims that constitutions change not only when an individual, office, or section of the city becomes greatly superior but also when opposite parts of the city become equals, and concludes his discussion of the general causes of faction and constitutional change with a few remarks about force and deception.

1304ᵇ1 Aristotle's middle class is apparently the hoplite class. The armed forces in a typical Greek city consisted of four arms: cavalry, hoplites, light infantry, and the navy (VI. 7. 1321ᵃ6–7, 8. 1322ᵇ1–2). The light infantry and the navy are drawn from the people (VI. 7. 1321ᵃ13–14, 19–21), and the cavalry is provided by the very rich (VI. 7. 1321ᵃ11). So, by a process of elimination, the class midway between the people and the wealthy must be the hoplite class—the class of citizens wealthy enough to provide themselves with heavy arms but not wealthy enough to maintain a horse.

1304ᵇ7–17 Aristotle says that constitutions are altered either by force or by deceit and then suggests an interesting symmetry in these two methods. Coercion is applied (1) from the start or (2) only later on, and deceit is used (3) only at the start or (4) both at the start and later on. In case (1) the new constitution is never accepted willingly; in cases (2) and (3) it is accepted willingly at the beginning but not later on; and in case (4) it is accepted willingly all along.

1304ᵇ12–15 The Four Hundred were a group of oligarchs that held power for four months in 411 BC during a particularly stormy period of Athenian history. Peisander, the spokesman of the oligarchs, persuaded the people that the king of Persia would switch sides in the Peloponnesian War and ally himself with Athens if they replaced their democracy with an oligarchy. But when the Athenian envoys led by Peisander attempted to negotiate an alliance with the Persian satrap Tissaphernes, they were rebuffed. The overthrow of the democracy was carried through none the less. Aristotle, contrary to Thucydides, implies that Peisander was aware from the beginning that there was little likelihood of a Persian alliance. (See Thuc. 8. 45–54, 8. 56, 8. 63–77, 8. 81–2, 8. 86, 8. 89–98; *AP* 29–33.)

CHAPTER 5

Aristotle turns now from the general causes of faction and constitutional change to those peculiar to specific constitutions, beginning with the causes peculiar to democracy. The chapter is divided into three parts corresponding to the constitutions into which a democracy changes: oligarchy (1304^{b}20–1305^{a}7), tyranny (1305^{a}7–28), or ultimate democracy (1305^{a}28–34).

1304^{b}20–1305^{a}7

Aristotle begins by describing how demagogues goad the notables into overthrowing democracies and installing oligarchies.

The Greek word *dēmagōgos*, which migrated into English as 'demagogue', is derived from *dēmos*, 'people', and *agōgos*, 'leader', and means literally 'leader of the people'. In one passage in this chapter Aristotle even uses the phrase 'the leaders of the people' (*hoi prostatai tou dēmou*) as a stylistic variant of *dēmagōgoi* (1305^{a}20–1). By extension the word *dēmagōgos* came to mean someone who behaves like a leader of the people; and in the next chapter Aristotle applies the term to those who, in seeking power among the few, imitate a leader of the many (6. 1305^{b}23–7).

Aristotle remarks that in ancient times the demagogues 'were drawn from those who were generals' whereas nowadays they need only be good public speakers (1305^{a}10–13). The reason a demagogue in Aristotle's day had to be a good public speaker is that ordinarily his power and influence rested, not on any executive office he held, but squarely on his ability to sway the assembly or the popular courts with a persuasive speech. The assembly and the popular courts are alluded to in the passage before us in the opposition of the public arena (*ta koinē(i)*) and the private suits (*ta idia(i)*).

Aristotle had a low opinion of demagogues. In his view the demagogue was a flatterer (*kolax*) of the people (11. 1313^{b}40–1). Flattery (*kolakeia*) is one of the vices discussed in the ethical treatises (*EN* II. 7. 1108^{a}26–30, IV. 6; *EE* II. 3. 1221^{a}7, III. 7. 1233^{b}29–34; *MM* I. 31). In the pleasures of social intercourse friendliness (*philia*) is the mean, and flattery and churlishness are the vices of excess and deficiency respectively. 'The flatterer and being flattered are pleasant; for the flatterer is one who appears to be an admirer and appears to be a friend' (*Rhet*. I. 11. 1371^{a}22–4). In truth he is neither. Unlike a true friend, he seeks only to please the object of his flattery, not to do him good; and the pleasure he gives is given not for its own sake but to garner benefit for himself (*EN* II. 7. 1108^{a}29, IV. 6. 1127^{a}8–10, X. 3. 1173^{b}31–1174^{a}1). Aristotle goes so far as to compare demagogues with the flatterers in a tyranny (IV. 4. 1292^{a}20–3). In the type of democracy in which demagogues flourish, the people collectively are a kind of tyrant; and the demagogues in such a democracy pander to this collective tyrant as the flatterers in a tyranny pander to one man.

Aristotle claims that democracies are overthrown for the most part because demagogues unjustly appropriate the property of the notables and force them in response to unite against the constitution. A Greek city did not have the devices of a modern state—property taxes, progressive income taxes, and inheritance (or death) taxes—for redistributing the wealth of its citizens. The Greeks took a dim view of direct taxes on citizens (though not on resident aliens) except in wartime emergencies. They regarded direct taxes on a citizen's person or property as something that no free man would tolerate. In their place a Greek city had liturgies and fines, the latter of which might involve the confiscation of all of a man's property. Thus, Aristotle describes the depredations instigated by the demagogues as consisting in the imposition of excessive liturgies and the confiscation of property (presumably after trial on some trumped-up charge).

Liturgies were compulsory public services performed by the wealthy citizens of a city. The more important liturgies were the trierarchy (the maintenance of a trireme for a year), the *choregia* (the provision of the chorus for the performance of a tragedy or a comedy), the *hestiasis* (the provision of a public banquet), the *architheōria* (the leadership of a sacred embassy), the *hippotrophia* (the maintenance of a cavalry horse), and the gymnasiarchy (the provision of gymnastic trainers and sometimes the runners for a torch race). All of these are mentioned in the *Nicomachean Ethics* (IV. 2. 1122ᵃ24–5, ᵇ19–23, 1123ᵃ22–4) and the *Politics* (IV. 3. 1289ᵇ35–6; V. 8. 1309ᵃ17–20; VI. 7. 1321ᵃ11, 35–9, 8. 1323ᵃ1).

1304ᵇ25–7 Cos is an island off the south-west coast of Asia Minor opposite Halicarnassus. We know nothing more of the overthrow of the democracy at Cos, though we hear that there was faction in Cos in 366 BC (Strabo 14. 2. 19; Diod. 15. 76. 2). (See Sherwin-White, pp. 65–6, 73, 75.)

1304ᵇ27–31 On the overthrow of the democracy at Rhodes see note to 3. 1302ᵇ23–4 above. What seems to have happened is that the demagogues needed money to pay the people for attending the assembly and serving on juries; for if the people did not attend, the demagogues would lose their influence. They raised at least some of the money they needed by preventing the disbursement of the money due the trireme commanders under their contracts with the city to build and fit triremes for the Rhodian navy. Since the trireme commanders were not paid, they were unable in their turn to pay their suppliers and workers, who sued the trireme commanders. To escape these lawsuits the trireme commanders banded together and overthrew the democracy. (See Newman, ad loc.)

1304ᵇ31–4 There were many cities scattered throughout the Greek world from Asia Minor to Sicily bearing the name of the hero Heracles. Which one is Aristotle referring to? An Heraclea is mentioned in four other passages in the *Politics* (6. 1305ᵇ2–12, 34–6, 1306ᵃ36–ᵇ1; VII. 6. 1327ᵇ14–15), but is further identified in only one (1305ᵇ36), the reference being to Heraclea on the Pontus (the Black Sea). Since the incidents related in these various passages are of little help in identifying the city or cities referred to, the simplest hypothesis, that the references are all to the same city, Heraclea Pontica, is generally favoured (see Newman, ad loc.). It was founded by Megara around 560 BC on the south coast of the Black Sea; and assuming the passage before us refers to this Heraclea, it was founded as a democracy but quickly became an oligarchy.

1304ᵇ34–9 On the overthrow of the democracy at Megara see the note to 3. 1302ᵇ31 above.

1304ᵇ39–1305ᵃI Cyme is also mentioned at II. 8. 1269ᵃI–3. There were three Cymes in the Greek world: Aeolic Cyme on the west coast of Asia Minor south-east of Lesbos, Euboean Cyme on the east coast of Euboea, and Italian Cyme (the Roman Cumae) on the west coast of Italy near Naples. We do not know which one Aristotle is referring to.

The Thrasymachus who overthrew the democracy at Cyme bears a famous name. Could he be the sophist from Chalcedon so savagely portrayed in Plato's *Republic*? Aristotle at any rate does not distinguish him from the sophist, to whom he clearly refers five times (*Soph. El.* 34. 183ᵇ32; *Rhet.* II. 23. 1400ᵇ19–20, III. 1. 1404ᵃ14, 8. 1409ᵃ2, 11. 1413ᵃ8). (See White, pp. 326–7.)

1305ᵃ7–28

Aristotle claims that 'in ancient times' (the seventh and sixth centuries BC) democracies changed, not into oligarchies, but into tyrannies, the tyrant usually being a former demagogue, and offers three reasons in explanation: (1) the demagogues were generals, (2) high office fell into the wrong hands, and (3) the people lived in the country.

From this explanation we can understand how Aristotle pictures the rise of tyranny from democracy. He envisages a democracy divided into two factions, a faction of the wealthy and a faction of the people. The people live in the country on their farms; the wealthy (presumably) in town. A general becomes a leader of the people—a 'demagogue' in the literal sense of the term—after gaining their respect by his prowess in war and their trust by his animosity toward the wealthy. He uses his military experience in the factional conflict between the people and the wealthy and eventually seizes power in the name of the people. He is able to remain in power because his followers, being busy on their farms in the country, are not around to hold him in check.

In Plato's similar but more vivid sketch of the rise of tyranny from democracy (*Rep.* VIII. 563e–566d), the demagogue becomes a tyrant at the moment he secures a bodyguard. Aristotle does not mention such a guard in the section before us, though he says later on that a tyrant differs from a king in having a guard of aliens rather than of citizens (10. 1311ᵃ7–8; see also *Rhet.* I. 2. 1357ᵇ30–6).

1305ᵃ15–18 The presidency (*prutaneia*) was a high office, and the president (*prutanis*) the high official who occupied it. Our knowledge of the office at Miletus is limited to what can be inferred from this passage. Athens and other cities (see VI. 8. 1322ᵇ28–9) had an office of the same name, but the nature of the office varied widely. We know nothing further about the event referred to.

1305ᵃ23–4 In the factional struggle that broke out in Athens after the Solonian reforms, Peisistratus led a third party, the party of (or beyond) the hills, against the party of the plain and the party of the coast. Using a ruse and relying on his military reputation, he was able in 561 BC to secure a bodyguard and make himself tyrant. (*Rhet.* I. 2. 1357ᵇ30–6; *AP* 13–14; Her. I. 59.)

1305ᵃ24–6 Theagenes became tyrant of Megara during the latter half of the seventh century BC. He married one of his daughters to the well-born and powerful Athenian, Cylon, supported Cylon's unsuccessful attempt to establish himself as tyrant of Athens, and was eventually driven out of Megara. (*Rhet.* I. 2. 1357ᵇ30–6; Thuc. I. 126. 3; Plut. *Gr. Q.* q. 18 (295 C–D).)

1305ᵃ26–8 Dionysius I rose to power in Syracuse during the Carthaginian invasion of Sicily in 406–405 BC. His rise followed the classical pattern. After distinguishing himself in battle, he put himself forward as a man of the people, denounced the wealthy in the assembly, and was elected as one of a panel of generals. By remaining aloof from the other generals and accusing them of betraying their country to the Carthaginians, he got himself elevated to 'general with supreme power' (*stratēgos autokratōr*). Then, employing a ruse, he persuaded the people to give him a bodyguard of six hundred soldiers. Once provided with the bodyguard, he openly proclaimed himself tyrant. He consolidated his power by convening an assembly and having his two most influential opponents executed, one of whom was the former general Daphnaeus. (Diod. 13. 91–6.)

1305ᵃ28–34

Aristotle notes finally that democracies change not only to oligarchies and tyrannies but also from one kind of democracy to another—from ancestral democracy to the newest sort. The ancestral democracy at Athens was the constitution of Solon (for which see II. 12. 1273ᵇ33–1274ᵃ7 and the note to VI. 4. 1318ᵇ6–1319ᵇ1). The 'newest sort', where 'the people are supreme even over the laws', is ultimate democracy (for which see IV. 4. 1292ᵃ4–37, 6. 1292ᵇ41–1293ᵃ10; VI. 4. 1319ᵇ1–32, VI. 5; and the notes to the two latter passages).

Aristotle implies that elective office is pursued with less zeal when candidates must satisfy a property qualification. The reason for the lack of zeal is that those who possess property are usually more interested in tending to it than in serving in public office (see VI. 5. 1320ᵃ27–8). Aristotle seems to think that the zealous pursuit of elective office in a democracy leads office-seekers to outbid each other with promises of greater and greater power for their electors—the people—the ultimate bid being all power to the people. Aristotle would have the separate tribes (subdivisions of the citizen body) elect the officials, his idea being perhaps that the interests of a tribe would not exactly coincide with those of the people as a whole.

CHAPTER 6

Aristotle discusses the causes of faction and constitutional change that are specific to oligarchy under two principal heads: constitutional change originating (1) from those outside the ruling circle and (2) from those within the circle. At the end of the chapter he mentions an additional cause: (3) mischance.

1305ᵃ36–ᵇ22

Constitutional change originating from those outside the constitution is attributed to four different causes: (*a*) the unjust treatment of the mass, (*b*) the narrowness of the ruling circle, (*c*) faction among the notables, and (*d*) the resentment of the mass toward their rulers.

1305ᵃ38–ᵇ1 The first case that Aristotle considers, in which an oligarchy is overthrown by the people because the oligarchs treat them unjustly, might seem to be a case of constitutional change originating in the ruling circle itself since the overthrow can be traced to unjust actions of the oligarchs and since (in Aristotle's example at least) the overthrow is led by an oligarch. But in classifying the case as he does, Aristotle is focusing on the fact that those who overthrow the oligarchy are the people, quintessential outsiders in an oligarchy.

Lygdamis was tyrant of Naxos, the largest island of the Cyclades, from around 545 to 524 BC. In the passage before us Aristotle tells us that Lygdamis came from the oligarchy itself, that he led the people against the oligarchy, and that he later became tyrant of Naxos. Other sources fill in a few details. The occasion of the faction against the oligarchy was an assault upon Telesagoras, a rich and popular citizen of Naxos, and his two daughters by some wealthy young men flown with wine. The people, with Lygdamis at their head, overthrew the oligarchy and (presumably) established a democracy. Later when Peisistratus was struggling to regain the tyranny of Athens, Lygdamis supplied him with men and money. After Peisistratus regained the tyranny, he repaid Lygdamis by conquering Naxos and installing him as tyrant. (Aristotle, fr. 558 (Rose 3rd edn.); *AP* 15; *Oec.* II. 2. 1346ᵇ7–12; Her. 1. 61, 1. 64.)

1305ᵇ1–12 The second case on Aristotle's list is one in which the narrowness of an oligarchy is attacked by rich men excluded from the ruling circle.

'The origin of faction initiated by others *also* takes different forms': what this sentence means is that just as factions initiated by those within the ruling circle have different sorts of origins (see 1305ᵇ22–1306ᵇ5), so *too* do factions initiated by others.

The constitutional provision preventing a father and a son, or an older and a younger brother, from holding office at the same time is based on the idea that the basic political unit is the family rather than the individual. By the narrowest interpretation of this idea each family that shares in the constitution is entitled to exactly one office-holder—the head of the household. By a slightly broader interpretation each privileged family is entitled to two—father and eldest son. Under such an arrangement the men from the privileged families who are left on the sidelines will be eager to get into the game themselves and can be expected to cause trouble until they do. In the three cities mentioned by Aristotle their agitation led to the constitution being loosened to various degrees. Heraclea on the Black Sea (see 1305ᵇ36 below and note to 5. 1304ᵇ31–4) became a looser oligarchy; Massalia (the modern Marseilles), more of a polity; and Istrus (also on the Black Sea), a democracy. At VI. 7. 1321ᵃ29–31 Aristotle describes a procedure at Massalia by which men outside the governing class were brought into it. The constitutional alteration at Massalia mentioned here may have been a result of the adoption of this selection process.

1305ᵇ12–22   Aristotle next considers the case in which the people, taking advantage of faction among the notables, overturn the oligarchy.

At Cnidus, a city on the long peninsula jutting from the southwest corner of Asia Minor, the people overthrew the oligarchy after the notables weakened themselves by internal dissension. As Newman points out (ad loc.), the overthrow at Cnidus is similar in one respect to that at Naxos and dissimilar in another. Although both oligarchies were overthrown by the people led by a notable, the cause of the overthrow at Cnidus was the people's contempt for the notables (see 3. 1302ᵇ25–7) rather than their oppression by them, as at Naxos. The notables at Cnidus were objects of contempt because they had weakened themselves by splitting into two factions.

1305ᵇ18–22   Aristotle notes finally that oligarchies—his example suggests he is still thinking of narrow oligarchies—are sometimes overthrown by the people out of simple resentment, even when the rulers rule well.

Erythrae is an Ionian city on the coast of Asia Minor opposite the island of Chios. The Basilidae, if their name can be trusted, were descendents of the original kings (*basileis*) of the city.

1305ᵇ22–1306ᵇ5

Aristotle turns now to the second of his principal heads: constitutional change originating within the ruling circle. He lists six sources of such change: (*a*) political rivalry, (*b*) financial ruin, (*c*) the formation of an inner circle within the ruling circle, (*d*) inability to manage the armed forces, (*e*) grievances, and (*f*) despotism.

1305ᵇ22–39   Political rivalry sparks constitutional change when some of the oligarchs, in seeking to triumph over their political rivals, become demagogues either within the ruling circle itself or in relation to the people.

1305ᵇ25–6 In 404 BC, after losing the Peloponnesian War, the Athenians were forced by the Spartan admiral Lysander to elect a provisional government of thirty oligarchs, known to history as the Thirty Tyrants, to manage the affairs of the city and to draft a new constitution. The leadership of the Thirty was soon seized by demagogues, who instituted a reign of terror. When Theramenes, a more moderate voice within the Thirty, began to oppose the excesses of his colleagues, he was summarily executed. Within nine months of their election the Thirty were deposed, and the democracy was restored soon after. The passage before us differs from two of our main sources for these events (Xen. *Hell.* 2. 3–4, and Diod. 14. 3–6) in portraying Charicles rather than Critias as the leader of the demagogues. The two men are paired in Xenophon's *Memorabilia* (1. 2. 31–7) and Lysias' *Prosecution of Eratosthenes* (55). (See also *AP* 34–8, and Plato, *Apol.* 32c–d.)

1305ᵇ27 On the Four Hundred see the note to 4. 1304ᵇ12–15. The Four Hundred split into two factions when they realized that they were about to be overthrown. The demagogues, led by Phrynichus among others, were implacable foes of democracy and justifiably feared for their lives if the oligarchy fell. (Phrynichus himself was assassinated even before it fell.) As a consequence, they were willing to pay any price, including the betrayal of Athens to the Spartans, to remain in power. The moderates, led by Theramenes and Aristocrates, favoured a kind of polity, the Five Thousand, under which full citizenship would be restricted to those who possessed heavy arms; and they hoped that their opposition to the demagogues would bring such a constitution into existence under their leadership (which it did). (*AP* 33, Thuc. 8. 89–90.)

1305ᵇ28–36 Aristotle passes now to constitutional change that comes about because oligarchs become demagogues in their relations with the people. He notes that demagogues are likely to arise in any oligarchy where, though only the wealthy hold office, the people elect the office-holders or sit on juries. For under such a constitutional arrangement an oligarch will be tempted to use demagoguery to win an election or to ruin a rival in court. As a result the people gain power at the expense of the oligarchs.

1305ᵇ29–30 Aristotle mentions Larissa, the principal city of Thessaly, three other times in the *Politics* (III. 2. 1275ᵇ26–30; V. 6. 1306ᵃ29–30, 10. 1311ᵇ17–20).

The function of a Guardian of the City (*politophulax*) is unclear. He seems to have been a high official similar to a general (II. 8. 1268^{a}21–3) charged among other things with guarding the city from enemies within (see VI. 8. 1322^{a}33–4).

1305^{b}33 Abydos, on the Asiatic coast of the Hellespont, probably became an oligarchy in 411 BC when it seceded from the Athenian Empire, to which it had belonged for over sixty years (Thuc. 8. 62).

1305^{b}36 For Heraclea Pontica see the note to 5. 1304^{b}31–4.

1305^{b}39–1306^{a}12 Aristotle next considers how a squandered fortune can undermine an oligarchy. Sometimes a ruined oligarch will promote the overthrow of an oligarchy in order to retrieve his fortune; at other times he will provoke an overthrow by his predations of public property.

1306^{a}1–2 The example of Hipparinus fits the chapter on oligarchy imperfectly since Dionysius I, the tyrant he helped to install, overthrew a democracy rather than an oligarchy. (For Dionysius see the note to 5. 1305^{a}26–8.) Hipparinus served with Dionysius on the panel of generals from which Dionysius rose to 'general with supreme power' and then to tyrant. Later Dionysius married Hipparinus' daughter Aristomache. Hipparinus' son Dion became a friend and pupil of Plato's and ultimately a foe of Dionysius' son and heir, Dionysius II. (Plut. *Dion* 3.)

1306^{a}2–4 On Amphipolis see the note to 3. 1303^{b}2–3. As the earlier passage indicates, the Amphipolitans came to regret their admission of Chalcidian colonists. We know nothing about Cleotimus and his activities beyond what can be inferred from the passage before us.

1306^{a}4–6 Aegina, an island in the middle of the Saronic Gulf a short sail from the Peiraeus, was a constant irritant to Athens. Chares was a famous fourth-century Athenian general who often employed mercenaries. We know of the transaction with Chares from no other source, though its nature may be conjectured: an individual wishes to retrieve his squandered fortune by installing a tyranny at Aegina and seeks aid from Chares and his mercenaries (perhaps while Chares was stationed at Corinth in 367 BC) promising pliant relations with Athens and a substantial reward for Chares himself. (See Newman, ad loc.)

1306^{a}8–9 On Apollonia Pontica see the note to 3. 1303^{a}36–8.

1306ᵃ9–12 As Newman points out (ad loc.), Aristotle is relaxing the Platonic maxim that it is impossible for a constitution to be altered when those who hold office are of one mind (*Rep.* VIII. 545d1–3). Aristotle thinks it possible but not easy. It is possible because, as he notes earlier in this very chapter, the people in Erythrae overthrew the oligarchy of the Basilidae 'even though those within the constitution managed things well' (1305ᵇ18–22). The example of Pharsalus shows that it is not easy.

Pharsalus is a city of Thessaly on the road from Larissa to central Greece. During the period when this passage was written the leading men at Pharsalus were friendly with Philip II of Macedon, and this friendship may have been an additional factor in the stability of the oligarchy (Hammond and Griffith, p. 539).

1306ᵃ12–19 Aristotle next considers the case in which an oligarchy is overthrown because it is structured as one oligarchy within another.

The Eleians occupied a region of the north-western Peloponnese. In 471 BC the many small cities in which they lived united into a single one called 'Elis' (Diod. 11. 54. 1). The inner circle of the oligarchy at Elis was particularly tight, for the life tenure of the elders and their dynastic election made access to their high office doubly difficult for outsiders. A dynastic election is presumably an election in which the candidates for an office are required by law to be sons or grandsons of the man who last held the office (see IV. 6. 1293ᵃ26–30).

One might infer from this cause of overthrow that Aristotle thinks that oligarchy is inherently unstable. For the oligarchy that Aristotle ranks highest and which he regards as 'the most well-tempered of the oligarchies' (VI. 6. 1320ᵇ21) has the very structure that he warns against, that of an oligarchy within an oligarchy. The higher officials in this well-tempered oligarchy compose a narrow circle within a wider one due to the fact that they must satisfy a larger property qualification than the lower officials (1320ᵇ21–9).

1306ᵃ19–31 Aristotle now describes several cases in which the oligarchs bring about their own downfall in dealing with the military requirements of war and the need for an armed guard in time of peace.

Aristotle thinks it difficult for an oligarchy to survive a war. The underlying reason, which seemed too obvious to Aristotle to require stating (but see Plato, *Rep.* VIII. 551d9–e4), is that the oligarchs are too few in number to constitute an effective fighting force. They have only two sources of additional troops: mercenaries or the people. If they hire mercenaries, the general who commands them is likely to make himself tyrant. If they call upon the people, they will need to give them something in return. What the people usually demand is 'a share of the constitution', that is, full citizenship, thus converting the oligarchy into a democracy.

In peacetime a city needs an armed guard to preserve order. In an oligarchy a problem arises with such a guard whenever the oligarchs split into two factions. For if the general commanding the guard belongs to one of the factions, the members of the other will feel threatened. But if the oligarchs attempt to resolve their problem by appointing a general who is neutral between the two factions, he is likely to make himself master of both.

For the distinction between the offices concerned with guarding the city and those concerned with war see VI. 8. 1322ᵃ33–4. That the commander of the guard is a general is stated at IV. 15. 1300ᵇ9–12.

1306ᵃ22–4 Timophanes was a general at Corinth at the time of its war with Argos and Cleonae around 365 BC. (Cleonae is eleven miles south-east of Corinth.) The Corinthians hired four hundred mercenaries and appointed Timophanes their commander. Timophanes used them to make himself tyrant, which distressed his younger brother, Timoleon. Although Timoleon had saved his brother's life on a previous occasion, he now participated in his assassination. Timoleon's act posed a delicate question for the Corinthians, Should he be celebrated as a tyrannicide or reviled as a fratricide? (Plut. *Timoleon* 4. The story is told slightly differently in Diod. 16. 65. 3–8.)

1306ᵃ24 On dynasty see the note to 3. 1302ᵇ17–18 above.

1306ᵃ29–31 We know nothing about these events in Larissa and Abydos beyond what can be inferred from this passage itself, and only Simus can be identified with any confidence. He is known to history as the man who betrayed Thessaly to Philip II of Macedon (Dem. *On the Crown* 48) and who consorted with prostitutes ([Dem.], *Against Neaera* 24, 108). (On Simus see Hammond and Griffith, pp. 525–6.)

Is Aristotle referring to the rise or the fall of Simus and Iphiades? He does not make it clear whether they are the neutral officers who rose to power in Larissa and Abydos or the leaders whom the neutral officers overthrew.

On Abydos see the note to 1305ᵇ33.

1306ᵃ31–ᵇ2 Aristotle next considers several cases in which faction breaks out within the governing class because an oligarch feels he has been wronged in connection with a marriage or dishonoured as the result of a lawsuit.

1306ᵃ34–6 Aristotle adds another example of a faction arising in connection with a marriage to the four mentioned at 4. 1303ᵇ37–1304ᵃ17.

The only information we have about the alleged injustice suffered by Diagoras and his overthrow of the oligarchy of horsemen at Eretria is contained in the passage before us. At IV. 3. 1289ᵇ33–41 Aristotle explains the connection between cavalry and oligarchy—the keeping of horses was expensive—and notes the use of cavalry in the wars between Eretria and its neighbour Chalcis, the two leading cities of the island of Euboea. (On Euboea see the note to 3. 1303ᵃ16–20.) In 490 BC Eretria was besieged and burnt by the Persian expedition that was soon to suffer a humiliating defeat at Marathon.

1306ᵃ36–ᵇ2 The punishment inflicted on Eurytion and Archias was particularly humiliating. The pillory was 'a wooden yoke placed on the back of the neck, which kept the head bowed down' (Newman, ad loc.). Being bound in such a yoke and exposed to public scorn was the sort of punishment usually reserved for thieves. Aristotle does not tell us whether the factional strife to which this demeaning punishment gave rise led to the overthrow of the oligarchies at Thebes and Heraclea. (On Heraclea see the note to 5. 1304ᵇ31–4.)

1306ᵇ3–5 In bringing to a close his list of cases of constitutional change originating among the oligarchs themselves, Aristotle notes that oligarchies are frequently overthrown by oligarchs who cannot bear the despotism of their colleagues.

The overthrow of the oligarchy at Cnidus to which Aristotle refers would seem to be distinct from the one at Cnidus referred to earlier at 1305ᵇ12–18 since the earlier reference attributes the overthrow to the people rather than to malcontents 'within the constitution'.

On Chios see the note to 3. 1303^{a}34–5.

1306^{b}6–16

The third avenue of change in oligarchies is mischance (*sumptōma*), which is simply chance (*tuchē*) by another name (see 3. 1303a3). (For the conjunction of 'chance' and 'mischance' see *Phys*. II. 8. 199^{a}1 and *Rhet*. I. 9. 1367^{b}24.) Chance, or mischance, plays an important role in the life of a city, though a wise lawgiver will seek to minimize its operation. In the section before us Aristotle notes that oligarchy and polity can fade away through mischance; in a later chapter he explains how to avoid such a mischance (8. 1308^{a}35–^{b}10). As he observes in another context, chance can work to preserve, as well as to undermine, an existing constitution (II. 11. 1273^{b}18–24). (On chance see the note to 3. 1302^{b}33–1303^{a}13.)

The mischance in question arises from a contingency that the lawgiver of an oligarchy or a polity fails to provide for. In an oligarchy or a polity there will always be a body of second-class citizens who own property including land but who are excluded from office and hence are not full citizens. The contingency is a steep rise in the value of their property 'due to peace or some other good fortune'. In time of peace the value of their farms would increase as they were able to spend their revenue on slaves and livestock rather than war (see Diod. 11. 72. 1). If this contingency occurs in an oligarchy or polity that has no law tightening the property qualification for office as the property of its citizens rises steeply in value, even the poorest landowner will eventually be able to satisfy it and become a full citizen; and the oligarchy or polity will be converted inadvertently into a democracy.

In his earlier discussion of the operation of chance Aristotle notes that the reverse also happens, that democracies change into oligarchies and dynasties by chance 'when the prosperous become numerous or their properties grow' (3. 1303^{a}10–13). It should be noted, however, that Aristotle employs different concepts of oligarchy in the two passages. In the earlier passage oligarchy is the rule of the prosperous, whereas in the passage before us it is the rule of the few. (For these differing definitions see the note to 1. 1301ᵃ28–35.)

1306ᵇ17–21 The absolutist type of democracy is that in which 'the multitude is supreme and not the law' (IV. 4. 1292ᵃ4–6). The absolutist type of oligarchy is that in which 'it is not the law that rules but the officials' (IV. 5. 1292ᵇ5–7).

CHAPTER 7

In this chapter Aristotle discusses four causes of faction and constitutional change specific to, or especially operative in, aristocracy: (1) the exclusivity of the rulers, (2) the disproportionate power of the wealthy, (3) the graspingness of the rulers, and (4) gradual unnoticed alterations. His prime example of aristocracy, the constitution based on virtue, is Sparta, as his prime example of democracy, the constitution based on freedom, is Athens. Elsewhere in the *Politics* he thinks it important to stress that the virtue especially honoured and cultivated at Sparta was not complete virtue— wisdom, temperance, bravery, and justice (for which see VII. 1. 1323ᵃ28–9)—but only military virtue (II. 9. 1271ᵃ41–ᵇ3; VII. 14. 1333ᵇ5–14, 15. 1334ᵃ40–ᵇ3; VIII. 4. 1338ᵇ11–16; following Plato, *Laws* I. 631a3–8, II. 666e1–667a5). Aristotle's illustrations from Spartan history will be more intelligible if this point is kept in mind.

1306ᵇ22–1307ᵃ5

Aristotle says that the exclusivity of the rulers causes faction 'above all' when conjoined with such factors as (*a*) unhonoured virtue, (*b*) great disparity of wealth, or (*c*) the wish of a great man to rule alone.

1306ᵇ25–7 This is a curious argument. Aristotle wishes to provide a reason for believing that the rulers in an aristocracy are few in number. The reason he offers is the fact that people commonly, though mistakenly, think that aristocracies are oligarchies. This fact, in Aristotle's view, is a good reason for believing that the rulers in an aristocracy are few because it is the fewness of the rulers in an aristocracy that explains the fact. (For another instance of such an argument see VII. 13. 1332ᵃ20–7.)

1306ᵇ27–31 Aristotle mentions three cases in which unhonoured virtue drives men to make a faction. In the first of these the rulers are challenged by men outside the constitution who claim to be their equals in virtue. Aristotle's example is an obscure episode of early Spartan history following the First Messenian War. The Spartans struggled for nineteen years in the last third of the eighth century BC to conquer the rich land of Messenia north-west of Laconia. When they succeeded, they annexed the territory and reduced its population to serfdom. The Maidens' Sons, according to several conflicting stories, were the offspring of irregular connections during the war. The epithet 'Maidens' Sons' (*Partheniai*) means literally 'sons of virgins' and signifies illegitimate rather than miraculous conception. Aristotle says that their fathers were Spartan Equals, or *homoioi*, but implies that the Maidens' Sons were not themselves Equals. Unhappy with their status (since only Equals were full citizens) and resentful because they had received none of the spoils of Messenia, the Maidens' Sons joined in a conspiracy, which the Equals dealt with by sending them off to Italy to found Taras, Sparta's one true colony. (For Taras see the note on 3. 1303ᵃ3–6; and for the *Partheniai* see Michell, pp. 85–8.)

1306ᵇ31–3 The second occasion on which unhonoured virtue is liable to spark faction is when a great man is dishonoured by a still greater. Aristotle's example is Lysander, the great Spartan admiral and statesman, who was dishonoured first by King Pausanias (the grandson of the Pausanias mentioned at 1307ᵃ4 below) and then later by King Agesilaus.

By the end of the Peloponnesian War Lysander had become, through his command of the Spartan navy, the most powerful man in Greece. It was his destruction of the Athenian fleet at Aigospotami on the Hellespont in 405 BC that brought Athens to her knees by severing her grain supply. After the Thirty Tyrants he had installed at Athens were deposed (see the note on 6. 1305ᵇ25–6 above), a faction of more moderate oligarchs retained control of the city while a democratic faction held the Peiraeus. The moderate oligarchs together with the Thirty (now living in Eleusis) sought and received his support. Lysander blockaded the Peiraeus with the aim of starving it into submission. At this point Pausanias intervened. According to Xenophon, he was envious of the fame and power that success would bring to Lysander (*Hell.* 2. 4. 29). Securing the necessary support in Sparta, Pausanias arrived in Attica with an army of his own and superseded Lysander. He abandoned Lysander's policy for one of reconciliation and worked out a settlement that restored democracy to Athens. (Xen. *Hell.* 2. 4. 24–43; Diod. 14. 33. 5–6; Plut. *Lys.* 21.)

Lysander saw an opportunity to regain power a few years later. When King Agis died in 398 BC, the succession was disputed. Agis' half-brother Agesilaus claimed the throne on the ground that the heir-apparent Leotychidas was not the son of Agis but of the Athenian Alcibiades. Lysander vigorously supported Agesilaus. He had been his lover and believed, not unreasonably, that he could exercise power through him. Agesilaus was small and lame and unimpressive in appearance and had given no indication of the ability and ambition that were to mark his long military career. But once Agesilaus was chosen king, Lysander was quickly disabused. During a campaign in Asia Minor Agesilaus showed that he was his own man by asserting his supremacy over Lysander. (Xen. *Hell.* 3. 3. 1–4, 3. 4. 1–10; Plut. *Lys.* 22–3; *Agesilaus* 2–3, 6–8.)

Having been dishonoured by a king from each royal house—Pausanias was an Agiad king; Agesilaus a Eurypontid—Lysander had sufficient provocation to seek an alteration in the Spartan kingship. Aristotle says that he attempted to abolish the kingship (1. 1301ᵇ19–20). Our other sources tell us that he attempted, not to abolish the kingship, but to reform it. These sources tell us that he wanted to abolish the hereditary kingship *of the Heracleidae*—of the two houses that claimed descent from Heracles—and to replace it with an elective kingship open to every Spartan (Diod. 14. 13; Plut. *Lys.* 24–5, 30). We can bring Aristotle into accord with this by supposing that in his desire for conciseness he simply omitted the limiting phrase.

Aristotle agrees with Lysander about the Spartan kingship. In his own critique of the Spartan constitution, he contends that a king should be chosen, not on the basis of lineage, but 'on the basis of his own life' (II. 9. 1271ᵃ18–26). He also notes, undoubtedly with Lysander in mind, that the admiralship, or *nauarchia*, is a cause of faction in Sparta since it is 'almost another kingship'. The admiralship resembled a Spartan kingship in that the Spartan kings were basically just hereditary and perpetual generals (II. 9. 1271ᵃ37–41; see also III. 14. 1285ᵇ26–8).

1306ᵇ34–6 The third and final case of unhonoured virtue causing faction is where a person of manly character is excluded from office. Aristotle's example is the conspiracy of Cinadon, which was formed soon after Agesilaus became king. The story is recounted by Xenophon in his *Hellenica* (3. 3. 4–11). Xenophon's narration is interesting for its information about the social structure of Sparta and its view of the Spartan governing class from below. The conspirators wished to foment an uprising of all the non-citizen classes in Sparta. Xenophon lists four such classes: (1) the Helots, who were Greek serfs who cultivated the land for the Spartans, (2) the New People, or *Neodamodeis*, who were Helots who had been freed by the state in reward for service in war, (3) the Inferiors, or *Hypomeiones*, who had lost the rights of full citizenship through their inability to contribute to the messes, or *phiditia* (see II. 9. 1271ᵃ26–37), and (4) the Perioikoi (literally 'dwellers around'), who lived in the towns around Sparta and served in the Spartan army. Cinadon is reported to have claimed that these non-citizens outnumbered the citizens a hundred to one and would be glad to eat them raw. The conspiracy was betrayed by an informer; and the conspirators were brutally punished and almost certainly executed, though Xenophon is silent about their ultimate fate.

Xenophon does not tell us which non-citizen class Cinadon belonged to. He says only that he was not an Equal. The exclusion from the honours of office that this entailed would be particularly galling for someone of a manly nature like Cinadon. When asked why he had acted as he did, Cinadon replied, 'To be inferior to no one in Lacedaemon'. For Aristotle manliness is conjoined with love of honour (*EN* IV. 4. 1125ᵇ11–12, *Rhet.* II. 17. 1391ᵃ22–3) and connected with a capacity to rule (*EN* IV. 5. 1126ᵇ1–2).

1306ᵇ36–1307ᵃ2 Aristotle turns now to the case where great disparity of wealth, rather than unhonoured virtue, gives rise to faction. Such disparity, he notes, develops especially in time of war. The Messenian War to which he refers in illustration is the Second Messenian War. In the First War Sparta conquered Messenia and reduced its population to serfdom (see the note on 1306ᵇ27–31 above). In the Second War, two generations later, she fought to suppress a rising of the conquered Messenians. Aristotle indicates that the hardships occasioned by the Second War were not evenly distributed among the Spartans, but does not explain why. Perhaps

some families were more dependent upon income from Messenia
than others and suffered more when this income was disrupted.
Whatever the reason, those Spartans whom the war had impover-
ished demanded a redivision of the land. Whether they got it or not
we do not know.

Our only reliable source for the Messenian Wars is the poet
Tyrtaeus, whose poems were composed for the military and political crises of the Second War. The poem 'Law and Order', or
Eunomia, of which only a few fragments survive, addresses the
political crisis. It seems to have recounted the history of Sparta up
to and including the poet's own day. His war poems are exhorta-
tions to battle. They glorify patriotism and death in battle and were
probably chanted on the march to the accompaniment of a flute.
(For Tyrtaeus see Easterling and Knox, pp. 128–33.)

1307ᵃ2–5   The next case is that of a great man who starts a faction
because he wishes to rule alone. Aristotle's first illustration is the
Spartan general Pausanias, who rose to greatness in the Persian
Wars. As regent for his young cousin, King Pleistarchos, he led the
combined Greek army to its crowning victory at Plataea in 479 BC
and led a Greek fleet in the recovery of Byzantium in 478 BC. The
first victory drove the Persians from the Greek mainland, and the
second opened the Black Sea to Greek commerce. These victories
also went to Pausanias' head. He began acting more like a tyrant
than a general and even aspired 'to become tyrant of Greece' (Her.
5. 32). In pursuit of this ambitious goal he entered into a treason-
able correspondence with Xerxes, the Persian king. Recalled to
Sparta to answer for his actions, he was acquitted of the graver
charges but lost his command of the allied fleet. He returned to
Byzantium in an unofficial capacity and resumed his intrigues.
When he was recalled a second time, he returned to Sparta and
attempted to instigate a rebellion of the Helots by offering them
freedom and citizenship (Thuc. 1. 132. 4). The ephors learned of
this and of his correspondence with Xerxes. Anticipating arrest,
Pausanias sought refuge in a temple, where he starved to death.
(Thuc. 1. 94–5, 1. 128–34; Her. 5. 32; Diod. 11. 44–6.)

Aristotle looks to the aristocracy at Carthage for a second example of faction begun by a great man striving to become a monarch.
Hanno, nicknamed 'the Great' for obscure reasons, was a leading
figure in Carthage during the middle third of the fourth century BC.

His wealth was so great that it was reputed to surpass that of the state. He plotted to make himself tyrant by poisoning the Elders (for which see II. 11. 1272ᵇ37–1273ᵃ2) during his daughter's wedding banquet and then, when this plot was foiled, by inciting an insurrection among the slaves. Betrayed and captured, he was subjected to terrible torture—eyes gouged out, every limb broken—before being crucified. To prevent reprisals the members of his family were also executed. (Justin 20. 5; 21. 4; Picard and Picard, pp. 131–41.)

1307ᵃ5–33

The focus shifts now from the causes of faction in aristocracies alone to the reasons polities, as well as aristocracies, are overthrown. Aristotle thinks the basic reason is a flaw in the constitution itself. His discussion of the flaw is based on the idea of Chapters 7 through 9 of Book IV that polities and so-called aristocracies are mixtures of at least two of the three factors of political significance: virtue, wealth, and freedom (IV. 8. 1294ᵃ19–20). (Sometimes, as here, he speaks of mixtures of oligarchy and democracy rather than of wealth and freedom.) He distinguishes three types of so-called aristocracy. The mixture of all three factors is Carthaginian-style aristocracy (IV. 7. 1293ᵇ14–16); the mixture of virtue and freedom is Spartan-style aristocracy (1293ᵇ16–18); and the mixture of wealth and freedom is ordinary aristocracy (1293ᵇ20–1). Given the connection of aristocracy and virtue (IV. 8. 1294ᵃ9–11), one wonders why a mixture that does not include virtue is called an aristocracy at all. The answer seems to be that education and good birth are intimations of virtue (III. 13. 1283ᵃ23–6, IV. 8. 1294ᵃ20–2) and that these are found in ordinary aristocracy 'because education and good birth go more with the more prosperous' (IV. 8. 1293ᵇ37–8). In Chapter 9 of Book IV Aristotle explains some of the ways in which a mixed constitution, and the Spartan constitution in particular, combines democratic and oligarchic elements.

So-called aristocracy is distinguished from true, or unmixed, aristocracy (IV. 7. 1293ᵇ1–7, 8. 1294ᵃ24–5)—the constitution of one's dreams (IV. 11. 1295ᵃ28–9) and presumably of the ideal city sketched in Book VII. Like Carthaginian-style aristocracy, true aristocracy is based on all three factors of political significance: virtue, wealth, and freedom. The difference between the two constitutions is that in Carthaginian-style aristocracy the good, the wealthy, and the freeborn are distinct groups whereas in true aristocracy they are exactly the same men (VII. 9. 1328^{b}33– 1329^{a}26).

Polity, like ordinary aristocracy, is a mixture of wealth and freedom. The two constitutions differ only in their relative weighting of the two factors. If wealth outweighs freedom, the constitution is an ordinary aristocracy; if the reverse, it is a polity (compare IV. 8. 1293^{b}31–8 with the passage before us). (Aristotle does not tell us what the constitution is called if the two factors are perfectly balanced.) Given the connection of polity and military virtue (III. 7. 1279^{a}37–^{b}4), the question arises, as a similar question arose about ordinary aristocracy, why a mixture that does not include military virtue is called a polity at all. The answer presumably is that the citizens of a constitution that mixes wealth and freedom will be rich enough to own heavy arms and that the effective use of heavy arms demands at least a modicum of military virtue. (For more on polity and aristocracy see the note on 1. 1301^{b}9.)

Aristotle observes that polities are more stable than ordinary aristocracies and offers a two-sided explanation. In a polity the wealthy will find it difficult to encroach on the many because the many have the strength of numbers, and the many will not be motivated to encroach on the wealthy, because they are content with an equal share. In an ordinary aristocracy, on the other hand, the wealthy become insolent and avaricious, which can easily spur the many to move against them.

What sort of flaw, or deviation from justice, in the constitution itself leads to the overthrow of an ordinary aristocracy? The sort of flaw that Aristotle mentions elsewhere (IV. 12. 1297^{a}6–13) and implies here is the allotment of disproportionate power to the wealthy (balanced sometimes by a grant of fake privileges to the many).

When a mixed constitution is overthrown, Aristotle says that it changes into either a democracy or an oligarchy. When the wealthy in an ordinary aristocracy overpower the many, the aristocracy becomes an oligarchy; when the many in a polity overpower the wealthy, the polity becomes a democracy. But Aristotle notes that an ordinary aristocracy can also change into a democracy, and a polity into an oligarchy, when the favoured party under the constitution creates a reaction in the less favoured by its unjust treatment of them.

1307ᵃ12–14 'For aristocracies differ from so-called constitutions ⟨i.e. polities⟩ in this respect, and it is due to this that some of them are less and some are more enduring': what this sentence is struggling to say is that aristocracies and polities differ in the way they mix freedom and wealth, and that it is due to the way they mix these two factors that aristocracies are less enduring than polities.

1307ᵃ21 'Either party': either *favoured* party.

1307ᵃ26–7 For equality according to worth see 1. 1301ᵇ26–1302ᵃ8 and the notes thereto.

1307ᵃ27–33 This episode from the history of Thurii is difficult to reconstruct. We know of it from no other source, and there seems to be a lacuna in the text at a critical juncture in Aristotle's narrative. The episode is offered as an example of a change from a mixed constitution to its opposite caused by a deviation from justice in the constitution itself. Since the constitution that is replaced is described as too oligarchical, it must have been an ordinary aristocracy. The deviation from justice in the constitution was its excessively high property qualification for office, which would have produced a very narrow governing class. The property qualification was lowered. What occasioned the lowering we are not told, but presumably it was agitation by those who were excluded from office by the high property qualification. In a sentence marked as an antithesis to the one about the property qualification being lowered, we are informed that the notables illegally acquired all of the land. At this point in the narrative (1307ᵃ31) the lacuna occurs. Possibly what filled it—this is only a guess—were words whose import was that the intended broadening of the citizen body was negated by the acquisition of all of the land by the notables. We are next told that the people had been employed in a war and, consequently, were trained warriors. They used this training to overpower the notables who were guarding the city and to regain their land. The implication is that the aristocracy became a democracy. Perhaps this was due to the lowered property qualification now having its intended effect of broadening the citizen body. Or perhaps the property qualification was eliminated entirely. The date of this episode is unknown, but Thurii was not founded until the middle of the fifth century BC (see the note on 3. 1303ᵃ28–33).

1307ᵃ34–40

Aristotle claims that in aristocracies the notables are too grasping, too often get their own way, and marry whom they choose; and he attributes their undesirable conduct to the fact that aristocratic constitutions are oligarchic. What does he mean here by 'are oligarchic'? Newman takes him to mean 'give office to a few' (note to 1307ᵃ34). The problem with this interpretation is that the fewness of the rulers in an aristocracy explains only why their undesirable conduct is permitted—the fewer the rulers, the more concentrated their power—not why they engage in it. The notables in an aristocracy are grasping and unbridled, not because they are few in number, but because they are unjust. On the other hand, a stronger interpretation, such as 'give office to a few who are wealthy (but not virtuous)', would erode the truth of Aristotle's universal statement that '*all* aristocratic constitutions are oligarchic'. Only ordinary aristocracies award office on the basis of wealth and freedom alone, and Aristotle is clearly thinking of more than these; for his first example is Sparta, whose constitution awards office on the basis of freedom and virtue (see the introductory note to 1307ᵃ5–33 above).

1307ᵃ35–6 The concentration of property into a few hands at Sparta is discussed in more detail at II. 9. 1270ᵃ15–39.

1307ᵃ38–9 In 398 BC Dionysius I, the tyrant of Syracuse, sought a marriage alliance with the people of Locri, a city on the east side of the toe of Italy. Earlier he had been rebuffed by the people of Rhegium, the city on the tip of the toe. The Rhegians insisted that the only maiden willing to wed him was the daughter of the public executioner, an insult for which they paid dearly ten years later. The Locrians, on the other hand, offered him the hand of Doris, a daughter of a man of the highest reputation. He married her on the same day that he married Aristomache. (Diod. 14. 44–45. 1, 107; Plut. *Dion* 3; for Aristomache see the note on 6. 1306ᵃ1–2 above.)

The first-born of this double wedding, Dionysius II, the son of Doris, succeeded his father as tyrant of Syracuse in 367 BC. He was driven out after twelve years and sought refuge at Locri. The Locrians accepted him as a refugee because of his connection with one of their leading families. Dionysius repaid them by seizing the acropolis and making himself tyrant. Though Dionysius was a licentious and predatory tyrant, Aristotle's description of his ten years' reign as the destruction of the city seems an exaggeration. Dionysius I destroyed Rhegium for insulting him; his son only preyed upon Locri. (Justin 21. 1–3; Strabo 6. 1. 8.)

1307ᵃ40–ᵇ25

Aristotle, unworried by inconsistency, now includes a general cause of constitutional change among those specific to aristocracy. That even small things cause constitutional change was said earlier at 3. 1303ᵃ20–5.

1307ᵇ6–19 Aristotle's description of the overthrow of the constitution of Thurii is unusually expansive. This is fortunate since we know nothing of it from any other source. Aristotle says that the constitution of Thurii changed to a dynasty but does not say what it changed from. However, by offering this episode as an illustration of a general principle about the overthrow of aristocracies, he implies that it changed from an aristocracy. His description of the overthrown constitution also suggests an aristocracy. He mentions four of its elements: a generalship, a body of officials who manage the affairs of the city, a board of advisers, and an assembly of the people. The advisers, or *sumbouloi*, whose function seems to have been to guard the laws, would be an oligarchic element if, as their name suggests, they were similar to pre-councillors, or *probouloi* (VI. 8. 1323ᵃ8–9). The body of officials also has the appearance of an oligarchic element. On the other hand, the assembly of the people and the law restricting the repeated tenure of the generalship are democratic elements. The overthrown constitution thus seems to have been a mixed constitution that combined wealth and freedom. Since it seems to have tilted toward its oligarchic elements, Aristotle would classify it as an (ordinary) aristocracy. It was overthrown by a faction of young military leaders who were able to garner support from the guards and the assembly. The guards, or *phrouroi*, were a contingent of soldiers used to enforce the laws and to guard the walls (see II. 5. 1264ᵃ26 together with Plato, *Rep.* III. 415d7–e3 and IV. 419a10–420a1).

The relation of this constitutional change at Thurii to the one mentioned earlier in this chapter at 1307ᵃ27–33 is a mystery. Though the episodes are distinct, the constitution overthrown in each episode seems to have been an ordinary aristocracy. It is replaced by a democracy in the one case and by a dynasty in the other, so there must have been a third change from democracy or dynasty back to aristocracy. (For dynasty see the note to 3. 1302ᵇ17–18.)

1307ᵇ19–24 'All constitutions are overturned sometimes from within themselves and sometimes from without, when an opposite constitution is either near by or far away yet possessed of power. ' This sentence is syntactically ambiguous. Does the temporal clause go with both halves of the phrase 'sometimes from within themselves and sometimes from without' or with the second half only? Is Aristotle contrasting two sorts of foreign intervention, by invitation of a faction within and by intrusion, or is he contrasting constitutional overthrow which does not involves a foreign power with that which does? Although some translators (Jowett, Barker) adopt the latter construal, Aristotle probably intended the former. If the latter were what he had in mind, his new point would stand in contrast to everything that precedes and could be expressed more clearly and concisely by omitting the first alternative entirely: 'Constitutions are sometimes overturned from without, when an opposite constitution . . .'. Furthermore, he supports his general observation by appealing to the history of the Athenian and Spartan empires; and what this history illustrates is that these two powers sometimes intervened by invitation and sometimes by intrusion. A faction intent on overturning the constitution of its city was not above inviting Athens or Sparta to intervene on its side: an oligarchical faction wishing to overturn a democracy would appeal to Sparta, and a democratic faction in an oligarchy would appeal to Athens (Thuc. 3. 82. 1). Athens and Sparta did not, however, always wait for an invitation but imposed democratic and oligarchic constitutions respectively upon their allies (IV. 11. 1296ᵃ32–6; Thuc. 1. 19; Isoc. *Paneg.* 106, *Panath.* 53–4; Xen. *Hell.* 3. 4. 7). A similar story can be told of the United States and the Soviet Union during the Cold War.

CHAPTER 8

In Chapters 8 and 9 the topic shifts from the destruction of constitutions to their preservation. Aristotle's treatment of the new topic is based on the general causal principle that opposites produce opposites: if A causes B, then the opposite of A causes the opposite of B. He does not pause to examine this principle or to question its applicability in the political realm. Probably the principle seemed too obvious to him to require defence, for he believed he could find instances of it all around. The advance of the sun in summer causes generation, and its retreat in winter causes destruction (*GC* II. 10. 336ᵃ30–ᵇ10). The hot causes iron to liquefy, and the cold causes it to solidify (*Meteor*. IV. 6. 383ᵃ8–10, 7. 384ᵇ2–15). In any case, Aristotle uses the principle in Chapters 8 and 9 without hesitation. He applies it to the causes of destruction of constitutions that he has just investigated and comes up with seventeen ways of preserving constitutions. Aristotle does not run through the causes of destruction seriatim, but Newman provides a table that matches each mode of preservation with a cause of destruction (vol. iv, pp. 569–70).

1307ᵇ30–40

Aristotle's first recommendation to the statesman or politician intent on preserving the constitution of his city is to guard against small infractions of the law. The sort of overthrow for which this is the antidote is presumably the sort that occurred at Ambracia (3. 1303ᵃ20–5) and Thurii (7. 1307ᵃ40–ᵇ19). If so, the infractions that should be guarded against include alterations, as well as violations, of the law; for the overthrow at Thurii, and probably also the one at Ambracia, stemmed from the former rather than the latter.

Aristotle attributes the failure to guard against the gradual overthrow of a city's constitution to fallacious reasoning on the part of the city officials. In his eyes the officials resemble an imprudent housewife who reasons that all her expenditures are small because each is small. They are led astray, Aristotle thinks, by the ambiguity of the word 'all', which can be taken either distributively or collectively. ('They all lifted the boulder', for example, can mean either that they each lifted the boulder or that they lifted the boulder together.) The fallacy arises because the very same sentence expresses either a valid or an invalid conclusion depending upon the interpretation of the word 'all'. If each infraction of the law is of small importance, it follows that all (distributively) are of small importance, but not that all (collectively) are of small importance. Collectively the infractions may be of great importance. (See II. 3. 1261ᵇ16–32, 5. 1264ᵇ15–22; VII. 13. 1332ᵃ36–8.)

The Stoic and Academic logicians, who were soon to come upon the scene, have an alternative and more plausible analysis of the fallacy. They trace the fallacy, not to the ambiguity of the word 'all', but to the vagueness of the word 'small'. On their analysis the trouble stems from the absence of a sharp boundary between what is and what is not small. As these logicians pointed out, the absence of such a boundary allows one to prove that any given number, no matter how large, is small. The absence of a sharp boundary between the small and the not-small means that if any number n is small, so too is $n + 1$. Thus, to prove that any given number is small, start with the true premiss that 1 is small and successively infer that 2, 3, 4, and so forth are small by appealing to successive instances of the universal generalization that $n + 1$ is small if n is small. This is the famous sorites paradox (D.L. 7. 82; Galen, *On medical experience* 16. 1–17. 3). The reasoning of the careless city officials, on one reconstruction at least, shares the same form. They underestimate the cumulative importance of infractions of the law because they think that a single infraction is of small importance and that if n infractions are of small importance, so too are $n + 1$.

1307ᵇ32–3 'For lawlessness creeps in unnoticed' is almost an exact quotation of Plato's *Rep.* IV. 424d3–4.

1307ᵇ40–1308ᵃ35

1307ᵇ40–1308ᵃ3 In Book IV Aristotle discusses a number of constitutional chicaneries cultivated in mixed constitutions (IV. 13. 1297ᵃ14–38). The purpose of such chicanery is to increase, behind a façade of fairness, the power of one group at the expense of another. A good example is to allow every free man to register as a full citizen when he reaches the appropriate age, but to impose a large fine on any full citizen who fails to attend the assembly or to show up for jury duty. A law to this effect has the illusion of fairness since it applies equally to all citizens and only penalizes them for failing to participate in the political life of their city. But the threat of a large penalty would frighten a poor man more than a rich one and would effectively deter many of the poor from registering as full citizens (IV. 13. 1297ᵃ24–9). The right to register as a full citizen under such a law is a false good from the standpoint of the poor; and from such false goods, Aristotle notes, true evil arises (IV. 12. 1297ᵃ10–11).

1308ᵃ3–24 Aristotle's third piece of advice, addressed to the high officials of an aristocracy or an oligarchy, is to be just to those outside the constitution and democratic toward those within.

Those outside the constitution are the free men who enjoy no political rights under it. They pose a threat to the stability of an oligarchy or an aristocracy since their free status provides a reasonable basis for claiming such rights. Those within the constitution, also called 'those who are alike' (*hoi homoioi*), are the members of the governing class (*politeuma*). These are the men who have the right to attend the assembly and to be jurors. The officials are a subset of those who are alike. Thus, in addition to staying on good terms with each other, the officials must mollify both those outside the constitution and those within the constitution but outside the circle of officials.

The best way to mollify the latter group, Aristotle suggests, is to allow them all to share in the offices; and one way to increase access to office is to adopt the democratic institution of short terms for offices. Aristotle mentions in passing that short terms for offices also reduce the opportunity for a demagogue in a democracy to make himself tyrant or for a coterie in an oligarchy to found a dynasty.

The causes of destruction to which the third way of preserving constitutions is a response are the insolence and greed of those in office (3. 1302ᵇ5–14); the dishonouring of one man of stature by another (7. 1306ᵇ31–6); and the division of the governing class of an oligarchy into an inner and an outer circle (6. 1305ᵇ2–22, 36–9, 1306ᵃ13–19, 31–ᵇ5).

1308ᵃ11–13 The claim of the mass for equal political rights is not, in Aristotle's view, a just claim, based as it is on numerical rather than proportionate equality (1. 1301ᵇ29–35; VI. 2. 1317ᵇ3–4). But he does think that such a claim on the part of those who are alike (*hoi homoioi*) is just. Does he mean to imply, then, that those who are alike are proportionately equal? Is so, by what standard of worth?

1308ᵃ17–18 That demagogues arise even among the few in an oligarchy who are alike (*homoioi*) was mentioned at 6. 1305ᵇ24–7.

1308ᵃ24–30 It is an interesting question whether Aristotle's fourth preservative of constitutions—fear of a foreign power—provides a counter-example to the causal principle underlying the discussion in Chapters 8 and 9. (For the principle see the introductory note to the present chapter.) Aristotle claimed earlier that constitutions are overturned 'when an opposite constitution is either near by or far away yet possessed of power' (7. 1307ᵇ19–24). Now he says that constitutions are preserved by their proximity to agents of destruction. Thus, in at least one case the very thing that destroys a constitution, rather than its opposite, also preserves it.

We read in Diodorus of a ruler who used fear of a foreign power to bolster his hold on power. In 395 BC after roundly defeating a Carthaginian army besieging Syracuse, Dionysius I secretly allowed the band of Carthaginian citizens, but not the mercenaries and allies of the Carthaginians, to escape under cover of darkness 'in order that the Syracusans because of their fear of them should never have leisure to claim their freedom' (Diod. 14. 75. 3).

1308ᵃ31–5 The fifth recommendation is directed at faction arising from the rivalries of the notables (for which see 4. 1303ᵇ19–1304ᵃ17 and 6. 1305ᵇ22–39). Aristotle tells us that there should be laws dealing with such rivalries and that officials should take steps to keep disputes from spreading beyond the original disputants. What sort of laws would be helpful he does not say.

1308ᵃ35–ᵇ10

Sometimes a polity or an oligarchy is overturned inadvertently because the wealth of a city has increased or decreased while the property qualification for full citizenship has remained the same (see 6. 1306ᵇ6–16). To meet this problem Aristotle's sixth recommendation is that the total property in a city be reassessed at regular intervals and that the property qualification be tightened or loosened in proportion to any increase or decrease of the assessed value of the total property. If the total property in the city has doubled in value, the property qualification should also be doubled.

This recommendation is based on three assumptions. First of all, Aristotle is assuming that oligarchy, polity, and democracy are defined in terms of the number of rulers under each: oligarchy is the rule of the few; polity is the rule of the middle class; and democracy is rule of the many (see 6. 1306ᵇ10–11). For he says that if the property qualification is not tightened when the wealth of a city increases, an oligarchy changes into a polity, and a polity into a democracy (1308ᵇ9–10). This would not happen if oligarchy were defined as the rule of the wealthy. Such an oligarchy remains an oligarchy no matter how many free men win a share of the constitution by becoming wealthy (III. 8. 1280ª1–2).

Secondly, Aristotle is assuming that any increase or decrease in the total wealth of the city is dispersed throughout the population. He is not considering the possibility that the increase or decrease might be due to the good or bad fortune of a single individual. Suppose that one man becomes rich as Midas by discovering a treasure buried on his property. This would not turn an oligarchy, defined as rule of the few, into a polity.

Finally, Aristotle is assuming that the population of the city remains constant. Suppose, for example, that the wealth of the city decreases by half because half of the population is carried off by a plague. If the property qualification were cut in half to match the decrease in wealth, the number of full citizens would remain constant but the ratio of full citizens to the totality of free men would double. An oligarchy would become a polity, and a polity would become a democracy. In such a situation the law that Aristotle recommends would destroy the constitution it was designed to preserve.

1308ᵇ6–10 Deciphered, what this sentence says is this. If the wealth of a city declines and the property qualification is not loosened, a polity (the rule of the middle class) will change into an oligarchy (the rule of the few), and an oligarchy will change into a dynasty (the rule of a handful). If, on the other hand, the wealth of a city increases and the property qualification is not tightened, an oligarchy will change into a polity, and a polity into a democracy (the rule of the many).

1308^{b}10–31

1308^{b}10–19 Aristotle's seventh recommendation, that potential troublemakers be banished abroad, answers to 3. 1302^{b}15–21 and 7. 1307^{a}2–5. It implies that internal banishment was not unknown in the Greek world, an implication confirmed by a passage in the *Laws* where Plato writes of 'banishments to temples at the boundaries of the country' (IX. 855c3–4).

1308^{b}20–4 The eighth recommendation is that an office be established to keep an eye on those citizens whose private lives are not in accord with the constitution they live under, for example, spendthrifts in an oligarchy (6. 1305^{b}39–1306^{a}9).

1308^{b}24–31 The ninth recommendation, a principle of equipoise, is offered as a remedy for the constitutional instability that occurs when one part of a city prospers while the other parts do not (3. 1302^{b}33–1303^{a}13, 4. 1304^{a}17–38, and 7. 1306^{b}36–1307^{a}2). According to the principle of equipoise, a good way to guard against this sort of instability is to combine and balance the opposing parts of the city: the worthy and the mass, the wealthy and the needy. Since this combining and balancing will only be possible when the opposing parts all have a share of the constitution, the principle would seem to be designed primarily for mixed constitutions.

1308^{b}31–1309^{a}32

1308^{b}31–1309^{a}14 Aristotle's tenth recommendation, that a city should have laws and administrative procedures to guard against peculation, is a response to the source of faction mentioned at 3. 1302^{b}5–10. Aristotle thinks that peculation is doubly dangerous in oligarchies. When oligarchs steal public property, it is not only resented by the many but it also awakens in them a second cause of resentment, their exclusion from office.

1308^{b}38–1309^{a}9 When Aristotle speaks of democracy and aristocracy existing together, what he seems to envisage is a mixed constitution under which both the many and the notables have political rights (see IV. 7. 1293^{b}14–18). He thinks that the notables and the many will be able to live in harmony under such a constitution only if office is not a source of profit. The many will not press their right to hold office if there is no profit to be gained from it; and if the many do not hold office, the notables will not suffer the indignity of taking orders from an inferior (VI. 4. 1318ᵇ35–7).

It is none too clear what Aristotle means in this passage by the notables. He replaces the opposition between the notables and the mass (1309ᵃ1) with that between the needy and the prosperous (1309ᵃ4–6), which suggests that the notables are simply men of wealth. On the other hand, the references to aristocracy would seem to indicate that they are men of virtue. Perhaps he means that they are men of both wealth and virtue. But if so, he does not credit them with complete virtue (unless the law against peculation is directed only toward the many); for men of complete virtue do not steal. He may be thinking of Spartan notables, who were men of only partial virtue (II. 9. 1271ᵃ41–ᵇ3; VII. 14. 1333ᵇ5–14, 15. 1334ᵃ40–ᵇ3; VIII. 4. 1338ᵇ11–16) and notoriously corruptible (*Rhet.* III. 18. 1419ᵃ31–6, Thuc. I. 131. 2). (On notability see the note on I. 1301ᵃ28–35 above.)

1309ᵃ10–12   What Aristotle is describing here is a transfer of money from one treasurer to another at the end of one term of office and the beginning of another. To prevent peculation, he recommends that the event be witnessed by the entire citizen body.

The first division of the citizens of a city is into tribes, and a brotherhood is a subdivision of a tribe (see Plato, *Laws* V. 745d–e, 746d). What Aristotle understands by a company is obscure.

1309ᵃ14–32   Aristotle's next two recommendations, that democracies should spare the wealthy and that oligarchies should care for the poor, are antidotes for the instability inherent in the two constitutions. From a socio-economic perspective there are two major groups in a city: the rich and the poor (IV. 4. 1291ᵇ7–8, V. 11. 1315ᵃ31–3, VI. 3. 1318ᵃ30–1). Oligarchy and democracy are deviant constitutions in which one or the other of these groups rules in its own interest (III. 7. 1279ᵇ4–10, 8. 1279ᵇ39–1280ᵃ5; IV. 4. 1291ᵇ7–13). But a policy that subordinates the interest of the one group to that of the other is bound to create enmity. By its very nature, then, each of these constitutions tends to generate a faction dedicated to its overthrow (see 5. 1304ᵇ20–1305ᵃ7 and 6. 1305ᵃ38–ᵇ1).

To forestall such faction Aristotle recommends that the rulers under each constitution protect and even promote the interests of the group not in power. That is to say, they should imitate the rulers under a correct, or just, constitution, who seek the common advantage rather than their own (III. 6. 1279ᵃ17–21). The pursuit of justice thus turns out to be the best policy for promoting the stability of democracy and oligarchy.

1309ᵃ18 On liturgies see the introductory note to 5. 1304ᵇ20–1305ᵃ7.

1309ᵃ23–6 The purpose of these two proposals, that property should pass by descent rather than by bequest and that no one should be permitted to inherit more than a single property, is to preserve a degree of parity among the holdings of the oligarchs. The needy who would rise to prosperity under such a scheme would be needy sons or other relations of the deceased. Aristotle's recommendations appear to be based on the law regarding inheritance outlined in great detail in Plato's *Laws* (XI. 922a–929d).

CHAPTER 9

This chapter continues Aristotle's discussion of the preservation of constitutions. The decision of the editor of the Greek text to divide the discussion into two chapters is not based on any textual clue and should be ignored.

1309ᵃ33–ᵇ14

Aristotle's thirteenth recommendation for preserving constitutions addresses the problem noted at 3. 1303ᵃ16–20, that constitutions are sometimes overthrown by high officials who are unfriendly to them. To avoid this problem he advises seeking three things in high officials: (1) friendliness toward the established constitution, (2) great ability, which seems to be a combination of experience (1309ᵇ5) and knowledge (1309ᵇ8), and (3) virtue and justice. Since justice is itself a virtue (III. 4. 1277ᵇ19, 13. 1283ᵃ38–9), what Aristotle means by 'virtue and justice' is evidently 'virtue and *especially* justice'. The virtue and justice one should look for is described as virtue and justice relative to the established constitution. This is the virtue and justice of a good citizen, not the virtue and justice of a good man, which is the same everywhere (III. 4. 1276ᵇ30–5). The justice of a good citizen is law-abidingness, the disposition (*hexis*) of a citizen to obey the laws of his city (*EN* V. 1. 1129ᵃ7, ᵇ11–14). But different kinds of constitution have different kinds of laws: democracies have democratic laws; oligarchies oligarchic laws (III. 10. 1281ᵃ37, 11. 1282ᵇ10–11; IV. 1. 1289ᵃ13–15, 9. 1294ᵇ6–7; V. 9. 1310ᵃ14–18). Consequently, what is just (*to dikaion*) varies from one constitution to another, and along with it the justice (*dikaiosunē*) of a good citizen. As Aristotle says in the section before us, there must also be differences in the virtue of justice (*dikaiosunē*) if what is just (*to dikaion*) is not the same in relation to all constitutions.

1309ᵃ39–ᵇ8   This is the first of two puzzles, or *aporiai*, generated by Aristotle's thirteenth recommendation. It is more a problem than a puzzle, the common problem of filling a post from among non-ideal candidates. There are only two candidates for a generalship, Aristotle supposes. One has great ability for the post but is wicked and hostile to the constitution; the other is a good man and friendly to the constitution but has no great ability as a general. Which should we choose? Aristotle says that greater weight should be given to the rarer of the three qualities. In the case of the generalship more weight should be given to military experience than to virtue. Aristotle pointedly does *not* say that more weight should be given to military experience than to friendliness to the constitution, though military experience is also rarer than such friendliness. The reason, no doubt, is that this would undermine his thirteenth recommendation, one purpose of which was to prevent the overthrow of a constitution by a general who is unfriendly to the established constitution. There seems to be something wrong with the principle that Aristotle advances, for a common property like loyalty may be as important in a general as the much rarer property of great ability.

What is wrong is that Aristotle's principle is a principle of search rather than of selection. If *A* and *B* are independent properties of some population and if *A* is rarer than *B* among the population, then it is more likely that any given *A* will be a *B* than that any given *B* will be an *A*. Thus, if one is searching for someone who is both *A* and *B*, an efficient policy is to search for *A* first. This interpretation is borne out by Aristotle's idea for filling the office of treasurer. In filling this office, he argues, one should pay more attention to virtue than to knowledge; 'for this office requires more virtue than the many have, while the knowledge required is common to all'. Aristotle seems to be saying that any candidate who has sufficient honesty for the job will be likely to have all the knowledge he needs. But this has nothing to do with the original puzzle, which concerned filling an office from among candidates none of whom has all the qualities desired in the office-holder.

1309ᵇ8–14 This second puzzle, or *aporia*, is a question about virtue: why does an office-holder need it if he has enough knowledge and experience to do the job well and is a friend of the constitution? Why does a treasurer need to be virtuous if he knows accounting and is a friend of the constitution? The answer one expects from Aristotle is that a man may know accounting and be a friend of the constitution and still be an embezzler. There does not seem to be much of a puzzle here.

What *is* puzzling is that Aristotle's answer, which comes in the form of a rhetorical question, is not that an office-holder without virtue might be evil or wicked (*ponēros*), but that he might be weak-willed (*akratēs*). A weak-willed man, in Aristotle's view, is only 'half-wicked' (*EN* VII. 10. 1152ᵃ17). Unlike the totally evil or wicked man, who acts on the basis of mistaken views about good and bad, the weak-willed man has correct views about good and bad, but fails to abide by them. 'The weak-willed man', Aristotle says, 'knowing that what he does is bad, does it as a result of passion' (*EN* VII. 1. 1145ᵇ12–13; see also I. 13. 1102ᵇ14–18, IX. 4. 1166ᵇ6–10, and *Anim.* III. 9. 433ᵃ1–3), whereas 'vice perverts us and causes us to be utterly deceived about the first principles of action' (*EN* VI. 12. 1144ᵃ34–6). The weak-willed man is like a city that disregards good laws; the evil or wicked man is like a city that observes bad ones (*EN* VII. 10. 1152ᵃ15–24).

Why does Aristotle think that an embezzling treasurer is weak-willed rather than wicked? Why does he assume that the embezzling treasurer knows how to serve the interests of his community? The notion that a weak-willed man is only half-wicked may provide the clue. For a man who is half-wicked is also half-good. Aristotle seems to be assuming, rather plausibly, that most citizens, by living in a community and belonging to a family, have at least half-formed characters and that, consequently, an embezzling treasurer who acts from wickedness rather than from weakness of will is the exception rather than the rule.

1309ᵇ14–18

As his fourteenth recommendation Aristotle recalls the great elementary principle 'so often mentioned' that the group that wants a constitution to remain should be stronger than the group that does not. This principle is in fact mentioned only one other time in the *Politics* (IV. 12. 1296ᵇ14–16), though Aristotle twice mentions a maxim that falls under it—the maxim that those sharing in a constitution should outnumber those who do not (IV. 13. 1297ᵇ4–6, VI. 6. 1320ᵇ25–8). The maxim is narrower than the great elementary principle in two respects. First of all, the group that supports a constitution can include those who do not share in the constitution as well as those who do. Men will often acquiesce in a constitution they do not share in if they are permitted to lead their own lives without interference (IV. 13. 1297ᵇ6–8, V. 8. 1308ᵇ34–8, VI. 4. 1318ᵇ14–21). And, secondly, strength can lie in might as well as in numbers. Those who share in a constitution can increase their relative strength without increasing their numbers, for example, by confiscating the arms of those outside the constitution (see 10. 1311ᵃ12–13 and Newman's note to 1311ᵃ12). Aristotle may think that his great elementary principle has been 'often mentioned' because he does not distinguish the principle sharply from the narrower maxim.

The principle offers one cure for the frequent overthrows of narrow oligarchies and the faction endemic in narrow aristocracies (3. 1302ᵇ25–33; 6. 1305ᵇ2–22, 36–9, 1306ᵃ12–19; 7. 1306ᵇ22–1307ᵃ5). It raises the spectre, however, of a conflict between the need for stability and the claims of justice; for a group might support a constitution precisely because it permits them to take advantage of another group. A democracy, for example, might garner support by allowing the poor to use their superior numbers to redistribute the property of the wealthy. Though such a policy would conform to Aristotle's principle, it would also, in his view, be extremely unjust (III. 10. 1281ᵃ14–17). (For a different interpretation of Aristotle's principle see Miller, pp. 285–93.)

1309^{b}14–15   That what is advantageous to a constitution preserves it seems more like a conceptual truth than an empirical observation. Would anything destructive of a constitution be regarded as advantageous to it?

1309^{b}18–1310^{a}2

Aristotle's fifteenth recommendation, that democracies and oligarchies should not lose sight of the mean, is based on a Platonic idea (*Rep.* VIII. 562b and *Laws* III. 701e), though the analogy of a hooked and a snub nose used to explain it is a distinctive Aristotelian touch. In this analogy a hooked and a snub nose are both deviations from a straight nose (the Greek notion of a perfectly shaped nose). Hooked and snub noses are analogous to oligarchic and democratic constitutions. But which constitution is the analogue of a straight nose? Does Aristotle think there is one constitution from which both oligarchy and democracy deviate? The view of Book III is that oligarchy and democracy are deviations of aristocracy and polity respectively (7. 1279^{b}4–6). So the question is whether Aristotle thinks otherwise elsewhere. The answer is that he does. For he sometimes regards polity as a mixture of freedom and wealth (IV. 8. 1293^{b}33–4); and he sometimes suggests that oligarchy, as well as democracy, deviates from polity (II. 6. 1265^{b}26–8, IV. 7. 1293^{b}20–1, VI. 6. 1320^{b}21–2). So it seems reasonable to conclude that in the passage before us the analogue of a straight nose, the mean from which oligarchy and democracy deviate, is the mixed constitution described in Chapters 8, 9, and 11 of Book IV.

Usually when the constitution of a city is destroyed, it is replaced by another constitution. The point that Aristotle makes by means of the analogy of the noses is that there is a more complete kind of destruction that leaves a city with no constitution at all. Aristotle first explains that a nose can be similarly destroyed. A hooked or a snub nose can deviate from straightness only so far and still remain a nose. Tightened too far in the direction of snubness a nose will be completely effaced; tightened too far in the direction of hookedness it will cease being a nose and become a beak. (The metaphor of tightening comes from the practice of tightening or loosening the strings of a lyre to produce a particular tone.)

Similarly, he argues, an oligarchic or democratic constitution can deviate from the mean by intensifying its basic principle only so far and still remain a constitution. An oligarchy tightens its basic principle, wealth, by increasing the amount of wealth required to qualify for full citizenship. If it tightens its principle too far, eventually only the wealthiest men will hold office and the oligarchy will become a dynasty in which these wealthy men are supreme rather than the law (IV. 6. 1293ᵃ26–34, VI. 6. 1320ᵇ29–33). A democracy, on the other hand, tightens its principle, freedom, by progressively stripping away those qualifications for full citizenship that go beyond free status: legitimacy, neither parent being an alien, and so forth (III. 5. 1278ᵃ28–34, VI. 4. 1319ᵇ6–11). Such a policy of minimization, carried too far, will eventually make citizens even of the rabble, who are easily manipulated by demagogues. The result is that the mass become supreme rather than the law (IV. 4. 1292ᵃ4–30, V. 5. 1305ᵃ28–32, VI. 4. 1319ᵇ1–32). Thus, the law breaks down in the ultimate forms of democracy and oligarchy. But where there is no law, there is no constitution (IV. 4. 1292ᵃ30–2). (Aristotle uses the same analogy to make a similar point in *Rhet.* I. 4. 1360ᵃ23–30.)

1309ᵇ35–1310ᵃ2   This passage is interesting for the example of excess that it offers. Though the levelling of property is a democratic rather than an oligarchic measure (II. 7. 1266ᵇ40–1267ᵃ1), Aristotle offers it as a cautionary tale to both democrats and oligarchs. This measure, Aristotle points out, destroys both oligarchy and democracy; for these constitutions presuppose a division of the population into rich and poor, which an equalization of property erases. The reason such a division of the population is presupposed is that oligarchy and democracy are deviant constitutions under which one of the two classes, the rich or the poor, rules in its own interest to the disadvantage of the other (III. 7. 1279ᵇ4–10).

Aristotle says that if property were levelled in either a democracy or an oligarchy, another constitution would come into existence; but it is unclear what constitution he thinks it would be. Aristotle examines the idea of levelling property at considerable length in connection with the model constitution of Phaleas (II. 7). The point he stresses is that such a levelling would do little by itself to cure the ills of political life. So Aristotle apparently does not believe that the constitution that would come into existence if property were levelled in an oligarchy or a democracy is a correct constitution. But the only deviant constitution in addition to oligarchy and democracy is tyranny.

1310^{a}2–12

Aristotle's sixteenth piece of advice is a remedy for the constitutional instability caused by demagogues in democracies (5. 1304^{b}20–1305^{a}7) and by their counterparts in oligarchies (6. 1305^{a}38–^{b}1). The advice is explicitly addressed to the sort of democracy 'where the mass is supreme over the laws' and by implication to the corresponding sort of oligarchy where a few wealthy men are supreme over the laws. The advice is directed, in other words, to the extreme, or ultimate, form of each constitution (IV. 6. 1292^{b}41–1293^{a}10, 30–4).

Aristotle would have the oligarchs swear, contrary to the oaths sworn by some of them, not to treat the people unjustly. But what is the standard of justice of this oath? It must be oligarchic rather than natural, or absolute, justice since the goal of the advice is the preservation of oligarchy rather than its conversion into a correct constitution. But to treat the people justly by the standard of oligarchic justice is to treat them lawfully. In other words, the oligarchs are to swear not to break the laws of their oligarchy in dealing with the people. This amounts to advising them not to let their constitution sink to the level of an extreme oligarchy where a few men are supreme over the laws. By implication this is also Aristotle's advice to the leaders of the people in a democracy.

What does Aristotle mean when he says that the leaders of an oligarchy ought both to hold and to make a show of holding (*hupolambanein kai hupokrinesthai*) a view contrary to the hostile opinion they now hold? The word *hupokrinesthai* is used of a person acting a part in a play (see *EN* VII. 3. 1147^{a}23) and strongly suggests dissimulation. Aristotle uses the same word when he advises the tyrant to play the part of a king (11. 1314^{a}40). But this suggestion of dissimulation in the second verb is countered by the idea of assent in the first. The two verbs together indicate that Aristotle's advice is twofold: the oligarchs should treat the people justly and should make a show of the fact. They need to make a show of the fact, for otherwise the people may be unaware of it.

One wonders how a demagogue or an oligarch can speak on behalf of the opposition and still maintain his position of leadership within his own party, particularly if he is not dissembling. The interpretation that has been offered of the content of the oath suggests an answer. In speaking on behalf of the opposite party a demagogue in a democracy or an oligarch in an oligarchy does not espouse the ideals of the opposite party but rather the virtue of adhering to the laws of the established constitution. Thus, he maintains his influence within his own party by defending the established constitution and placates the opposition by opposing all attempts to overstep the law to their detriment.

1310ᵃ12–36

Aristotle's seventeenth and final recommendation, that citizens should be educated in harmony with the constitution they live under, is intended to forestall the faction and constitutional change that is due to the law being flouted. Aristotle describes such faction and constitutional change at 3. 1302ᵇ25–33 and 7. 1307ᵃ27–33.

What is it to be educated in harmony with a constitution? Although Aristotle devotes an entire book of the *Politics* to an outline of an education in harmony with the best constitution, he provides only a few clues about the nature of an education in harmony with a deviant constitution. The immediately preceding recommendation and the discussion surrounding the current one indicate that an education in harmony with democracy should cultivate an understanding of democracy, should counter the excesses rabid democrats are prone to, and should promote good relations with the rich. An education in harmony with oligarchy should be along the same lines, *mutatis mutandis*.

1310ᵃ14–19 Aristotle says that the most beneficial laws will not benefit a city unless people are habituated and educated in the constitution and points out that a city, as well as an individual, can be weak-willed. There are three ideas here. The first is that beneficial laws will not benefit a city unless they are obeyed (IV. 8. 1294ᵃ3–7). This is the point of mentioning weakness of will. The second idea is that laws will not be obeyed unless people are habituated and educated to obey them (II. 8. 1269ᵃ20–1; *MA* 10. 703ᵃ29–34). The third idea is more subtle. For Aristotle does not say that people should be habituated and educated in the laws, but that they should be habituated and educated in the constitution. Why? Presumably because the laws of a city reflect its constitution (IV. 1. 1289ᵃ13–25). A democracy has democratic laws; an oligarchy has oligarchic laws. Aristotle notes in another context that when a constitution changes, people's habits often lag behind, giving force to the old laws and giving the new constitution the cast of the old (IV. 5. 1292ᵇ11–21). The people need to be educated and habituated in the new constitution in order for the laws that express it to be observed.

The idea that a city with a democratic or an oligarchic constitution can be weak-willed is at odds with Aristotle's account of weakness of will in an individual. Democracy and oligarchy are deviant constitutions, and the laws that accord with deviant constitutions are bad laws (III. 11. 1282ᵇ8–13). But Aristotle says that 'the weak-willed man is like a city that votes for all the *right* decrees and has *good* laws, but never uses them' (*EN* VII. 10. 1152ᵃ19–21). Thus, a weak-willed man is not like a democracy or an oligarchy that disregards its laws. Such a city should be likened rather to an irresolute thief; and Aristotle would call a person with the principles of a thief, not weak-willed (*EN* VII. 8. 1151ᵃ10–28, 9. 1151ᵃ29–ᵇ4), but vile (*EN* II. 6. 1107ᵃ8–17).

1310ᵃ19–25   The excesses to be guarded against in oligarchy and democracy are luxury and licence respectively. Aristotle's account of these excesses follows the much fuller account in Book VIII of Plato's *Republic* and raises some questions that only the *Republic* answers. Why does Aristotle say that it is the sons of the rulers, not the rulers themselves, who live in luxury in present-day oligarchies? A reader of the *Republic* will know the answer. The sons are spending the money their miserly fathers accumulated (*Rep.* VIII. 554a5–8, 556b8–c1).

1310ᵃ25–36   Democracy is thought to be defined, Aristotle says, by two things: the supremacy of the majority and freedom. He goes on to say that those who define democracy this way think that freedom means doing whatever one wishes (compare *Rep.* VIII. 557b4–6) and to imply that by 'the majority' they mean 'the majority of free men'. Majority rule *per se* is not distinctive of democracy. Under every constitution the citizens make their decisions by majority rule (IV. 8. 1294ᵃ11–14). What distinguishes democracy from other constitutions is the standard by which full citizenship is allotted, namely, free status. This is implicit in Aristotle's amplification of the definition, for it is only those who claim full citizenship on the basis of free status who think that the just is equality (1. 1301ᵃ28–31).

The problem Aristotle notices is that the two parts of this definition of democracy conflict. The champion of democracy so defined believes both that every free man should have an equal voice in the political decisions of his city and that every free man should enjoy the freedom to do whatever he wishes. But the rabid democrat who defines freedom as being able to do whatever one wishes will be loath to be ruled by anyone, even by a majority of his fellow citizens (VI. 2. 1317ᵇ11–15; *Rep.* VIII. 562b9–563e1). As Aristotle says in the passage before us, the rabid democrat thinks it slavery to live in harmony with the constitution.

Aristotle thinks the conflict arises from a bad definition of freedom and implies that it would disappear under a good definition. But in the passage before us he does not tell us what a good definition of freedom would be, nor does he provide many clues elsewhere (but see *Met.* A. 2. 982ᵇ25–6, Λ. 10. 1075ᵃ18–23, and Irwin, pp. 421–2). His one comment that living according to a democratic constitution is not slavery but safety is unhelpful. For it is inconsistent both with his definition of democracy and with his account of natural slavery. By his own (not the disputed) definition democracy is a *despotic* constitution under which the poor oppress the rich (III. 6. 1279ᵃ17–21, 7. 1279ᵇ8–9). Despotic rule (*despotikē archē*) is the rule of a master over slaves (III. 4. 1277ᵃ33–5, 6. 1278ᵇ32–7; VII. 14. 1333ᵃ3–6). Thus, for some, living according to a democratic constitution *is* slavery. And according to Aristotle's account of natural slavery, the natural slave finds safety in slavery (I. 2. 1252ᵃ30–1). Hence, it is inconsistent of Aristotle to oppose safety and slavery and to imply that what provides safety cannot be slavery.

CHAPTER 10

Chapters 10 and 11 are devoted to the things that destroy and preserve monarchies. The discussion is structured as before. Since Aristotle accepts the principle that opposites produce opposites (see 11. 1313ᵃ18–19 and the introductory note to Chapter 8), he thinks the measures that preserve monarchies can be inferred from the things that destroy them; so he investigates destruction (in Chapter 10) before turning (in Chapter 11) to preservation.

1310ᵃ39–ᵇ7

Aristotle says that what happens to kingships and tyrannies is similar to what he has already related about constitutions. For, he explains, kingship accords with aristocracy and is overthrown for the same reasons it is; and tyranny is a combination of ultimate democracy and oligarchy and is destroyed for the same reasons they are. The accord between kingship and aristocracy is explained below at 1310ᵇ31–4; the relation of tyranny to ultimate democracy and oligarchy is explained at 1311ᵃ8–22.

The distinction Aristotle implies between monarchies and constitutions comes as a bit of a surprise since he usually counts monarchy as a constitution (see, for example, IV. 8. 1294ᵃ25–7). It must have some importance for him, for it crops up three more times in the remainder of Book V (10. 1311ᵃ22–5, ᵇ37; 12. 1315ᵇ40–1). But what is its importance? It seems to be an expression of an earlier theme of the *Politics*, that political rule—that is, rule among equals who take turns ruling and being ruled—is distinct from both despotic and kingly rule (I. 5. 1254ᵇ2–6, 7. 1255ᵇ16–20, 12. 1259ᵃ37–ᵇ17; III. 4. 1277ᵇ7–13). Despotic rule is characteristic of a tyranny, and kingly rule of a kingship (IV. 10. 1295ᵃ15–17). Thus, if the distinction in the passage before us corresponds to the earlier one, political rule (*politikē archē*) is characteristic of a constitution proper, a *politeia*. Such a correspondence is supported by a remark in Book III: 'When there came to be many similar in virtue, they no longer endured ⟨kingship⟩ but sought something common and established a constitution' (15. 1286ᵇ11–13). Presumably the common thing (*koinon ti*) sought by these peers was a community (*koinōnia*); and since they established a constitution (*politeia*), they must have been seeking a political community (*politikē koinōnia*). By this line of reasoning, then, a monarchy, not being a constitution, is not a political community. So the point behind the distinction between monarchies and constitutions is that monarchy is fundamentally different from other systems of government: it belongs to a different genus. Thus, Aristotle has a good reason for splitting Book V as he does and discussing monarchy separately from the other systems.

The idea that the constitutional and the political are closely linked is promoted by the Greek language itself. For the Greek words for constitution and political, *politeia* and *politikos* respectively, share the same stem. This means that the opposition between monarchies and constitutions is also to some extent a part of the Greek language. So we should not be surprised to discover that years before Aristotle wrote the section before us Isocrates expected to be understood when he complained of the Spartans that 'they wage war against constitutions, and help to establish monarchies' (*Paneg.* 125).

The word *politeia* is thus trebly ambiguous. In the broadest sense of the term it denotes a genus whose species include kingship and tyranny along with aristocracy, oligarchy, polity, and democracy; in a narrower sense it signifies only the four non-monarchical species; and in the narrowest sense it refers to just one species—so-called constitution, or polity.

1310ᵇ7–31

Aristotle pauses to discuss the origin and nature of monarchy before launching into his main topic, how monarchies are destroyed. He begins with the origin, though it would seem more logical to begin with the nature.

1310ᵇ9–12   Three different accounts of the origin of kingship are to be found in the *Politics*. In the section before us Aristotle claims that kingship arises to protect the worthy from the people. In Book I by contrast he thinks of kings as patriarchs rather than protectors. The first cities, he says, were kingships because they preserved the patriarchal structure of the households from which, by way of the intermediate stage of the village, they sprang (I. 2. 1252ᵇ15–27). According to his third account the awarding of a crown is an act of reciprocation. Men are made kings out of gratitude for benefits conferred (III. 14. 1285ᵇ3–9, V. 10. 1310ᵇ34–40).

1310ᵇ12–14   That the tyrant begins his career as a champion of the many was almost a platitude of Greek political thought (see, for example, Her. 3. 82. 4 and Plato, *Rep.* VIII. 565c–d). Aristotle says that, as a king protects the worthy (*hoi epieikeis*) from the people, a tyrant champions the people against the notables (*hoi gnōrimoi*). Although he sometimes conjoins *epieikēs* and *gnōrimos* in what appears to be an attempt to elucidate the one adjective by means of the other (VI. 4. 1318^b35), they are not exactly synonyms. Strictly speaking, the worthy are men of virtue (II. 11. 1273^b3; III. 10. 1281^a12, 28; *EN* IX. 8. 1169^a16–18), whereas the notables may be men of either wealth or virtue (IV. 8. 1293^b38–40; V. 7. 1307^a29–31; VI. 4. 1319^b12–14, 7. 1321^a39–41; and see the note to 1. 1301^a28–35 above). Aristotle does not say that kings protect the wealthy from the people, though he does say that tyrants champion the people against the wealthy (among others).

1310^b14–26 This is Aristotle's classification of the various well-trodden paths to tyranny. He says that men have acquired the power to become tyrants in three ways—as demagogues, as kings, and as high officials—and indicates that high officials in ancient democracies (that is, those of the seventh and sixth centuries BC) followed one route and those in oligarchies another. In ancient democracies the nascent tyrant garnered his power by holding an office of long tenure, whereas in oligarchies he acquired his power by holding several high offices at the same time—for this is presumably what Aristotle means when he speaks of oligarchies making 'some one individual supreme over the greatest offices' (see II. 11. 1273^b8–9 and III. 16. 1287^a6–8).

1310^b26–31 Aristotle's examples of men who trod the three paths to tyranny, with the exception of Dionysius I, are all from the age of tyrants of the seventh and sixth centuries BC. Pheidon, we are informed, converted the kingship of Argos into a tyranny. Herodotus tells us that he established the system of measures for the Peloponnesians and insolently installed himself as president of the Olympic Games (6. 127).

Phalaris was tyrant of Acragas on the southern coast of Sicily (the later Roman Agrigentum and modern Agrigento) for sixteen years in the first half of the sixth century BC. He was renowned for his cruelty, especially for roasting people alive in a hollow bronze bull (Pindar, *Pythian* I. 95–6). In the *Nicomachean Ethics* he is associated with cannibalism—Aristotle attributes to him an appetite to eat a child—and is offered as an example of bestiality (VII. 5. 1148^b19–24, 1149^a13–14), the moral state that is as subhuman as heroic virtue is superhuman (VII. 1. 1145ᵃ15–33). In the passage before us Aristotle says that Phalaris established a tyranny from an office of honour without saying what that office was. The fable of the Horse and his Rider narrated in the *Rhetoric* (II. 20. 1393ᵇ8–23) suggests that it was 'general with supreme power' (*stratēgos autokratōr*). The fable was supposedly conceived when Phalaris was general with supreme power in Himera, a city opposite Acragas on the northern coast of Sicily, and was seeking a bodyguard. The purpose of the fable was to warn the people of Himera that such a bodyguard would lead to their enslavement by Phalaris.

Panaetius, the first Sicilian tyrant, was a warlord as well as a demagogue; and it was through his command of the army that he overturned the oligarchy in Leontini (12. 1316ᵃ34–7, Polyaen. 5. 47). Leontini (the modern Lentini) is twenty miles north-west of Syracuse.

Cypselus was the founder of a tyranny at Corinth that retained its power for over seventy years (12. 1315ᵇ22–4). Herodotus sums up his reign, which began around the middle of the seventh century BC, in two sentences: 'Many of the Corinthians he banished, many he deprived of their goods, and still more, by far, of their lives. He ruled for thirty years, died in prosperity, and was succeeded in the tyranny by his son Periander' (5. 92). Aristotle takes a more favourable view of Cypselus. He claims at 12. 1315ᵇ27–8 that Cypselus lived without a bodyguard during his entire thirty-year reign, thus implying that Cypselus' rule did not generate a host of potential tyrannicides. That would not be true of the predatory and sanguinary tyrant Herodotus describes.

For Peisistratus and Dionysius I see the notes to 5. 1305ᵃ23–4 and 5. 1305ᵃ26–8 above.

We can add our own examples from the twentieth century. Both Stalin and Hitler rose to absolute power from what Aristotle calls positions of honour. Stalin used his position of general secretary of the Soviet Communist Party to win supreme power in the Soviet Union (Bullock, pp. 125, 341). Hitler exploited his position as chancellor to attain similar power in Germany, though it was Hitler's gifts as a charismatic speaker, as a demagogue, that carried his party to the electoral victory in 1932 from which his chancellorship followed (Bullock, pp. 274, 341).

1310ᵇ31–40

The topic now shifts from the origin of monarchy to its nature. In this and the two following sections, Aristotle explores the nature of monarchy by examining (1) the kinship between kingship and aristocracy, (2) the differences between kingship and tyranny, and (3) the similarities between tyranny on the one hand and oligarchy and democracy on the other.

Aristotle thinks that kingship and aristocracy are alike because both are in 'accord with worth' (*kat' axian*). The word *axia* is a key term in Aristotle's political philosophy and sometimes has a broad and sometimes a narrow sense. In the section before us he uses the word in a narrow sense in which it signifies one specific standard of worth, the aristocratic (see also III. 5. 1278ᵃ19–20), rather than in the broad sense of his theory of justice where it is a mere placeholder for an unspecified standard of worth (see *EN* V. 3. 1131ᵃ24–9 and the note to 1. 1301ᵃ25–ᵇ4 above).

Though Aristotle relates kingship to aristocracy through its standard of worth, the standards of kingship and aristocracy do not seem to be exactly the same. For when Aristotle explains the standard he attributes to kingship—when he explains what he means by *axia*—it turns out that the standard includes, not only individual or family virtue, the standard of aristocracy (IV. 8. 1294ᵃ9–11), but benefits and ability as well. How are these supplements to be understood? The first is possibly redundant since the conferring of benefits can be regarded as a sign of virtue (*Rhet.* I. 9. 1366ᵃ36–ᵇ1). As Aristotle says, the conferring of benefits 'is the work of good men' (III. 15. 1286ᵇ11; see also *EN* VIII. 11. 1161ᵃ11–15). The second, ability, or *dunamis*, is probably added because a king, unlike a random member of an aristocracy, will need to be a military leader if he is to provide the sort of benefits that win a man a kingship: preventing enslavement, setting free, founding a city, and acquiring territory. If this is correct, kings are held to a higher standard than aristocrats, as indeed Aristotle maintains elsewhere (see the note to 1. 1301ᵇ26–9 above).

Newman thinks the second supplementary item is power rather than ability (vol. i, p. 541; vol. iv, p. x). The word *dunamis* frequently has this sense in the *Politics* (see, for example, III. 15. 1286ᵇ28; V. 4. 1304ᵃ24, ᵃ34, 7. 1307ᵇ21, 8. 1308ᵇ18), but not I think here. For in the other passages where *aretē* and *dunamis* are distinguished, virtue is distinguished from ability, not power (III. 13. 1284ᵃ6–7, V. 9. 1309ᵃ33–9, and VII. 3. 1325ᵇ10–14).

The specific virtue Aristotle has in mind when virtue is opposed to ability is justice (see especially 9. 1309ᵃ36). Since kingship is a correct form of constitution, the justice in question is the justice that prevents a ruler from putting his own advantage ahead of the common advantage (see III. 12. 1282ᵇ16–18). It is natural, or absolute, justice rather than justice relative to a particular form of constitution (9. 1309ᵃ36–9); and it can be the justice either of an individual or of a family. Aristotle mentions virtue of family as well as individual virtue because some men inherit their kingships rather than earn them on the basis of their own qualities (III. 14. 1285ᵃ14–16, ᵇ26–8).

Aristotle speaks of kings conferring benefits on cities or nations. What is the difference between a nation and a city, between an *ethnos* and a *polis*? The basic difference is size. As a village is too small to realize the end of a city, namely, good life (I. 2. 1252ᵇ15–30), a nation is too large (VII. 4. 1326ᵇ2–5; see also *EN* IX. 10. 1170ᵇ31–2). Aristotle says that it is not easy for a very large city to possess a constitution (1326ᵇ5), perhaps implying that for a nation to possess one is impossible. The insurmountable problem is one of knowledge and communication. If there is to be a political community where citizens rule and are ruled in turn, they will need to know each other's characters so that they can decide lawsuits correctly and elect the right men to office; but it will not be possible for the citizens to know each other well if there are too many of them (VII. 4. 1326ᵇ12–20; see also Plato, *Laws* V. 738e). Moreover, in the absence of modern means of communication, proclamations from the rulers of a city can reach no further than the voice of a herald (VII. 4. 1326ᵇ5–7, III. 3. 1276ᵃ24–30).

It may have been Aristotle's study of nations that led him to distinguish constitutions proper from monarchies. For if nations lack constitutions and are ruled by monarchs, monarchy cannot be a form of constitution.

1310ᵇ37–40 Examples of men who became kings by conferring benefits on their cities or nations.

Codrus was a legendary king of Athens, though Aristotle apparently accepts his historicity. He seems more a figure of legend in

Plato, who associates him with Alcestis and Achilles (*Symp.* 208d). Aristotle says that Codrus became king by preventing the enslavement of his compatriots but does not say whom the threat came from. Presumably he is thinking of the Dorians.

Cyrus the Great, the founder of the Persian Empire (559–529 BC), freed the Persians from the Medes (see Plato, *Menexenus* 239d–e).

The Lacedaemonian kings referred to are presumably the original founders of the dual kingship, Agis and Eurypon, the eponymous kings of the two royal lines.

The story of the acquisition of the kingship of the Macedonians by Perdiccas I (in the middle of the seventh century BC) is told by Herodotus (8. 137–9).

The Molossians inhabited Epirus, the north-western part of Greece. The Molossian kings traced their line back to Neoptolemus, the son of Achilles (Plut. *Pyrrhus* 1).

1310^b40–1311^a8

Aristotle turns now to the differences between kingship and tyranny, and begins by reiterating the basic difference: a king is a guardian of the common interest, a tyrant of his own (III. 7. 1279^a32–4, ^b4–7). To this basic difference Aristotle appends two others: kings and tyrants differ in their aim and in the character of their guard. He does not mention two further differences emphasized elsewhere, that a king rules over willing subjects, whereas a tyrant rules by force over unwilling subjects (III. 14. 1285^b2–3, V. 10. 1313^a3–10), and that a king rules according to law whereas a tyrant rules despotically according to his own mind (IV. 10. 1295^a15–17).

These various differences are not unconnected. The subjects of a king are willing to submit to his rule because he is a guardian of their interests; and since they are willing subjects, he does not, like a tyrant, need a guard of mercenaries to secure his throne, but only a guard of citizens to enforce the law (III. 14. 1285^a25–9, 15. 1286^b27–33). And the idea that a tyrant pursues his own private interest follows from the idea that his aim is pleasure, for pleasure is the very paradigm of a private interest.

A king, in Aristotle's view, guards the common interest by

protecting the rich and the poor from one another. He protects the poor from the insolence, or *hubris*, of the rich (see *Rhet*. II. 16), and the rich from the injustice of the poor, in particular from a redistribution of their property among the poor (III. 10. 1281ᵃ14–17, VI. 3. 1318ᵃ24–6). (On *hubris* see the note to 3. 1302ᵇ5–10 above; and for another conjunction of injustice and insolence see 12. 1316ᵇ22 below.)

The distinction of kings from tyrants is to be found already in Thucydides (1. 13. 1), but the explanation of the distinction along the lines of the five differences listed above is an invention of Socrates and Plato. That a tyrant, unlike a king, rules over unwilling subjects contrary to law is attributed to Socrates by Xenophon in the *Memorabilia* (4. 6. 12; see also Plato, *Stat.* 276e, 291e1–5). That a tyrant, unlike a king, needs a bodyguard of mercenaries and leads a life dominated by the bodily pleasures is part of Plato's famous description of tyranny and the tyrant in the *Republic* (VIII. 567d5–e2, IX. 587b14–c3). And that a tyrant, unlike a king, is concerned with the public interest only in so far as it advances his own private interest is foreshadowed in the thought expressed in the *Statesman* that a king gives each man his due, whereas a tyrant maims or murders anyone he wishes (301c6–d6).

All three differences between kingship and tyranny mentioned in the passage before us require examination. First of all, the presence of a guard of aliens is not an invariable mark of tyranny and presumably is not intended as such. For Aristotle notes that the tyrant Cypselus reigned without a bodyguard for thirty years (12. 1315ᵇ27–8). Thus, his view must be that tyranny is usually, but not invariably, associated with alien mercenary guards. The fact about the tyranny of Cypselus was worth remarking precisely because it represented an exception to a general rule.

Next, Aristotle's idea that tyrants aim at pleasure is an inadequate account of the motivation of tyrants. We have notable exceptions to this idea among the tyrants of our own time. Hitler was a vegetarian, neither smoked nor drank, and was reputed to be impotent (Bullock, pp. 421, 423). Stalin, though a heavy drinker and a glutton, seems to have derived more pleasure from toying with, bullying, and humiliating the guests at his table than from eating and drinking (Khrushchev, pp. 264, 297–305; Bullock, pp. 868, 950, 1027). One person who knew him said: 'This passionate politician has no other vices [beyond a craving for power]. He loves neither money nor pleasure, neither sport nor women. Women, apart from his own wife, do not exist for him' (quoted by Bullock, p. 201).

The claim that tyrants aim at pleasure, and kings at what is noble, does not seem to be an empirical generalization based upon an examination of the motivation of kings and tyrants but an inference from Aristotle's appraisal of the moral character of kings and tyrants, in conjunction with his view about the aims of good men and bad. Aristotle thinks that tyrants aim at pleasure because he thinks that is what bad men aim at. (For the motivation of the good and the bad, see *Top.* I. 13. 105ᵃ27–8; *EN* III. 8. 1116ᵇ30–1, 12. 1119ᵇ15–16; IV. 1. 1121ᵇ7–10; X. 9. 1180ᵃ10–12; and *EE* III. 1. 1230ᵃ26–32.)

A better way of discovering the aim of tyrants is suggested by Aristotle himself in the *Nicomachean Ethics*. When he wishes to discover the different conceptions that men have of happiness, he examines the lives they lead (*EN* I. 5). Following this method one would infer that a person whose life is focused on the acquisition and retention of power aims at power for its own sake. Aristotle mentions power (*dunamis*) as a good that some men seek (VII. 1. 1323ᵃ36–8; *EE* VII. 15. 1248ᵇ27–9; see also *Rhet.* II. 17. 1391ᵃ20–30), and he notes that mastery (*to kratein*) is the goal of some constitutions (II. 9. 1271ᵇ3; VII. 2. 1324ᵇ7, 1325ᵃ4, 14. 1333ᵇ14; see also Plato, *Rep.* IX. 581a9). It is surprising that he never considers the possibility that power and mastery, rather than pleasure, might be the primary aim of a tyrant.

One need not attribute the same aim to every tyrant. A man who inherits a tyranny may have a different aim from the man who established it, just as a man who inherits a fortune may have a different aim from the man who built it. Hermann Göring, who hoped to succeed Hitler, had a greater appetite for high living than his leader (Bullock, p. 936). That the founders and the inheritors of tyrannies may have different aims is implied by Aristotle's own remarks when he contrasts the tenacity of the former with the apolaustic lives of the latter (1312ᵇ20–5).

Finally, there is Aristotle's idea that a tyrant pursues the public interest only in so far as it advances his private interest. His idea is that the public interest and a tyrant's private interest, though they may occasionally coincide, are always distinct. This idea is difficult to evaluate because of the unclarity of the notion of the public interest. But Thomas Hobbes has an interesting argument against it: 'Now in Monarchy', he argues, 'the private interest [of the monarch] is the same with the publique. The riches, power, and honour of a Monarch arise onely from the riches, strength and reputation of his Subjects. For no King can be rich, nor glorious, nor secure; whose Subjects are either poore, or contemptible, or too weak through want, or dissention, to maintain a war against their enemies . . .' (*Leviathan*, ch. 19, p. 97).

It might be thought that Hobbes's argument does not address the point at issue since he speaks of a king rather than a tyrant. But for Hobbes kingship and tyranny are the same. He rejects the Platonic-Aristotelian division of monarchy into a correct and a deviant form, and claims that tyranny is simply monarchy that is disliked: 'they that are discontented under *Monarchy*', he writes, 'call it *Tyranny* . . .' (ch. 19, p. 96). Furthermore, his argument makes no appeal to the moral character of the monarch, and is intended to hold whether the monarch be a saint or a monster.

Stalin provides a good illustration of the issue dividing Hobbes and Aristotle. Stalin came to personify the Soviet Union, to identify with its power and prestige, and to vigorously defend its interests. If the public interest is identified with the national interest, Stalin's private interest and the public interest of the Soviet Union seem to be the same, and Hobbes seems to be right. But while promoting the national interest of the Soviet Union Stalin had little concern for the welfare of individual Soviet citizens including the members of his own household, and was actively hostile to the welfare of millions. If the public interest of the Soviet Union is identified with the interest of individual Soviet citizens taken distributively rather than collectively, then the public interest and Stalin's private interest diverge, and Aristotle is right against Hobbes.

1311^{a}8–22

This section, a continuation of Aristotle's discussion of the nature of monarchy, is devoted to the evils of tyranny. It begins with the remark that tyranny has the same end as oligarchy. Since Aristotle has just said that pleasure is the aim of a tyrant, the remark that wealth is the end of tyranny is unexpected. What is the relation between the aim (*skopos*) of a tyrant and the end (*telos*) of tyranny? It must be that of end-to-means since, as Aristotle says, it is by means of wealth that a tyrant maintains his guard and his luxury (see also Plato, *Rep.* IX. 580e2–581a1). There is a similar relation between the end of kingship, presumably virtue (*aretē*) (1310ᵇ32–3), and the aim of a king, the noble (*to kalon*); for the noble is attained through the exercise of virtue (see *EN* III. 9. 1117ᵇ7–9, IX. 8. 1168ᵇ25–8).

Aristotle claims that tyranny combines the worst features of oligarchy and democracy—the oligarchic hostility to the people and the democratic hostility to the notables—and lists six practices it adopts from the two constitutions. His list is an extension of one begun by Plato, whose description of tyranny in the *Republic* incorporates the three oligarchic practices, though not under that label (VIII. 568d4–569b5).

The confiscation of heavy arms, the first item on Aristotle's list, would be a delicate operation. No hoplite would surrender his equipment (consisting of helmet, breastplate, greaves, shield, sword, and spear) willingly. It might be needed for defence against domestic, as well as foreign, enemies; and, furthermore, it was an expensive acquisition on the hoplite's part. A confiscation of such equipment required a ruse of some sort. A military review might be held to get the hoplites to appear with their equipment. At some point in the review they would be ordered to stack their equipment, and then through some trick or other lured away from it so that it could be impounded unnoticed (*AP* 15; Xen. *Hell.* 2. 3. 20).

An armed citizenry is always a threat to a tyrant. This is one reason the right to bear arms is enshrined as the Second Amendment of the United States Constitution. During the ratification period one writer explained the proposed amendment as follows: 'As civil rulers, not having their duty to the people duly before them, may attempt to tyrannize, and as the military forces which must be occasionally raised to defend our country, might pervert their power to the injury of their fellow-citizens, the people are confirmed by the next article [what is now the Second Amendment] in their right to keep and bear their private arms' (originally published 18 June 1789, quoted in Halbrook, p. 76).

The two other oligarchic practices adopted by tyrannies are the mistreatment of the rabble and their dispersion away from the town. Aristotle does not indicate what sort of mistreatment he has in mind, though heavy taxation is one possibility (see 11. 1314ᵃ40–ᵇ4). The point of dispersing the rabble away from the town is to dilute their power by increasing their distance from their ruler and from one another.

The three ways in which tyrants imitate democracies are in making war against the notables, executing them, and exiling them. The first of these refers to an attack upon the notables as a group, in league perhaps with the rabble, in contrast to the execution and exile of individuals one by one (see 5. 1304ᵇ20–4, 9. 1310ᵃ4–5).

Tyrants take these measures against the notables, Aristotle says, because it is from the notables that conspiracies against them arise. An instance of this maxim from modern times is the conspiracy against Hitler of 20 July 1944, carried out by Claus Count von Stauffenberg, a member of an old and distinguished family in southern Germany (see Hoffmann).

The famous story of the stalks of grain comes from Herodotus (5. 92). Aristotle retells it earlier in the *Politics* (III. 13. 1284ᵃ26–33), reversing the roles of Periander and Thrasybulus. According to Aristotle's retelling, Thrasybulus, the tyrant of Miletus, sent a messenger to Periander, the tyrant of Corinth, asking for advice about governing. Wanting to relay his answer in a manner incomprehensible to the messenger, Periander walked through a field of grain breaking off the tallest stalks. The messenger duly reported this odd behaviour to Thrasybulus, who understood the advice at once. It was still current in Elizabethan England, as the following passage from *Richard the Second* makes plain:

> Go thou, and like an executioner,
> Cut off the heads of too fast-growing sprays,
> That look too lofty in our commonwealth;
> All must be even in our government.   (3. 4. 33–6)

1311ᵃ22–31

Aristotle finally reaches the topic of this chapter, the things that destroy monarchies. As with constitutions proper he first lists these things and then gives historical examples of them. But he does not give historical examples of every item on his list, and he feels free to add to the list as he goes along.

Though the opening words of this section refer back to the

opening words of the chapter ($1310^a40–^b2$), the section as a whole looks back to the causal analysis of Chapter 2. In spite of the brevity of the section before us compared to the earlier chapter, the two closely correspond. Chapter 2, however, mentions three causes, not two. The cause that is not reiterated is 'the disposition of those who form factions' (2. 1302^a20). Men are disposed to form factions if they think they are being treated unjustly by those in power (2. $1302^a22–31$). Such a disposition is a general cause of constitutional change (2. 1302^a23), which may be why Aristotle omits it from his analysis in the present chapter. He may wish to focus on the specific, rather than the general, causes of the overthrow of monarchies.

The specific causes of the destruction of monarchies are the same, or nearly the same, as the specific causes of constitutional change. Aristotle's statement that the ends of those who attack monarchies are wealth and honour corresponds to his statement in Chapter 2 that the 'things for which men form factions are profit and honour and their opposites' ($1302^a31–2$). He lists three origins of change in monarchies—injustice, fear, and contempt—and then subdivides the first of these into insolence and deprivation of private property. If the genus is replaced by its two species, there are four species in all: insolence, deprivation of private property, fear, and contempt. In Chapter 2 Aristotle lists seven origins of constitutional change: profit and honour (reappearing as origins of change), insolence, fear, superiority, contempt, and disproportionate growth ($1302^a34–^b3$). Deprivation of private property on the short list corresponds to profit on the long, since profit must come either from public or private property (3. $1302^b5–10$). This leaves three items whose absence from the short list requires explanation: honour, superiority, and disproportionate growth. Disproportionate growth is absent since it is not a cause of change in monarchies; superiority seems to have been omitted by inadvertence since it is alluded to in the next chapter ($1315^a8–14$); and honour, though not mentioned as an origin of change, does appear as a final cause.

1311ᵃ31–ᵇ36

Aristotle distinguishes between an attack upon the person and upon the throne of a monarch. An attack upon the person (*epi to sōma*, literally upon the body) aims not at power but at the physical destruction of the man (see 11. 1315ᵃ24–7). As Aristotle expresses it, such an attack is for revenge, not for superiority (1311ᵃ34–6). Attacks upon the throne (*epi tēn archēn*, literally upon the rule) aim at power. They are of two sorts. They aim either at replacing the monarch with another monarch (1312ᵃ8–9) or at replacing the monarchy with a constitution proper (12. 1316ᵃ29–34). The different aims of an attack on the throne correspond to the different aims of faction under a constitution proper. Such a faction sometimes wishes to overturn the established constitution; other times it wishes to seize power under it (1. 1301ᵇ6–13).

1311ᵃ32–6   Aristotle claims that attacks upon monarchs that are responses to their insolence are upon the person of the monarch rather than his throne, and in the sentence that connects insolence with anger and anger in turn with revenge offers what appears to be an argument in support of this claim. Anger is defined in the *Rhetoric* as 'a desire associated with pain for conspicuous revenge because of conspicuous belittling by those who have no good reason to belittle oneself or those near to one' (II. 2. 1378ᵃ31–3; see also *Top*. VIII. 1. 156ᵃ32–3 and *Anim*. I. 1. 403ᵃ29–ᵇ1). Since insolence is a form of belittlement (*Rhet*. II. 2. 1378ᵇ22–5), it is, as Aristotle says in the passage before us, a cause of anger. But anger is always directed toward individuals such as Callias and Socrates rather than toward kinds (*genē*) such as thief or sycophant (*Rhet*. II. 2. 1378ᵃ33–5, 4. 1382ᵃ4–5). Thus, if Aristotle thinks of different individuals filling the same office as similar to different individuals instantiating the same kind, he has an argument for his claim that the anger to which insolence gives rise can only be relieved by revenge visited on an individual.

Aristotle is not as helpful as he might be about the many kinds of insolence, or *hubris*. The discussion that follows seems, however, to be based upon a division of insolence into that which has a physical dimension (*eis to sōma*: rendered at 1311ᵇ7 as 'upon the person' but literally 'upon the body') and that which does not, the former kind being divided in turn into sexual violations of one sort or another and physical assaults. Thus, Aristotle's examples of attacks upon monarchs caused by insolence of the non-physical variety (1311ᵃ36–ᵇ6) are followed by examples of attacks caused by sexual violations (1311ᵇ6–23) and physical assaults (1311ᵇ23–36). (See also 11. 1315ᵃ15–16; and for the general concept of insolence, or *hubris*, see the note to 3. 1302ᵇ5–10 above.) In the *Laws* Plato divides insolence into five kinds along different lines (X. 884a–885a).

1311ᵃ36–ᵇ6 Examples of attacks on monarchs caused by insolence of the non-physical variety.

1311ᵃ36–9 Peisistratus, tyrant of Athens, had three sons: Hippias, Hipparchus, and Thessalus. When he died in 527 BC, he was succeeded by his eldest son, Hippias. Harmodius was a handsome Athenian youth beloved by the older Athenian Aristogeiton. As Plato describes their relation, the passion (*erōs*) of Aristogeiton was answered by the steadfast affection (*philia bebaios*) of Harmodius (*Symp.* 182c4–7). (On Greek bisexuality see the note to 4. 1303ᵇ20–6.) The fatal situation developed when Hipparchus too developed a passion for Harmodius and began making unwelcome advances. When his overtures were repulsed not once but twice, Hipparchus became angry and contrived to get back at Harmodius through Harmodius' sister. The girl was first invited to be a basket-bearer in the procession at the Panathenaic festival and then rejected as unworthy on the ground that her brother was effeminate (*AP* 18. 2). In revenge, Aristogeiton and Harmodius conspired with a few others to assassinate the sons of Peisistratus at the festival. Thinking their plot had been betrayed, Aristogeiton and Harmodius were forced into action at the festival prematurely. Acting alone, they were able only to kill Hipparchus. Hippias kept a cool head and preserved both his life and his throne. Harmodius was killed by the guards on the spot; Aristogeiton escaped but was captured, tortured, and executed. Four years later in 510 BC Hippias was driven from Athens with the aid of Sparta, after which Aristogeiton and Harmodius were celebrated as tyrannicides. (Her. 5. 55–6, 6. 109, 6. 123; Thuc. 1. 20, 6. 53–9; *AP* 18.)

1311ᵃ39–ᵇ1 On Periander, tyrant of Ambracia, see the notes to 3. 1303ᵃ23 and 4. 1304ᵃ31–3 above. He was a nephew of Periander, tyrant of Corinth.

1311ᵇ1–3 Philip II of Macedon was assassinated at Aegeae (the early capital of Macedon) in 336 BC on the brink of his invasion of Asia Minor. He was succeeded by his son, Alexander, destined for greatness.

Pausanias was a young man who had caught Philip's (one) eye and then found this eye straying to another young man also named Pausanias. Out of jealousy the first Pausanias scurrilously attacked the second and drove him to seek death in battle. Attalus was an uncle of Cleopatra, the newest of Philip's many wives, and a friend of the deceased Pausanias. Knowing that the surviving Pausanias was the cause of his friend's death, Attalus invited him to dinner, got him dead drunk, and handed him over to his mule skinners for sexual misuse. When the poor fellow realized what had happened to him, he complained to Philip. Because Attalus was Philip's uncle-in-law and one of the two generals of his advance force in Asia Minor, Philip hesitated to take action against him and, as a consequence, drew the anger of Pausanias upon himself. Pausanias killed him with a dagger at a dramatic moment of the Panhellenic festival celebrating the marriage of the king's daughter to her uncle, Alexander king of Epirus. Before the assassin could escape he was dispatched by Philip's bodyguard. (Diod. 16. 91–4.)

Philip's tomb has recently been excavated at Vergina (the ancient Aegeae), and the bones found in the tomb—the remains of a cremation—may actually be Philip's. A skeleton reconstructed from the bones and labelled as Philip's is on exhibit at the archaeological museum in Thessaloniki. (For the tombs at Vergina see Hammond 1994, pp. 179–82.)

As the only contemporaneous account of Philip's assassination that has survived, the sentence before us is of great historical interest. But it is interesting for other reasons as well. First of all, it provides the best evidence we have concerning the date of composition of the *Politics*. We can infer from the sentence that Aristotle was working on at least one part of the *Politics* after 336 BC during the last fourteen years of his life. Secondly, the sentence reveals something about Aristotle the writer. For he is reporting the assassination of someone he knew. His father had been the court physician of Philip's father, Amyntas III; and he himself had served as Alexander's tutor when Alexander was a youth (D.L. 5. 1–4; Plut. *Alexander* 7). He thus has an opportunity for a personal comment or aside of the sort he makes in the *Nicomachean Ethics* about Plato's Academy (I. 6. 1096ª11–17). But the writer does not let his mask slip an inch. The sentence is written with the clinical detachment characteristic of the *Politics*.

There is one further reference to Philip at *Rhet.* II. 23. 1397ᵇ31–1398ª3.

1311ᵇ3–4 Amyntas the Little is otherwise unknown. His boast was presumably that he had enjoyed the sexual favours of the young Derdas.

1311ᵇ4–6 Evagoras, king of Salamis in Cyprus from 411 BC until his assassination in 374 BC, was renowned for Hellenizing his city. Aristotle, it should be noted, expresses no scepticism about a eunuch having a wife. (Diod. 15. 47. 8.)

1311ᵇ6–23 Examples of attacks upon monarchs caused by their insolence in matters having to do with sex.

1311ᵇ8–20 Archelaus II, king of Macedon from circa 413 to 399 BC, is famous, or rather infamous, for the unfavourable judgement passed on him by Plato in the *Gorgias*. Archelaus serves as Plato's paradigm of an arch-criminal whose incurably corrupt soul dooms him to suffer unending punishment in Hades, an eternal object lesson for others (525b–d). He is doomed to such a fate in Plato's view because of the way he cut his way to the throne. As Plato tells his story, Archelaus was an illegitimate son of Perdiccas (king of Macedon from circa 452 to 413 BC) by a slave owned by Perdiccas' brother Alcetas, which meant that in justice Archelaus was Alcetas' slave (see *Laws* XI. 930d). Though it is not said explicitly, it is implied that Alcetas had the first claim to succeed Perdiccas, and Alcetas' son Alexander the next claim after Alcetas. Archelaus began his ascent to the throne by inviting his uncle and his cousin to his house and then murdering them—murders made more horrible in Greek eyes by two facts: they were murders of a master and his son by their slave and of two guests by their host. To these two victims Archelaus added a third, his 7-year-old half-brother, the legitimate son of Perdiccas, whom he pushed into a well and drowned. (*Gorg.* 470d–471d.)

Plato's unfavourable view of Archelaus does not seem to have been widely shared by other contemporaries of the monarch. Archelaus was praised by Thucydides for building forts and straight roads, organizing mounted and hoplite forces, and doing more to strengthen his kingdom for war than all eight kings preceding him put together (2. 100. 2). And the poets Euripides, Agathon, and Timotheus joined his Hellenizing court. Euripides wrote his masterpiece, the *Bacchae*, while a guest of Archelaus. (We discover below at 1311ᵇ30–4 that Euripides was in fact a causal factor in the attack on Archelaus. Decamnichus became a leader of the conspiracy against Archelaus because the king allowed Euripides to repay Decamnichus for a remark about the poet's halitosis with a flogging.) Aristotle tells us that Socrates declined an invitation to join the brilliant circle around Archelaus, not because he thought the inviter was a bloody murderer, but because he thought the invitation insolent. According to Aristotle, Socrates claimed that insolence, or *hubris*, consists just as much in the inability of those who are treated well to repay as it does in the inability of those who are treated ill (*Rhet.* II. 23. 1398ᵃ24–6; see also D.L. 2. 25).

In the section before us Aristotle reveals still another side of Archelaus' complex personality. The arch-criminal, dynamic warlord, and patron of the arts now appears as lecher. For this is what the complaints of Crataeas and Hellanocrates amount to. Hellanocrates complained that Archelaus engaged in sexual intercourse with him out of insolence (*hubris*) rather than erotic desire (*erōtikē epithumia*). He was irked, in other words, to discover that for Archelaus he was just another sexual conquest and not an object of passionate love.

1311ᵇ13 Elimeia is a region of central Greece directly south of Macedonia.

1311ᵇ20–3 Cotys, king of Thrace, was assassinated in 359 BC (Hammond 1986, p. 514).

1311ᵇ23–36 Examples of attacks upon monarchs that avenge insolence in the form of blows.

Aristotle claims that such attacks are made not only on monarchs but even on office-holders and royal dynasts, and gives an example of such an attack upon dynasts before giving one upon a monarch.

1311ᵇ26–30 The overthrow of the dynasty of the Penthilidae at Mytilene on the island of Lesbos took place at an unknown date before 650 BC. The Penthilidae derived their name from their ancestor Penthilus, whom they believed to be an illegitimate son of Orestes, the legendary matricide (Strabo 13. 1. 3). The Penthilus mentioned by Aristotle is obviously not the man from whom the family took its name. The family is referred to with loathing by the two sixth-century poets of Lesbos, Sappho (fr. 71 Loeb) and Alcaeus (frs. 70, 75 Loeb). (Andrewes, p. 92.)

1311^{b}30–4 Since Euripides died in 406 BC and the attack on Archelaus took place in 399 BC, Decamnichus was evidently a man who could smoulder for a long time.

1311^{b}36–1312^{a}39

In the following sections Aristotle discusses attacks upon monarchs motivated by fear (1311^{b}36–40), contempt (1311^{b}40–1312^{a}14), love of honour (1312^{a}21–39), and multiple causes (1312^{a}15–20).

1311^{b}36–40 Example of an attack upon a monarch caused by fear.

Xerxes, king of Persia from 486 BC to 465 BC, led the great invasion of Greece of 480 BC. Darius was the eldest of his three sons, and Artapanes was the leader of his bodyguard. Aristotle says that Artapanes was fearful, not because he had hanged Darius, but because he had done it without an order from Xerxes. The implication is that such an order would not have been out of the question, which in turn implies that Xerxes had come to believe, fairly or unfairly, that his son was guilty of some grave offence, such as conspiring against him, for which hanging would be the proper penalty. Aristotle does not tell us why Artapanes decided to act on his own without authorization from Xerxes. After murdering Xerxes Artapanes was himself killed, and Xerxes was succeeded by his youngest son Artaxerxes, who ruled Persia for forty years. (For a different account of Xerxes' assassination see Diod. 11. 69.)

1311^{b}40–1312^{a}14 Examples of attacks on monarchs caused by contempt for the man (1311^{b}40–1312^{a}8) or contempt for the danger (1312^{a}8–14).

1312^{a}1–4 Sardanapalus was a legendary Assyrian monarch. Aristotle neglects to mention that in the famous story about Sardanapalus to which he here alludes the monarch was not only doing woman's work among women but also wearing the make-up, jewels, and clothes of a courtesan, mimicking a female voice, and rolling his eyes lasciviously (Athen. XII, 528e–530c; Diod. 2. 23–7; Justin 1. 3). In the *Nicomachean* and *Eudemian Ethics* Sardanapalus is introduced as an exponent of the life of bodily pleasure (*EN* I. 5. 1095^{b}19–22; *EE* I. 5. 1216^{a}16–19).

1312^{a}4–6 Dionysius II of Syracuse and Dion were closely related, though not by blood. Dionysius I had married two women on the same day (see the note to 7. 1307ᵃ38–9 above). Dionysius II was a son of his Locrian wife, Doris. Dion was a brother of his other wife, Aristomache, and also the husband of Aristomache's daughter Arete. (Aristomache's other daughter Sophrosyne was given to Dionysius II, her half-brother.) Dion was thus both a brother-in-law and an uncle of Dionysius II. Conflict was inevitable.

Aristotle does not mention the most famous person involved in the conflict between the two men—Plato. As a young man of around 20, Dion had become a friend and pupil of the 40-year-old philosopher on the latter's first trip to Sicily in 387 BC; and when Dionysius II succeeded to the throne upon the death of his father twenty years later, Dion persuaded the new monarch to invite Plato to return to Syracuse with the (unrealistic) goal of making the young ruler, who was then about 30, a philosopher. During Plato's visit a breach that was never to close opened between uncle and nephew when an incriminating communication between Dion and Carthage, the traditional enemy of Syracuse, was revealed. Dion was banished from Sicily for conspiracy though allowed to continue drawing the income from his large estate.

Aristotle's statement that Dion resolved to attack Dionysius after observing the contempt with which he was regarded by his subjects and his perpetual drunkenness—he is said to have once kept a drinking party going continuously for ninety days (Plut. *Dion* 7. 4)—implies that Dion made his resolution while residing in Syracuse. But if so, he waited a long time to act on it, for almost ten years separate his banishment from his return. Aristotle continues the story at 1312ᵃ33–9 below. (Plato, *Ep.* VII; Plut. *Dion.*)

1312ᵃ12–14 Astyages, king of the Medes, was overthrown by his vassal Cyrus in the middle of the sixth century BC. The story of his overthrow is told by Herodotus (1. 108–30). For Cyrus see the note to 1310ᵇ37–40 above.

1312ᵃ14 There were at least two Thracian monarchs named 'Seuthes': Seuthes I, son of Sparadocus (Thuc. 2. 101. 5) and Seuthes II, son of Maisades (Xen. *An.* 7. 2. 32). The one mentioned by Aristotle is presumably the latter, the minor monarch of the first part of the fourth century BC who plays a major role in the last book of Xenophon's *Anabasis*. (The identification is based on Xen. *Hell.* 4. 8. 26.) The attack upon Amadocus to which Aristotle refers is otherwise unknown.

1312ᵃ15–20 Attacks on monarchs from multiple causes.

1312ᵃ16 The Ariobarzanes to whom Aristotle refers is probably the Persian satrap who led the Satraps' Revolt circa 362 BC (Diod. 15. 90; on the identification of Ariobarzanes see the note to 15. 90. 3 in the Loeb edition). In referring to what appears to be the same event, Xenophon in the *Cyropaedia* adds the further item of information that Ariobarzanes was Mithridates' father (8. 8. 4).

1312ᵃ17–20 Some editors think this passage is out of place and should follow the word 'drunk' at 1312ᵃ6, since the phrase 'for this reason' fits a single cause such as contempt better than the multiple causes to which Aristotle has just turned (Newman, ad loc.).

'Boldness is bravery that possesses power' (see also I. 9. 1258ᵃ10–11). The bravery of which boldness is here taken to be a species cannot be true bravery, for true bravery is a mean between boldness and cowardice (*EN* II. 7. 1107ᵃ33–ᵇ4; *EE* III. 1. 1228ᵃ26–ᵇ3). So unless Aristotle is nodding, it must be one of the five other kinds of bravery that he distinguishes (*EN* III. 8. 1116ᵃ15–17; *EE* III. 1. 1229ᵃ11–12). Of these, the best candidate seems to be the one listed third in the *Nicomachean Ethics*, spirit, or *thumos* (III. 8. 1116ᵇ24–1117ᵃ9; *EE* III. 1. 1229ᵃ20–9). It is none too clear what Plato and Aristotle mean by *thumos*; but it seems to be something like assertiveness combined with a strong sense of self-worth (see especially VII. 7. 1327ᵇ23–1328ᵃ7). If all of this is correct, Aristotle is claiming, not implausibly, that boldness is an assertive sense of self possessing power.

1312ᵃ21–39 Examples of attacks upon tyrants due to the pure love of honour.

1312ᵃ36–9 Aristotle may have heard these words from Dion's own lips. Dion was banished from Syracuse the same year that Aristotle, a youth of 17, entered Plato's Academy (D.L. 5. 6); and during his banishment Dion lived in Athens and also attended the Academy (Plut. *Dion* 17. 1, 47. 2, 52. 2). Thus, when Dion sailed for Sicily in 357 BC with 800 mercenaries (Plut. *Dion* 22. 3–5, 25. 1), he and Aristotle would have known each other for ten years.

Though Aristotle was undoubtedly impressed by Dion's audacity in marching against the ruler of one of the strongest cities in Europe with such a small army (see Diod. 16. 9. 1–2), to associate Dion with those who attack tyranny solely for honour and glory seems wrong. To begin with, Aristotle had earlier traced the origin

of Dion's attack on Dionysius to contempt (1312ᵃ4–6). Furthermore, Dion was spurred to action, after living in style on the Greek
mainland for ten years, by two actions of Dionysius. In Dion's
absence Dionysius had given Dion's wife Arete (his own half-
sister) to another man and had sequestered Dion's property (Plut.
Dion 18. 1, 19. 5, 21. 1–3; Plato, *Ep.* VII. 345c4–347e5). (The loss
of his income seems to have upset Dion more than the loss of his
wife, whom he had not seen in ten years.) Thus, his attack upon
Dionysius seems to have four distinct causes: honour, contempt,
insolence, and confiscation of private property. Aristotle returns a
third time to the story of Dion at 1312ᵇ16–17 below.

The twentieth century provides better examples than Dion of
men and women who have opposed tyranny from the pure love of
honour. One such example is the White Rose resistance to Hitler
led by the students Hans and Sophie Scholl at the University of
Munich in the summer of 1942 and the winter of 1943. Their resistance, in which several other students and the professor of philosophy Kurt Huber participated, consisted in the distribution of a
series of six leaflets known as The White Rose Letters opposing
Hitler and the war and calling for passive resistance and sabotage.
The third leaflet uses a passage from the very chapters of the
Politics we are discussing to describe Nazi tyranny (11. 1313ᵇ11–28;
Scholl, p. 84). All the participants were arrested and executed.
(Scholl, Moll.)

1312ᵃ39–1313ᵃ17

The remainder of this chapter is devoted to the destruction of
monarchies rather than simply of monarchs; and since the two
types of monarchy are destroyed in different ways, Aristotle considers them separately—first tyranny (1312ᵃ39–ᵇ38) and then kingship (1312ᵇ38–1313ᵃ16).

1312ᵃ39–ᵇ9 Tyranny is sometimes destroyed from outside, just
like a constitution proper (7. 1307ᵇ19–24), when some opposite
constitution, such as democracy or kingship or aristocracy, is
stronger. Kingship is opposite to tyranny because it is the correct
constitution of which tyranny is the deviation (III. 7. 1279ᵇ4–5); and
aristocracy is opposite to tyranny due to the kinship of aristocracy
and kingship (1310ᵇ31–4). As Aristotle expresses it in the passage

before us, kingship and aristocracy are opposite to tyranny 'because of the opposition of the constitution'. But why is ultimate democracy opposite to tyranny? Aristotle argues, rather surprisingly, that ultimate democracy is opposite to tyranny because it *is* tyranny. By parity of reasoning, tyranny is opposite to itself. But perhaps what Aristotle has in mind is that tyranny and ultimate democracy are at opposite poles among deviant constitutions. Both are tyrannies, but tyranny proper is rule by a single man whereas ultimate democracy is rule by a tyrannic assembly composed of many men (1312ᵇ34–8; IV. 4. 1292ᵃ4–13).

1312ᵇ6–9 Aristotle classifies Sparta as an aristocracy at IV. 7. 1293ᵇ16–18 and takes this classification for granted in Chapter 7 above. Thucydides says that Sparta overthrew tyrannies everywhere in Greece apart from Sicily (1. 18. 1). In particular, Sparta overthrew the tyranny in Athens (see the note to 1311ᵃ36–9 above). Syracuse was well governed in Aristotle's view during the period from 466 BC to 413 BC when it was an aristocracy (see the note to 4. 1304ᵃ27–9 above).

1312ᵇ9–17 The period of good government in Syracuse was preceded by the tyranny of Gelon and his brothers and succeeded, after a few years of democracy, by the tyranny of Dionysius I and II (see the notes to 3. 1302ᵇ31–3, 3. 1303ᵃ38–ᵇ2, and 5. 1305ᵃ26–8 above). Gelon is remembered for the large role he played in the destruction of the Carthaginian expedition led by Hamilcar, which landed on the north coast of Sicily in 480 BC at the same time that Xerxes was invading Greece (*Poet.* 23. 1459ᵃ24–6; Her. 7. 153–67). He died within two years of his great victory and was succeeded by his brother Hieron, who ruled for ten years (12. 1315ᵇ37) and of whose rule we hear something at 11. 1313ᵇ13–15 below. We know nothing about Gelon's son beyond what Aristotle tells us here. He is omitted from the list of tyrants at 12. 1315ᵇ34–8, where Thrasybulus is said to have ruled Syracuse upon Hieron's death for eleven months. Perhaps Gelon's son was the nominal ruler during this period and Thrasybulus his regent (Newman, ad loc.). (Diod. 11. 67–8.)

1312ᵇ16–17 Aristotle resumes his account of Dion's campaign against Dionysius II (see the note to 1312ᵃ36–9 above) and compresses four tumultuous years into one sentence. Dion landed on the south coast of Sicily and marched on Syracuse gaining supporters along the way so that his small army had grown large by the time he reached the city's walls. As luck would have it, Dionysius was away in Italy, which allowed Dion to gain the support of the people of Syracuse and make a triumphal entry. Dionysius' guard retained possession of the citadel and were soon joined by the tyrant. The citadel held out for several years, though Dionysius himself did not wait that long to sail into exile at Locri (see the note to 7. 1307ᵃ38–9 above). Dion was elected 'general with supreme power' (*stratēgos autokratōr*), but the people's support was always equivocal and unsteady due to Dion's aristocratic leanings and his connections through marriage with Dionysus. He never mastered the political problems of Syracuse. The moral education he had received at Plato's hands eventually faltered, and he acquiesced in the murder of a political rival. Dion was himself assassinated by mercenaries in the employ of another rival for power, an Athenian named Callippus, who had been one of his comrades, a commander of mercenaries in his expeditionary force, and his host in Athens. (Plut. *Dion*.)

1312ᵇ17–25 Aristotle claims that the main reason tyrannies are overthrown is that the man on the throne is regarded with contempt. Similarly he had noted in earlier chapters that democracies are overturned chiefly because of the licence of their demagogues (5. 1304ᵇ20–1), and polities and aristocracies chiefly because of deviations from justice in their constitutions (7. 1307ᵃ5–7).

Aristotle's proof that contempt for the tyrant is the chief cause tyrannies are overthrown implies that a man who founds a tyranny leads a different sort of life from a man who inherits one. The latter, Aristotle says, leads a life of enjoyment, becomes contemptible, and is overthrown. The former retains his throne because he does not become contemptible, which implies that he does not lead a life of enjoyment. Aristotle does not tell us what sort of life he does lead, but it would seem to be a life focused on the acquisition and retention of power (see the note to 1310ᵇ40–1311ᵃ8 above).

1312ᵇ21–5 When Aristotle states that those who inherit tyrannies lose them straight away, he is probably thinking of Dionysius II, even though Dionysius had been tyrant of Syracuse for ten years when Dion launched his campaign against him. Aristotle only claims the general truth of his statement. Periander, the heir of Cypselus, was a notable exception (12. 1315ᵇ22–6).

1312ᵇ25–34   What does Aristotle mean when he says that anger is a part (*morion*) of hatred? He cannot mean that anger is a kind of hatred; for in his classification of psychological qualities he appears to treat anger and hatred as co-ordinate species of the same genus. Anger and hatred are each a kind of passion, or *pathos* (*EN* II. 5. 1105ᵇ21–3; *MM* I. 7. 1186ᵃ12–14; *Rhet.* III. 19. 1419ᵇ25–7). Furthermore, in the passage before us, anger is contrasted with hatred, not subordinated to it.

The reason Aristotle offers for saying that anger is a part, or *morion*, of hatred is that anger causes the same actions as hatred. And in his discourse on hatred, or enmity, in the *Rhetoric* (II. 4. 1381ᵇ37–1382ᵃ15) he says that anger is productive of enmity (1382ᵃ1–2). But a cause of a thing may be part of its definition (*Anim.* II. 2. 413ᵃ16–20). (Every definition of a thing mentions at least one of its four causes.) Thus, when Aristotle says that anger is a part, or *morion*, of hatred, his thought may be that anger is an efficient cause of hatred and as such a part of its definition.

The main difference between hatred and anger in Aristotle's view is that hatred, unlike anger, is directed at kinds as well as individuals. (See the definition of anger in the note to 1311ᵃ32–6 above.) As Aristotle says, everyone hates the thief and the sycophant (*Rhet.* II. 4. 1382ᵃ6–7). This may be the explanation of his claim that hatred, unlike anger, is not accompanied by pain. He may think that a kind is not the sort of thing that can cause either pleasure or pain. In any case, the other differences between hatred and anger mentioned in the passage before us are consequences of this last one. Anger is more conducive to action than hatred because it is less calculative, and it is less calculative because pain impedes calculation.

1312ᵇ30–1   On the overthrow of the Peisistratids see the note to 1311ᵃ36–9 above.

1312ᵇ34–8   Although the ultimate forms of democracy and oligarchy are discussed at some length in Book IV (see 4. 1292ᵃ4–37, 5. 1292ᵇ5–10, 6. 1293ᵃ30–4, 11. 1296ᵃ1–4, and 14. 1298ᵃ29–33), in Book V they are only mentioned in connection with tyranny.

1312ᵇ37–8   When Aristotle calls ultimate oligarchy and extreme democracy parcelled-out tyrannies, his language suggests the tyranny of the petty officials of a modern bureaucratic state. But this is not what he has in mind. He is not thinking of the administrative offices that a full citizen of a Greek city would be called upon to fill from time to time, which would be pretty much the same whether the constitution is moderate or extreme. He is thinking rather of the assembly of full citizens in an extreme democracy or the ruling circle in a narrow oligarchy (IV. 4. 1292ᵃ11–30, 6. 1293ᵃ30–4). It is these bodies that are tyrannical, not their individual members. Their tyranny is parcelled out in the sense that their decrees are passed by a vote of their members.

1312ᵇ38–1313ᵃ10   The topic shifts now to the destruction of kingship. Aristotle claims that it is usually destroyed by one or the other of two internal causes: faction or a turn toward tyranny. The sort of faction to which he refers is faction among those who share in the kingship, that is to say, faction within the royal house or among the king's retainers.

1313ᵃ3–5   When Aristotle says that 'Kingships do not spring up any longer now', he does not mean to imply that they no longer exist; for he was acquainted with at least three surviving kingships: the Macedonian, Lacedaemonian, and Molossian (1310ᵇ39–40; 11. 1313ᵃ23–33).

1313ᵃ10–16   Aristotle appends a third cause of the overthrow of kingships that is special to those that are hereditary as distinct from elective (III. 14. 1285ᵃ14–16, 1285ᵇ3). In support of the principle that such kingships are overthrown when the king becomes contemptible and behaves insolently, he appeals to the fact that this is what happened in the past, though he does not cite any cases.

1313ᵃ14–16   When a king loses the favour of his subjects, he must become either a tyrant or a private individual.

CHAPTER 11

Turning now from the destruction of monarchy to its preservation, Aristotle devotes a perfunctory paragraph to the preservation of kingship before unveiling his infamous Handbook for Tyrants. This Handbook is divided into two parts corresponding to the two ways of preserving tyranny, the traditional Way of Repression (1313ᵃ34–1314ᵃ29) and the more enlightened Way of Moderation (1314ᵃ29–1315ᵇ10). No tyrant is overthrown until one or more individuals have both the wish to overthrow him and the ability. The Way of

Repression seeks to deprive anyone who might harbour such a wish of the power to act on it; the Way of Moderation seeks to forestall the formation of the wish.

1313ᵃ18–33

Aristotle's single thought regarding the preservation of kingship, that moderation is the key to its survival, addresses only one of the three causes of destruction enumerated in the last chapter (10. 1312ᵇ38–1313ᵃ16). One way in which kingship is destroyed, he said, is 'when kings attempt to govern more tyrannically, claiming supremacy over more and more things and contrary to law' (10. 1313ᵃ1–3). The remedy he now offers, which, as Newman points out (ad loc.), comes from Plato's *Laws* (III. 690d5–692c8), is to restrict the range of the king's authority. His authority being restricted, a king will be less despotic than an absolute monarch, more on a level with his subjects, less envied by them, and in consequence less threatened by overthrow.

One problem with this remedy is that it does not cohere well with Aristotle's conception of kingship. Aristotle thinks that kingship is justified only when the virtue of the king is superior to that of his subjects (see the note to 1. 1301ᵇ26–9 above). Thus, the more equal in character a king is to his subjects, the less his rule is justifed and the less willing his subjects will be to submit to it (10. 1313ᵃ3–9). Furthermore, the notion that the durability of a kingship is increased by restricting the range of the king's authority raises a question about absolute kingship, the constitution that comes first in Aristotle's hierarchy of constitutions. The range of authority of an absolute king is unrestricted: such a king is 'like a god among men' and rules over everything according to his own wish unrestricted by law (III. 13. 1284ᵃ3–17, ᵇ25–34; 16. 1287ᵃ1–3, 8–10). Does Aristotle think, then, that absolute kingship is bound to be short-lived?

1313ᵃ24 For the Molossian kingship, which still existed in Aristotle's day, see the note to 10. 1310ᵇ37–40 above.

1313ᵃ25–33 For the dual kingship of Sparta and the ephorate see the note to 1. 1301ᵇ19–21 above. Theopompus was a Eurypontid king of Sparta (circa 720–675 BC) and a leader in the First Messenian War (for the war see the note to 7. 1306ᵇ27–31).

1313ᵃ34–1314ᵃ29

In this section Aristotle discusses the Way of Repression. In ancient as in modern tyranny the Way of Repression seeks to produce demoralized, isolated, and powerless individuals, though Aristotle describes its products in somewhat different terms. He refers to the demoralization of the subjects of tyranny by the expressions *phronein mikron*—to think small (1313ᵇ9–10, 1314ᵃ16, 29)—and *mikropsuchos*—small-souled or small-minded (1314ᵃ16–17)—and he speaks, not of social isolation, but rather of what gives rise to it—distrust.

Aristotle stresses the fact that the measures of the Way of Repression are those of a master (*despotēs*) of slaves. He says that the tyrant who follows the Way of Repression rules despotically (*despotikōs*) (1314ᵃ20–1) and that his subjects live like slaves (1313ᵇ9), and he refers to the mastery (*to despotikon*) of his tyranny (1314ᵃ8–9). Since our word 'despot' is derived from *despotēs*, it is convenient to use it and its adjective and adverb as translations of the corresponding Greek words; but the Greek words are stronger than the English and in the *Politics* at least always signify a relationship like that of master to slave. The correlative of ruling despotically is being ruled like a slave (IV. 11. 1295ᵇ19–21). Although Aristotle thinks that all deviant constitutions are despotic (III. 6. 1279ᵃ18–21), he regards some as more despotic (*despotikōterai*) than others (IV. 3. 1290ᵃ28, V. 10. 1310ᵇ19). The tyranny described in the Way of Repression is despotic to the maximum degree short of literal slavery (see IV. 10. 1295ᵃ17–23).

It is worth noting that when Aristotle describes the 'city of our dreams' in Book VII (for the expression see VII. 4. 1325ᵇ36), he endorses the aims of the Way of Repression in relation to real slaves. To provide the citizens of his ideal city with the leisure for politics and philosophy (I. 7. 1255ᵇ35–7) Aristotle proposes to have all the farming done by slaves 'who are neither all of the same race nor of high spirit' (VII. 10. 1330ᵃ25–7). He wants slaves who are spiritless and racially isolated for the same reason the repressive tyrant wants subjects who are demoralized and socially isolated. He wants to prevent the slaves from seeking a new order (VII. 10. 1330ᵃ28).

The Way of Repression is not simply a tyrant's guide to retaining

power, though it can be read that way. Aristotle is repelled by the
repressive tyrant and his methods, and expresses his repulsion. He
says explicitly that his methods are vile (1314ᵃ12–14), and in the last
sentence of Chapter 11 he implies that his character is vicious
(1315ᵇ10). But more importantly he passes judgement on the
repressive tyrant constantly throughout the Way of Repression by
noting who his friends and enemies are. The tyrant, he says, is a
friend of the vicious (1314ᵃ1–2) and an enemy of the outstanding,
the proud-hearted, the worthy, the dignified, and the free (1313ᵃ40–
1, 1314ᵃ3–4, 6, 19). Since it is a principle of Aristotle's ethical
philosophy picked up from ordinary life that 'like is a friend to like'
(III. 16. 1287ᵇ33; *EN* VIII. 1. 1155ᵃ32–5, IX. 3. 1165ᵇ13–23; *EE* VII.
1. 1235ᵃ4–12, 20–5), the character of the tyrant is clear. Though he
likes to think of himself as the one man in the city who is dignified
and free (1314ᵃ5–7), to Aristotle's eyes his dignity is spurious and
his freedom illusory.

1313ᵃ34–ᵇ6 For Periander's advice to cut off the outstanding
stalks see the note to 10. 1311ᵃ8–22 above.

The Way of Repression advises doing away with some of the
most important social and cultural institutions of a Greek city. The
public meals, or *sussitia*, were eating clubs to which each member
contributed a fixed amount of produce and money. In Sparta
the clubs had around fifteen members, new members requiring a
unanimous vote of the old (Plut. *Lycurgus* 12. 1–10). Aristotle, like
Plato before him (*Rep.* III. 416e3–4; *Laws* VII. 806d7–807a3),
approves of the institution and wants it in his ideal city (VII. 10.
1330ᵃ3–8). The political clubs, or *hetairiai*, were cliques of the rich
and powerful (see Thuc. 3. 82. 6 and 8. 48. 3). Education, or *paideia*,
in the classical period was the education of a child, or *pais*, from
his sixth or seventh year until early manhood—until 21 in Aristotle's ideal city (VII. 17. 1336ᵇ37–40)—and consisted of gymnastics,
music, and letters (VIII. 3. 1337ᵇ23–5; Plato, *Prot.* 325c5–326e5).
The schools, or *scholai*, were scholarly (*scholastikoi*) as distinguished from civic (*politikoi*) associations (Plato, *Gorg.* 452e4)—
presumably groups of men, like the circles around Isocrates,
Plato, and Aristotle, who gathered for the study of philosophy or
rhetoric.

Aristotle thinks that these institutions generate pride and trust.
They generate trust because they allow people to get to know each

other; and, Aristotle says, 'knowledge increases trust'. He cannot mean that the better one knows a person the more one trusts him, for one might discover that the person is completely untrustworthy. He must mean rather that the better one knows a person the better one knows whether he is to be trusted. Knowledge increases trust among the trustworthy. Aristotle does not say how the institutions generate pride, but Plato provides a clue. He thinks that philosophy and gymnastics instil pride (*Symp.* 182b7–c4, *Rep.* III. 411c4–7). The repressive tyrant is hostile to pride and trust because pride makes a man want to conspire against him—no proud-hearted man will endure the servility of despotism—and trust makes conspiracy possible. As Aristotle remarks below, 'a tyranny is never overthrown until some men trust each other' (1314^{a}17–19).

1313^{b}6–16   The next measure of the Way of Repression is to require those residing in town to be always in sight and to hang around the doors of the palace. Aristotle cannot mean that the tyrant is to require this of everyone living in town. For who would do the work? When Xenophon discusses the corresponding Persian custom in the *Cyropaedia* (8. 1. 6–8, 16–20), he explicitly limits its applicability to those 'who are able to be maintained by the labour of others' (8. 1. 16); and the same restriction is surely to be understood here. It is the prosperous that the tyrant wants within eyeshot. He has two reasons for this. First, he wants to know what the prosperous are up to so that any plots against him can be forestalled. (For information about the activities of everyone else he relies on a network of spies.) And, secondly, he wants the prosperous to think small and to feel insignificant, so that they will be too dispirited to challenge his rule. They come to feel insignificant because, in being required to be at his beck and call, they are treated like slaves (see Isoc. *Paneg.* 151). This feeling of insignificance that the tyrant wishes to engender might be compared with the pervasive sense of insecurity that Stalin's Great Purge of the 1930s created in the Soviet Union. 'The population', one authority writes, 'had become habituated to silence and obedience, to fear and submission' (Conquest 1990, p. 447).

1313^{b}18–25   Aristotle says that it is characteristic of a tyrant to make his subjects poor to prevent them from (among other things) maintaining a guard. This implies that the tyrant's bodyguard of foreign mercenaries was not necessarily the only armed force in a

Greek tyranny—that there might also be a force of armed citizens. Such a force would of course be a perpetual threat to the tyrant's power. We do, oddly enough, hear of such a force existing in Syracuse during the tyranny of Gelon and his brothers (Diod. 11. 67. 2–5).

The enormous labour required to construct the pyramids is described by Herodotus (2. 124–5). The chief offering of the Cypselids, the tyrants of Corinth, was a golden statue of Zeus at Olympia, to which Plato alludes in the *Phaedrus* (236b3–4). (For the Cypselids see 12. 1315ᵇ22–9 below.) The colossal temple of the Olympian Zeus at Athens, fifteen of whose columns are still standing, was begun by the tyrant Peisistratus in the sixth century BC and completed seven centuries later by the Roman emperor Hadrian. Polycrates was tyrant of the island of Samos from about 535 to 522 BC. Herodotus describes three famous works on Samos: an underground aqueduct, a mole in front of the harbour, and 'the largest of all the temples we know of' (3. 60).

1313ᵇ25–9 One reason for the heavy taxation at Syracuse was the heavy expenditures demanded by the (unsuccessful) campaigns of Dionysius I to drive the Carthaginians from Sicily.

A person with no property of his own must work for someone else, which in Greek eyes was a kind of limited slavery (I. 13. 1260ᵃ41–2, VIII. 2. 1337ᵇ19–21). Thus, a tyrant who came to possess all the property in his city through taxation or expropriation would make his subjects his virtual slaves twice over. Economic slavishness would be added to their political slavishness.

The idea that the tyrant wages war so that his subjects will need a leader and not have time to conspire against him comes from Plato (*Rep.* VIII. 566e–567a).

1313ᵇ29–32 When Aristotle says that it is characteristic of a tyrant to distrust his friends, or *philoi*, most of all, he means to include the tyrant's own family among the distrusted. For the Greek word *philos* signifies relatives as well as close acquaintances. Xenophon has Hieron remark on the propensity of tyrants to be assassinated by their wives, brothers, and children (*Hieron* 3. 7–9).

1313ᵇ32–1314ᵃ4 Aristotle says that tyranny and ultimate democracy are alike in the position they accord women and slaves and in the honour they bestow on flatterers. Though he regards the reign of women in the household as an evil of tyranny on a par with lack of discipline among slaves, he never explains how tyranny fosters such a reign. Does he think that men, once they become accustomed to the servility of tyranny in the public arena, readily submit to the domination of their wives in the domestic sphere? Aristotle does not explain why slaves flourish under a tyranny either, but in this case Plato provides the answer. The tyrant regards the slaves in his city as potential allies against the free men, and encourages their loyalty by enlisting some of them into his bodyguard (*Rep.* VIII. 567e3–7).

The susceptibility of tyrants (and of other powerful persons) to flattery is as much a phenomenon of modern as of ancient times. People in positions of power—especially (but not exclusively) if they are insulated from public and private criticism—tend to develop inflated opinions of their own worth, ability, and knowledge (see Plato, *Apol.* 21b1–22a6, *Rep.* IV. 426d1–e3) with the result that flattery appears to them as no more than simple truth. Stalin came to regard himself as a genius not only in domestic and foreign affairs and in military matters but in linguistics as well (Khrushchev, pp. 605–8; Bullock, p. 1059).

1314ᵃ4–5   The history of the Soviet Union is replete with instances of this proverb, of using one thug to get rid of another. The most famous involves the last three men to head the Soviet secret police during Stalin's reign. When Genrikh Yagoda, head of the secret police from 1934 to 1937, fell from favour, Stalin appointed the 'malignant dwarf' Nikolai Yezhov to head the secret police and gave him the job of eliminating Yagoda and his men. When Yezhov in his turn lost Stalin's confidence, Stalin replaced him with the odious Lavrenti Beria, whose first task was the elimination of Yezhov and his colleagues. Beria was himself executed in 1953 in the struggle for power following Stalin's death. (Conquest 1985, Knight, pp. 87–90.)

1314ᵃ29–1315ᵇ10

The Way of Moderation, the topic of the third part of this chapter, is the way of pretence. The tyrant who takes this path tries to win his subjects' acquiescence in, if not their active consent to, his rule by 'beautifully playing the part of a king'. Though he plays the part, he does not become a king. In introducing this second way Aristotle says that 'The tyrant must guard one thing only, his power, so that he may rule not only when his subjects wish it but also when they do not.' But a monarch who can rule even when his subjects do not wish it, is not a king. For as Aristotle remarks at the end of the preceding chapter: '[W]hen his subjects do not wish it, a king will straight away not be a king. But the tyrant is a tyrant even when his subjects do not wish it' (1313^{a}14–17). Thus, the advice of the Way of Moderation is not to be, but only to appear to be, a king (1315^{a}41–^{b}2).

The advice of the second way is naturally couched in the language of appearing and seeming—*phainesthai* (1314^{b}15, 18, 23–4, 31, 33, 39; 1315^{a}3, 21, ^{b}1) and *dokein* (1314^{a}39, 40, ^{b}7). But there is a complexity here because *phainesthai* is a verb with a large repertoire of uses. In particular, it has one sense when coupled with an infinitive and another when coupled with a participle. When coupled with an infinitive it usually means that the object denoted by its subject *appears* to be doing (but may actually not be doing) whatever is signified by the infinitive (*Top.* I. 1. 101^{a}3–4). Thus, *phainetai t' alēthē legein* means 'He appears to speak the truth (but may be lying)'. In the section before us *phainesthai* is used with an infinitive only once (1315^{b}1). Most occurrences of the word are coupled with a participle. So coupled it usually means (in Aristotle at least) that the object denoted by its subject is *observed*—that is, *appears to the senses*—to do whatever is signified by the participle (*Cael.* II. 13. 295^{b}19–21). Thus, *touto phainetai gignomenon* means 'This is observed to occur' (see *Meteor.* II. 2. 354^{b}14, 9. 369^{b}17–18). Aristotle uses *phainesthai* with a participle five times in the Way of Moderation (1314^{b}15, 23–4, 31, 39; 1315^{a}21). Where it is used with a participle or where one is understood, I have translated it as 'is seen'. All other occurrences are translated as 'appears'.

These grammatical points underline the two aspects of Aristotle's advice in the Way of Moderation. First there is the advice that the tyrant create a public persona. He should be seen doing the things that kings do. This is captured by *phainesthai* with the participle. But the man to whom the Way of Moderation is addressed will likely remain a tyrant. His public persona will mask a character that remains at heart tyrannical. He will appear to be a man he is not. This second aspect is captured by the other occurrences of *phainesthai* and by the three occurrences of *dokein* (translated 'seems') referred to above.

It is precisely this element of pretence that distinguishes Aristotle's advice to the tyrant in the Way of Moderation from that of Xenophon in *Hieron* (chs. 9–11) and of Isocrates in *Helen* (32–7) and in *To Nicocles*. The tone of the Way of Moderation is closer to that of Machiavelli's *The Prince* than it is to these works of his older contemporaries. Though Aristotle's Handbook for Tyrants stands between these earlier works and *The Prince*, it reflects the former less than it foreshadows the latter, especially Machiavelli's advice to a prince to always appear merciful, truthful, humane, sincere, and religious whether he be so in reality or not since 'everyone sees what you seem to be, few know what you really are . . .' (*Prince*, ch. 18). Machiavelli nevers refers to the *Politics* in *The Prince*, but he does display familiarity with it elsewhere. There is a clear (though inaccurate) reference to Chapters 10 and 11 of Book V in *The Discourses*. 'Among the primary causes of the downfall of tyrants', Machiavelli writes, 'Aristotle puts the injuries they do on account of women, whether by rape, violation or the breaking up of marriages' (III. 26). (The reference is inaccurate because by Aristotle's account the sexual relations that caused the downfall of Greek tyrants were almost entirely with young men. Of all the cases he mentions, only one involves a woman (10. 1311ᵇ4–6).) Thus, the echo of the Way of Moderation that a reader sometimes catches in *The Prince* may not be entirely coincidental and may reflect some direct borrowing on Machiavelli's part.

1314ª40–ᵇ18   Taxing and spending

Aristotle has just said that the tyrant who follows the Way of Moderation will do some of the things a true king would do and will *seem* to do others (1314ª39). He now says that such a tyrant must *seem* to take thought for the public funds and that a tyrant who renders an account of his receipts and expenditures would *seem* to be a head of household, an *oikonomos*, thus implying that the tyrant's concern for the public funds is not genuine and that he is not really an *oikonomos*. Both of these implications make sense. For it is Aristotle's view that an *oikonomos* rules his household as a king rules his kingdom—'household management', he says, 'is a kind of kingship of the household' (III. 14. 1285ᵇ31–3; see also I. 12). Thus, only a true king is a real rather than a feigned *oikonomos* in relation to his city. Similarly if a tyrant really did take thought for the public funds (*ta koina*) rather than merely seem to, he would be ruling for the common advantage (*to koinon sumpheron*) and be a true king rather than a tyrant (III. 7. 1279ᵃ33–4, V. 10. 1311ᵃ2–4).

In advising the tyrant to play the king, Aristotle does not say where pretence should end and reality begin. Should the tyrant's account of his receipts and expenditures, for example, be honest? Is the Way of Moderation consistent with the tyrant secretly siphoning some of the public revenues into his own pocket? Aristotle does not answer these questions explicitly, but he also never insinuates that the tyrant's accounting might be fraudulent. Indeed, Aristotle never advises or suggests anything in the Way of Moderation that would trouble a true king. When he advises the tyrant to play the king, he evidently means for him to act like a king. If this is so, the king-like tyrant differs from a true king only in his motivation: he is power-hungry. What he desires above all else is to retain power—unlike the true king, who has his eye on the noble (*to kalon*) and the common advantage (III. 7. 1279ᵃ33–4, V. 10. 1311ᵃ5). Thus, the king-like tyrant acts honestly because in his struggle to retain power he regards honesty as the best policy; the true king acts honestly because he is an honest man. On this interpretation the two men differ in their moral dispositions but—with one exception—not in their actions. The exception is when their subjects no longer wish them to rule. The true king willingly surrenders his throne; the king-like tyrant shows his teeth and claws.

Aristotle advises the tyrant not to squander public funds on courtesans, aliens, and craftsmen. The aliens to whom he refers would be such men as the Athenian poets Euripides and Agathon whom Archelaus II invited to his Macedonian court (see the note to 10. 1311ᵇ8–20 above), and the craftsmen would be the makers of the tyrant's luxury goods—his clothes, jewellery, furniture, and so forth.

The tyrant's worry while abroad on campaign for the safety of his property at home is also noted by Xenophon's Hieron (*Hieron* 1. 12).

1314ᵇ18–23 Personal qualities

Aristotle advises the king-like tyrant to appear not bad tempered but dignified and to cultivate a reputation for military virtue. The tyrant is evidently permitted a bad temper if it is masked by an even-tempered public persona. The importance of military

excellence is also stressed by Machiavelli, who claims that 'a prince
. . . should have no other object, no other thought, no other subject
of study, than war . . .'—he 'should never turn his mind from the
study of war; in times of peace he should think about it even more
than in wartime' (*Prince*, ch. 14).

1314^b23–7 Insolence

That tyrants are often overthrown because of their insolence
or that of the men around them was stressed in the last chapter
(1311^a32–^b36), but this is the first time Aristotle has attributed
the fall of a tyrant to the insolence of the women in his house-
hold. Plato refers to the insolence of women in the *Laws* (VI.
774c7).

1314^b28–36 Carousing

The tyrant is advised to live a life of moderation or at least to do his
drunken carousing in private. One might think that the tyrant
should worry about the envy that ostentatious revelry that continues for many days running is sure to elicit in the onlookers. That,
after all, is the reason for the ostentation—the revellers wish to be
admired as happy and blessed—and envy is a cause of faction (4.
1304^a36–7). Perhaps Aristotle warns only about the contempt the
revelry will generate because envy, being slavish (IV. 11. 1295^b21–
3), does not pose much of a threat to a tyrant.

1314^b36–8 Building programme

A repressive tyrant undertakes great building projects in order to
make his subjects poor (1313^b18–25). Aristotle advises the king-like
tyrant to engage in such projects, not as a tyrant, but as an overseer,
or *epitropos*. The point is that an *epitropos* is a servant of others. By
supervising the work of the household, an *epitropos* secures for his
master the leisure needed for politics and philosophy (I. 7. 1255^b35–
7; *MM* I. 34. 1198^b12–20). Thus, a tyrant who acts as if he were an
epitropos acts as if he were serving the public rather than his private
interest.

1314^b38–1315^a4 Religion

The tyrant is advised to appear zealous in religion so that his
subjects will be comforted by the thought that he fears divine
retribution should he step outside the law. Aristotle does not
believe in divine retribution himself (*Met. Λ*. 9), so he presumably

allows the tyrant's (and the true king's) public religiosity to mask private scepticism.

1315ᵃ4–8   Honours and dishonours

Machiavelli offers the very same advice in *The Prince*. Not only does he advise a prince 'to show himself an admirer of talent, giving recognition to men of ability and honouring those who excel in a particular art' (ch. 21) but he also says that princes 'should delegate unpleasant jobs to other people and reserve the pleasant functions for themselves' (ch. 19). This last piece of advice was already a commonplace in ancient times. Thus, Xenophon has Simonides tell Hieron 'that a ruler should assign to others the punishment of those in need of coercion while reserving for himself the awarding of prizes' (*Hieron* 9. 3).

1315ᵃ8–14   Lieutenants

The tyrant is advised to exercise caution both in giving power and in taking it away. In giving power, the advice is not to raise anyone so high that he becomes a rival for the throne. As Machiavelli warns, 'the man who makes another powerful ruins himself' (*Prince*, ch. 3). If powerful subordinates are absolutely necessary, timid characters are safer than bold ones, and two are safer than one, since they will be rivals of each other. In taking power away, the tyrant is advised to do it gradually.

Aristotle thinks this advice on giving power and taking it away is applicable to almost any constitution. Here it is addressed to kings as well as tyrants, and in an earlier passage (8. 1308ᵇ10–16) similar advice was offered to democrats and oligarchs.

1315ᵃ14–31   Insolence again

Aristotle advises the tyrant to avoid insolence above all in administering physical punishment and in his sexual relations with young men. Aristotle has said nothing so far about insolent punishment, though he may be thinking of cases like the one mentioned at 6. 1306ᵇ1–2 above (see the note to 1306ᵃ36–ᵇ2). He has already advised the tyrant to delegate the task of punishment to others (1315ᵃ7–8). Now he adds that the tyrant should be seen to administer such punishment paternally. There are two ideas behind this advice. First, there is Aristotle's theory that punishment is a kind of therapy (*EN* II. 3. 1104ᵇ16–17; *EE* II. 1. 1220ᵃ35–6), which is administered for the sake of the person who is punished (*Rhet.* I. 10. 1369ᵇ12–13). And, secondly, there is the idea that the relation of a father to his children should resemble that of a king to his subjects (I. 12. 1259ᵃ37–ᵇ1). Thus, to be seen administering punishment paternally is to be seen acting like a king and for the benefit of the malefactor. For insolent sexual relations see 10. 1311ᵇ8–20 above and note.

Aristotle warns the tyrant against insolence because of the full-blooded response it may arouse. In the last chapter he had asserted that insolent treatment stirs up spirit, or *thumos*, claiming 'that men give way to violent feelings (*tois thumois*) most of all because of insolence' (1312ᵇ29–30). Invoking Heraclitus he now adds the further point that the spirited element of a person, in reacting to insolence, is indifferent to the fate of the person himself.

1315ᵃ31–40   The rich and the poor

Ideally the tyrant, like a true king (10. 1310ᵇ40–1311ᵃ2), should secure the allegiance of both parts of his city, the rich and the poor. But if he cannot, he is advised to ally himself with the stronger of the two. In giving this latter advice, Aristotle is tacitly appealing to the 'great elementary principle' that the group that favours the status quo should be stronger than the one that does not (see 9. 1309ᵇ14–18 and note). There is an echo of this advice in Machiavelli, who thinks, however, that the stronger group is always the larger. 'It follows', he writes, 'that those [tyrants] who have the public as a whole for their friends and the great ones for their enemies are the more secure, in that their violence is backed by a greater force than it is in the case of those who have the populace for an enemy and the nobility for a friend' (*Discourses*, 1. 40). The two measures that Greek tyrants traditionally used to increase their power relative to their subjects were the strengthening of their guard with freed slaves (Plato, *Rep.* VIII. 567e3–7; Xen. *Hieron* 6. 5) and the confiscation of heavy arms (see the note to 10. 1311ᵃ8–22 above).

1315ᵃ40–ᵇ10   Conclusion

Aristotle claims that the tyrant who follows the Way of Moderation will rule over better men and will be himself a better man. Such a tyrant, he says, 'will be either nobly disposed toward virtue or at least half-good'. Why should this be? Why does Aristotle think that a tyrant will improve his character by playing the king? The answer lies in his view that the moral virtues are acquired by doing the things that accord with them: 'We become just by doing just things; temperate by doing temperate things; and brave by doing brave things' (*EN* II. 1. 1103ᵃ34–ᵇ2, 2. 1104ᵃ33–ᵇ3; II. 4). By this theory a tyrant who does the things that kings do should begin to develop the moral character of a king. At the worst, he will become half-good; at the best, he will become 'nobly disposed toward virtue', which seems to imply that he will become wholly good and ultimately cease to be a tyrant.

We can see now exactly how the advice of the Way of Moderation differs from that of *The Prince*. Unlike Machiavelli Aristotle never suggests that by acting contrary to virtue a tyrant can make his rule longer lasting, more secure, and better for his city. He would never write, as Machiavelli does, that 'a prince who wants to keep his post must learn how not to be good, and use that knowledge, or refrain from using it, as necessity requires' (*Prince*, ch. 15). Nor would he tell a tyrant in relation to the moral virtues that 'when you have them and exercise them all the time, they are harmful to you; when you just seem to have them, they are useful' (*Prince*, ch. 18). Aristotle would not say these things because his goal in the Way of Moderation is to draw the tyrant as closely as possible to the rule of a king.

CHAPTER 12

This chapter has two unrelated parts, a list of the longest tyrannies and a critique of Plato's account of constitutional change in Book VIII of the *Republic*. Some scholars think the first part was not written by Aristotle and bracket it as an interpolation. There are three reasons for doubting its authenticity: the omission of the tyranny of Dionysius I and his successors from the list in spite of the fact that it lasted (with one interruption) for over fifty years; the intrusive mention of oligarchy in the section of Book V devoted to monarchy; and the inclusion of tyranny among constitutions, or *politeiai*, at 1315ᵇ11, which is unusual in Book V though not unprecedented (see 10. 1312ᵃ39–40) (Newman, ad loc.). The last two grounds are not very weighty, but the omission of the tyranny of Dionysius and his successors is hard to understand in view of its prominence in the rest of Book V. One reason for thinking the passage authentic, on the other hand, is that, in stressing the moderation of the longest tyranny and of the founder of the second longest, it connects the durability of a tyranny with the Way of Moderation and thus provides a fitting conclusion to Aristotle's discussion of the latter.

The critique of Plato in the second part of the chapter presents a different sort of problem. Though it is clearly authentic, it does not fit within the structure of Book V. First of all, it is not in its natural place within an Aristotelian discourse. Aristotle's practice is to begin, rather than end, his discussion of a topic by reviewing the ideas of his predecessors. And, secondly, it directly follows a sentence that appears to bring Book V to a close (1315ᵇ40–1316ᵃ1). It seems to be an independent essay (and an unfinished one at that) which Aristotle or his editor tacked on to Book V as an appendix because he could find no other place for it.

1315ᵇ11–1316ᵃ1

1315ᵇ11–22   The tyranny of the Orthagorids

The century-long tyranny of Orthagoras and his descendants—not just sons (see Her. 6. 126)—at Sicyon, a few miles west of Corinth, was established in the middle of the seven century BC. The author of the passage before us, Aristotle or his surrogate, evidently thinks its history demonstrates the superiority of the Way of Moderation to the Way of Repression. For he begins by attributing its durability to its moderation and subservience to the laws—a tyranny that is subservient to law is close to a kingship (IV. 10. 1295ᵃ15)—and then goes on to mention two respects in which it exemplifies the advice of the Way of Moderation: the currying of favour by the tyrants and the military prowess of Cleisthenes (for the advice see 11. 1314ᵇ21–3, 1315ᵇ3–4). As an illustration of the moderation of Cleisthenes, the story is told that he not only crowned the man who had the courage to award the victory in a competition to someone other than Cleisthenes himself but that he apparently even set up a statue in the judge's honour. (If Stalin had been the tyrant, the judge would have been shot.)

Cleisthenes, the most distinguished of the tyrants of Sicyon, had two distinguished Athenian descendants. He was a grandfather of

Cleisthenes, the Athenian statesman (mentioned at III. 2. 1275ᵇ36 and VI. 4. 1319ᵇ21), and a great-great-grandfather of Pericles (mentioned at II. 12. 1274ᵃ8–9). (Her. 5. 66–8, 6. 126–31; Andrewes, pp. 58–61).

1315ᵇ22–9   The tyranny of the Cypselids

Cypselus founded the tyranny around 657 BC. Its durability, like that of the longest tyranny, is attributed to the moderation and political prowess of the rulers, though the qualities that are combined in Cleisthenes—moderation and military prowess—seem to be divided between Cypselus and Periander. Since Periander is the prototype of the repressive tyrant (11. 1313ᵃ34–7), the tyranny of the Cypselids is not really a good example of the Way of Moderation. For Cypselus, Periander, and Gorgus (Periander's half-brother) see the notes to 3. 1303ᵃ23, 10. 1310ᵇ26–31, and 10. 1311ᵃ8–22 above.

1315ᵇ29–34   The tyranny of the Peisistratids

The tyranny of the Peisistratids was noted for its moderation until its final years when Hippias, Peisistratus' eldest son and successor, became repressive in reaction to the assassination of his brother Hipparchus (Her. 5. 55; AP 19. 1–2). Our ancient sources are unanimous in their praise of Peisistratus' rule. Herodotus says that 'without disturbing the existing offices or changing laws, he administered the city according to the established customs ruling nobly and well' (1. 59. 6)—a judgement echoed by Thucydides (6. 54. 5). Similarly, in the *Constitution of Athens* we read that Peisistratus, in managing the affairs of the city, acted 'moderately and more politically than tyrannically' (16. 2). Nothing of this sort is said so directly in the passage before us, but earlier in the chapter it was noted that Peisistratus appeared before the Areopagus in answer to a lawsuit (1315ᵇ21–2). (The charge was murder, but his accuser was afraid to appear (AP 16. 8; Plut. *Solon*, 31).) His appearance before the Areopagus is noteworthy because the respect for the law that it demonstrates is uncharacteristic of a tyrant (IV. 10. 1295ᵃ15). The testimony about Peisistratus is so uniformly favourable that it has even been suggested that Aristotle used his reign as a model in composing the Way of Moderation (Andrewes, pp. 108–9). For more on the Peisistratids see the notes to 5. 1305ᵃ23–4, 10. 1311ᵃ36–9, and 11. 1313ᵇ18–25 above.

1315ᵇ34–9　For the tyranny around Hieron and Gelon see the notes to 3. 1302ᵇ31–3, 3. 1303ᵃ38–ᵇ2, and 10. 1312ᵇ9–17.

<h2 style="text-align:center">1316ᵃ1–ᵇ27</h2>

Aristotle attributes the ideas about constitutional change examined in this section to the character Socrates of the *Republic*. For whom does this character speak in his view—the author of the dialogue or the philosopher upon whom the character is modelled? Though Aristotle does not say in the passage before us, he makes it plain elsewhere (II. 12. 1274ᵇ9 and IV. 7. 1293ᵇ1) that he takes him to be speaking for Plato rather than the historical Socrates.

Aristotle has four main criticisms of Plato's account of constitutional change: (1) Plato does not assign a distinctive change to his first and best constitution; (2) he mistakenly thinks that constitutional change follows a single pattern; (3) he sometimes attributes constitutional change to the wrong cause; and (4) he traces the change of each type of constitution to a single cause when there are in fact a variety of different causes.

1316ᵃ1–17　Criticism of Plato's account of the change from aristocracy to timocracy

The downfall of Plato's first and best constitution, also called 'aristocracy' (*Rep.* VIII. 544e7, 545c9, 547c6), stems from a failure of its programme of eugenics. The programme requires a bit of applied mathematics, the details of which are obscure, involving a cosmic number. The ideal city begins its decline—which is inevitable since everything that comes into being ultimately perishes—when the rulers through some sort of miscalculation breed the young guardians at the wrong time (*para kairon*). These young guardians produce inferior offspring, who neglect the educational system when they grow up and become rulers themselves. As a result, the ability of the rulers to judge the (metallic) nature of men deteriorates; and people who lack a proper guardian's character become guardians. This leads to faction among the guardians, which is resolved by transforming the aristocracy into a timocracy (*Rep.* VIII. 545c8–547c5).

Aristotle focuses on three things in Plato's account of the change of his best constitution: the notion that nothing endures but everything changes in a certain cycle, the cosmic number, and the idea that some men are resistant to education. He then asks an rhetorical question, Why should this change be distinctive (*idios*) of Plato's best constitution rather than of all the other constitutions and, indeed, of everything that comes into existence? Unfortunately, it is unclear exactly what Aristotle's criticism is, for his rhetorical question is ambiguous. It can be taken to be about the cause of the change or the nature of the change. Since the question follows upon an analysis of the causal chain leading to the downfall of the best constitution, it is natural to suppose that it is about the cause of the change. This is the way Newman interprets the question in his first note on the passage. Aristotle, he says, 'holds that the overthrow of the best constitution should be traced to causes not only special to constitutions in general as distinguished from other things, but special to it'. Aristotle believes, according to this interpretation, that Plato has traced the cause of change of his best constitution, not to a special, but to a universal cause, a cause that applies to everything that comes into being. This universal cause would presumably be the fact that nothing endures but everything changes in a certain cycle. But if this is Aristotle's objection, it is not a good one. For such a universal cause is always concurrent with a special cause. And Plato *has* traced the downfall of his best constitution to a special cause—namely, to a failure of its programme of eugenics. Since no other constitution has such a programme, no other constitution changes for the same reason the best constitution changes.

The other possibility is that Aristotle's rhetorical question is about the nature of the change rather than its cause. Without noting (or apparently noticing) the ambiguity, Newman in his second note on the passage before us says that Aristotle's question implies 'that to omit to assign a *mode* of change special to itself to an entity so supreme as the best constitution . . . is a very serious omission' (my italics). The reason for thinking that Aristotle's question concerns the nature of the change rather than its cause is that this is what his words, taken literally, mean. This is shown by a parallel passage in *De Generatione et Corruptione* in which Aristotle considers the view that growth is change from something that has magnitude only potentially—that is, from a point or a void—to something that has magnitude actually, and claims, using the same language he uses in the *Politics*, that 'such change is not distinctive (*idios*) of growth but of coming-to-be' (I. 5. 320ᵇ29–30). Clearly Aristotle is making a point here about the nature of a sort of change rather than its cause. The problem with this second interpretation is that Aristotle has not explained why the best constitution should have a distinctive mode of change. Under this second interpretation his rhetorical question presupposes an undefended and questionable idea. It seems, then, that Plato would have a good reply to whichever of the two objections Aristotle is making.

On the cosmic number see Aubonnet, ad loc.

1316ᵃ14–17   It is unclear what Aristotle is talking about here. Plato says nothing in the *Republic* about time being an agent of change or about a turnabout (*tropē*), though this latter notion does occur in the *Statesman* (270c2, d4, 271b7).

1316ᵃ17–39   Criticism of Plato's view that constitutional change follows a single pattern

Aristotle has both an internal and an external criticism of the Platonic sequence of constitutional change. In this sequence aristocracy changes to timocracy (also called 'the Laconian constitution'), timocracy to oligarchy, oligarchy to democracy, and democracy to tyranny (called 'monarchy' at 1316ᵃ24) (*Rep.* VIII. 545c9, 550c8–9, 555b8–9, 562a10–b1). Aristotle's external criticism treats this sequence as an hypothesis about constitutional history subject to empirical investigation. Such investigation, Aristotle thinks, shows that any given constitution can change into almost any other. Thus, Plato's sequence is refuted by history.

This criticism seems misguided. For clearly Plato was not writing as an historian when he composed Book VIII of the *Republic*. The constitutions he discusses are only vaguely associated with historical cities, the only positive identification being that of timocracy with Sparta and the cities of Crete (*Rep.* VIII. 544c3). Furthermore, his description of the deterioration of the first and best constitution is speculative and a priori, and cannot be intended as constitutional history. Although he believes that his ideal city is possible (*Rep.* V. 472d9–473b3, VI. 499a11–c6) and even conjectures that it has existed somewhere on earth at some time (*Rep.* 499c7–d6), he does not claim to have any experience of, or to have heard any reports about, such an historical city. But if the first term of the sequence is not historical, the historicity of the entire sequence is undermined. The sequence is clearly determined by psychology rather than history. In constructing it Plato had his eye, not on the constitutional history of historical cities, but on various configurations of the parts of the soul. Each constitution is such a configuration writ large, and the constitutions are ordered from best to worst according to Plato's evaluation of the corresponding psychological configurations. That Plato would be unmoved by Aristotle's historical counter-examples does not mean that an examination of Plato's speculations about constitutional development from an historical point of view would be pointless. But the interesting question, given the speculative nature of the Platonic sequence, is not whether constitutional history followed the Platonic pattern in every Greek city but whether it followed it in any.

Aristotle's internal criticism focuses on tyranny. Aristotle claims that Plato has left three questions unanswered: (1) Will tyranny change? If it does change, (2) Why will it change? and (3) Into which constitution? Aristotle says that these are not easy questions for Plato because their answers are indeterminable. But instead of explaining this indeterminability Aristotle proceeds to answer the third question. He claims that if the continuity and cyclical nature of constitutional change is to be preserved, as Plato seems to envisage (*Rep.* VIII. 546a2–7), tyranny must change into aristocracy. Though Aristotle implies that this answer is absurd, he does not explain why. He is evidently assuming that constitutional change for Plato is always change for the worse—a natural assumption since Plato never mentions any other sort in Book VIII of the *Republic*. If Plato is making this assumption, then he will have a hard time answering Aristotle's three questions. If all change is change for the worse, how could tyranny, the worst possible constitution, change at all? A fortiori how could it change into the best constitution? And since it is also part of Plato's theory that constitutional decline is always caused by personal decline among the rulers, what cause could there be for tyranny to change, given that tyrants have reached the limit of personal decline? We should consider the possibility that Plato never intended these questions to be answered. The fact that they are unanswered and unanswerable can be taken as one more indication that his sequence of constitutional change is just another Platonic myth.

1316ᵃ18–20 When Aristotle says that all constitutions change more often to their opposite than to the one close by, which constitutions is he counting as opposites and which as close by? Since he is correcting Plato, he must be thinking of constitutions in relation to Plato's sequence. One constitution will be close to another if it is next to that other in Plato's sequence. The pairs of opposites are presumably kingship and tyranny, aristocracy and democracy, and timocracy and oligarchy (see 7. 1307ᵃ23–7, 10. 1312ᵇ4–9). But note that the last pair of opposites are also close to each other.

1316ᵃ29–34   For the tyranny at Sicyon see the note to 1315ᵇ11–22 above.

The tyranny of Antileon was not continuous with that of Phoxus, the other tyrant at Chalcis mentioned by Aristotle (4. 1304ᵃ29–31). The tyranny of Phoxus was followed by a democracy, that of Antileon by an oligarchy. This is all we know about the two tyrannies.

For the tyranny of Gelon's house see the note to 3. 1303ᵃ38–ᵇ2 above.

Charilaus reigned as a Eurypontid king of Sparta from around 780 to 750 BC (Her. 8. 131). Aristotle refers to him as a king rather than a tyrant at II. 10. 1271ᵇ25, and evidently thinks of him as a king who became a tyrant (see 10. 1310ᵇ18–20 and 1313ᵃ1–3).

Aristotle's claim at II. 11. 1272ᵇ29–33 that there was never a tyranny at Carthage has led some scholars to bracket the last three words of this sentence.

1316ᵃ34–9   For Panaetius see the note to 10. 1310ᵇ26–31 above. Cleander was assassinated in 498 BC after reigning as tyrant at Gela for seven years (Her. 7. 154–5, Andrewes, pp. 129–30). Anaxilaus was tyrant at Rhegium from 494 to 476 BC (Her. 6. 23, 7. 165, 170; Andrewes, pp. 130–3). Though Aristotle counts Rhegium as a Sicilian city, it is actually on the Italian side of the Straits of Messina.

1316ᵃ39–ᵇ6   Criticism of Plato's account of the change from timocracy to oligarchy

Aristotle thinks that Plato has assigned the wrong cause for this change. Plato says that oligarchy develops from timocracy when the rulers (1) begin to value money more than virtue, (2) become money-lovers and money-makers, and (3) institute a property qualification for office (*Rep*. VIII. 550d3–551b7). Aristotle claims that there is a change to oligarchy, not because the rulers become money-lovers and money-makers, but because (4) the large property-holders think it unjust for those who do not own property to share equally in political office with those who do. These large property-holders would be among the rulers of the timocracy Plato describes, since only the rulers own property under this constitution (*Rep.* VIII. 547b2–c4). Furthermore, the only reason that these property-holders can have for preferring the oligarchic conception of justice to the timocratic is that they value wealth more than (military) virtue (see the note to 1. 1301ᵃ25–ᵇ4 above). But this means that Aristotle's criticism amounts to no more than the claim that step (2) in Plato's causal chain should be replaced by (4). It is difficult to see why Plato should oppose this small revision.

It is odd that Carthage should be called a democracy, since it is classified as an aristocracy at IV. 7. 1293ᵇ14–16. But the constitution did have some democratic features (II. 11. 1273ᵃ6–13).

1316ᵇ6–27   Criticism of Plato's account of the change from oligarchy to democracy

Plato attributes the downfall of oligarchy to the wholehearted pursuit of wealth by its rulers. Their greed drives them to lend at high rates of interest to the intemperate among the young, who are reduced to penury and lose their civic rights. While thus creating bitter enemies for themselves among the disenfranchised, they allow their children to cultivate a taste for luxury and to grow physically and mentally lax. When the poor realize just how weakened and soft their rulers have become, they rise against them and take power themselves (*Rep.* VIII. 555b3–557a8).

Aristotle criticizes this account on two grounds. He criticizes Plato first for saying that an oligarchic city is two cities, one of the rich and one of the poor, when this is true of every city where men are unequal in wealth or virtue. This criticism implies that Plato thinks that only oligarchic cities split into opposing sections. But this implication is false. Though Plato is especially emphatic in Book VIII about the bifurcation of oligarchy (*Rep.* 551d5–7) and of the oligarchic man (*Rep.* 554d9–e1), he stresses earlier on in the dialogue that only his ideal city is a true unity and that every other city fragments into two or more cities (IV. 422e9).

Aristotle's second, more substantive, criticism is that Plato attributes the downfall of oligarchies to a single cause, the impoverishment of some of the citizens, even though oligarchies change for a variety of different reasons. Aristotle's discussion in fact supports the stronger criticism that such impoverishment is neither a necessary nor a sufficient condition of the downfall of oligarchy; for he claims that oligarchies sometimes change even though no one in the propertied class has become any poorer, and that they do not always change when some of the leading oligarchs become poor. Two additional causes of change are mentioned: an increase in the number of the poor from sources other than the propertied class and faction among the oligarchs. Aristotle does not explain how the poor can increase in number without drawing from the propertied class, but there are only two possibilities—the birth rate of the poor exceeds their death rate, or bastards, aliens, and freedmen are made (second-class) citizens (see III. 2. 1275ᵇ35–7, 5. 1278ᵃ26–34; V. 3. 1303ᵃ38–ᵇ1; VI. 4. 1319ᵇ6–10). They would be only second-class citizens since the poor are, of course, excluded from political office in an oligarchy.

1316ᵇ23–5 Aristotle here transfers a remark that Plato makes about the citizens of a democracy—they are free and do whatever they wish—to the property-holders in an oligarchy (*Rep.* VIII. 557b4–6).

1316ᵇ25–7 The discussion of the Platonic sequence of constitutional change breaks off suddenly and unexpectedly. The new objection that Plato has not considered the possibility that different forms of oligarchy and democracy change for different reasons is not developed, and nothing is said of Plato's account of the change of democracy into tyranny.

BOOK SIX

This book, like its predecessor, is a manual on practical politics. The person for whom it is intended is the lawgiver (5. 1319^{b}33) who wishes to establish, preserve, or straighten out a democracy or an oligarchy (1. 1317^{a}33–5, 5. 1319^{b}33–5).

CHAPTER I

1316^{b}31–1317^{a}18

Aristotle begins this introductory section by recalling three topics that were discussed earlier: (1) the number and nature of the various varieties of each of the three elements of a constitution— the deliberative, the official, and the judicial—(discussed in IV. 14–16); (2) which variety of each element goes with which constitution (discussed in various places throughout IV. 14–16); and (3) the destruction and preservation of constitutions (discussed in V). He then goes on to mention three new topics that need to be examined: (1) the mode of organization appropriate and advantageous to each subspecies of constitution, (2) the various hybrid constitutions, and (3) how to establish each subspecies of constitution.

To understand the first of the new topics, we need to understand the difference between being appropriate (*oikeios*) and being advantageous (*sumpherōn*) to a constitution. A mode of organization is appropriate (*oikeios*) to a constitution if it follows from the principle of that constitution (1317^{a}9–10, 29–31, 35–7; and for the use of the word in another context see I. 9. 1257^{a}6–13). It is advantageous (*sumpherōn*) to a constitution, on the other hand, if it is preservative of it (II. 9. 1270^{b}20–2; V. 9. 1309^{b}14–15; *Rhet.* I. 7. 1365^{b}26). The appropriate and the advantageous can conflict; for, as Aristotle likes to point out, institutions that are appropriate to a constitution when carried to an extreme often destroy it (5. 1319^{b}33–1320^{a}4; V. 9. 1309^{b}18–37).

The third topic, how to establish each subspecies of constitution, is not very different from the first; for the best way to establish a given constitution is to establish the institutions that are both appropriate and advantageous to it. Thus, we should not be surprised to find that Aristotle tends to conflate the two topics in the body of Book VI and mentions only one of them in winding up his discussion (5. 1320ᵇ16–17, 7. 1321ᵇ1–3).

The second topic introduces the notion of a hybrid constitution. Hybrid constitutions are produced by combining elements appropriate to different constitutions—an aristocratic judicial element, for example, with oligarchic deliberative and official elements. It is unclear just how many hybrid constitutions Aristotle thinks there are, for it is unclear whether he thinks there are four types of each of the three elements or six. He usually writes as though there were only four types: democratic, oligarchic, aristocratic, and constitutional (that is, appropriate to a polity) (IV. 16. 1301ᵃ10–15). But one comment of his implies that there is also a monarchic type of official element (IV. 15. 1299ᵇ20–4). There are sixty hybrid constitutions if there are four types of each element. Each of the four types of deliberative element can be combined with one or another of four types of official element, and each of these sixteen combinations can be combined in turn with one or another of four types of judicial element. This yields sixty-four combinations in all, four of which have elements all of the same type and hence are not hybrids. If there are kingly and tyrannic types in addition to the basic four, there are 210 hybrids—216 combinations of the six types of element minus the six pure forms.

The actual contents of Book VI are a bit different from what the introduction leads us to expect. First of all, we are led to expect that the first and third topics will be treated separately and in relation to every subspecies of constitution; but in the body of Book VI the two topics are conflated and discussed only in relation to the various species of democracy and oligarchy. Secondly, the topic of the various hybrid constitutions is introduced only to be abandoned; nothing more is heard of it in the remainder of Book VI. And, finally, nothing in the introduction leads us to expect a discussion of offices. The actual contents of Book VI are as follows:

A. Introduction (1. 1316ᵇ31–1317ᵃ18).
B. Democracy:

As this Table of Contents makes plain, Aristotle expresses a good deal more interest in democracy in Book VI than in oligarchy. He spends four times as many words on the one as on the other and devotes more than half of the entire book to democracy.

Book VI is closely tied to the two preceding books. It contains ten backward references to these books (1. 1316ᵇ35–6, 1317ᵃ13, 24, 38; 2. 1317ᵇ34; 4. 1318ᵇ7, 1319ᵇ5; 5. 1319ᵇ37; 8. 1321ᵇ6, 10); its concluding chapter resumes the discussion of offices begun in IV. 15; and its other chapters address one of the topics of the programme of IV. 2—'in what way the man who wishes to do so should establish these constitutions, I mean each kind individually of democracy and again of oligarchy' (1289ᵇ20–3).

1317ᵃ10–16 Which constitution is suited to which sort of population was discussed in IV. 12.

1317ᵃ18–39

In this section Aristotle explains why there are various species of democracy. His explanation is analytical rather than historical and is addressed to the lawgiver who wishes to bring a democracy into being and thus needs to understand the different ways a democracy can be structured. Aristotle says there are two reasons that democracies differ in kind: peoples differ, and democratic institutions combine in different ways. The way in which Aristotle accounts for the various species of democracy in terms of these two differentiae calls to mind the method of multiple simultaneous differentiation, which he introduces in his biological works (*PA* I. 3. 643ᵇ9–26). This method is based on two ideas answering two questions: (1) How are the species of a genus alike? and (2) How do they differ? The first idea is that each species of a genus shares with every other many generic attributes, not just one (*HA* I. 1. 486ᵃ14–25). Thus, all birds have feathers, a beak, two eyes, two legs, two wings, and so forth. The second idea is that the various species of a genus possess their multiple generic attributes to differing degrees—possess them 'more or less', as Aristotle expresses it (*HA* I. 1. 486ᵃ25–ᵇ17; *PA* I. 4. 644ᵃ16–18, ᵇ7–15; IV. 12. 692ᵇ3–8). Thus, different species of birds have longer or shorter feathers, longer or shorter legs, more or less crooked beaks, and so forth (*PA* I. 4. 644ᵃ19–21; III. 1. 662ᵃ33–ᵇ16; IV. 12). There are four reasons for thinking that Aristotle is using this method in Book VI. First, in dividing democracy into species he introduces multiple (two) generic differentiae. Second, he applies them simultaneously. Third, in saying that democracies differ because they include a larger or smaller portion of the people and a larger or smaller number of democratic institutions, he indicates that they differ because they possess the two generic differentiae to different degrees. Fourth and finally, he emphasizes that democracies that so differ differ, not simply in being better or worse, but in kind—they are, as he puts it, 'not the same'.

It is worth noting that the method that Aristotle seems to be using to classify the various species of democracy can be used to classify constitutions in general. For every constitution is defined by the political community it determines and by its institutional arrangements. The generic constitutions—democracy, oligarchy, and so forth—are defined first. Each of these is defined by the sort of persons it makes full citizens and by the nature of its institutions. Thus, a constitution is a democracy if a larger or smaller proportion of the people, the *dēmos*, qualify for full citizenship under it and if it has a larger or smaller number of democratic institutions; it is an oligarchy, on the other hand, if full citizenship is restricted to a larger or smaller proportion of the rich and if it has a larger or smaller number of oligarchic institutions. Each species of a given genus is defined, in turn, by a determinant measure of each of the two generic differentiae of the generic constitution. The best type of democracy, for example, has the smallest body of full citizens and the smallest number of democratic institutions (4. 1318ᵇ6–1319ᵃ4). The use of 'the more and less' might seem to produce as many species of democracy as there are of bird, but Aristotle keeps the number low by counting groups of individuals rather than the individuals themselves. In the chapter before us, for example, he distinguishes only three different peoples, or *dēmoi.*

1317ᵃ22–9 That democracies are different because peoples are different was mentioned earlier at IV. 4. 1291ᵇ15–28, 6. 1292ᵇ22– 1293ᵃ10, and 12. 1296ᵇ24–31. The three peoples to whom Aristotle refers—the mass of farmers, the mass of artisans, and the mass of labourers—were in his eyes and those of his contemporaries of successively lower social status (I. 11. 1258ᵇ35–9, III. 5. 1278ᵃ8–25, VIII. 2. 1337ᵇ8–15). Artisans (*banausoi*) were skilled workers such as cobblers and carpenters (IV. 4. 1291ᵃ1–4, *Met. B.* 996ᵃ33–4); labourers (*thētes*) were unskilled manual labourers who were hired for the day (I. 11. 1258ᵇ25–7, Plato, *Stat.* 290a4–5).

1317ᵃ35–8 That democracies and oligarchies are destroyed when their fundamental principles are followed unswervingly was discussed earlier at V. 9. 1309ᵇ18–35.

1317ᵃ39 Though Aristotle says he is going to discuss the axioms (*axiōmata*), the ethical character (*ēthē*), and the ends of democratic constitutions, he runs the first and third topics together and never reaches the second one.

CHAPTER 2

This chapter has two parts, the first devoted to the principles of democracy, and the second to the institutions through which these principles are realized (for the distinction compare II. 9. 1269ᵃ32–4).

1317ᵃ40–ᵇ17

In this philosophically rich and complex section on the principles of democracy Aristotle (1) distinguishes two marks, or signs, of freedom, (2) mentions a democratic argument in connection with each, and (3) argues in his own voice that proletarian democracy is the usual outcome of egalitarian democracy.

Aristotle begins by announcing that freedom is a fundamental principle, or *hupothesis*, of democracy. But what is a fundamental principle of a constitution? Is it a first, or underived, principle as opposed to a derived principle, or is it a principle, derived or underived, as opposed to an institution? When we examine

Aristotle's use of the word in the rest of the *Politics*, we find that it often signifies a first, or underived, principle that expresses the end, or goal, of a constitution (II. 2. 1261ᵃ15–16, 5. 1263ᵇ29–32, 9. 1271ᵃ41–ᵇ3; VII. 9. 1329ᵃ21–4). This is consistent with Aristotle's explanation of the word in the *Posterior Analytics* and with some of his remarks in his ethical works. In the former he says that an *hupothesis* is, among other things, a first, or underived, principle (*An. Post.* I. 2. 72ᵃ14–21, 10. 76ᵇ27–30, 19. 81ᵇ14–15; see also *Met. Δ*. 1. 1013ᵃ14–16); and in the latter he says that the end, or goal, of an action is a starting-point just like the *hupotheseis* of geometry (*EN* VII. 8. 1151ᵃ16–17; *EE* II. 10. 1227ᵃ8–9, 11. 1227ᵇ28–30). In one passage in the *Politics*, however, the word clearly signifies the principles of a constitution in general, not just its first, or underived, principles. Aristotle says that 'a person might refer all the measures characteristic of tyranny (*ta turannika*) to these fundamental principles (*hupotheseis*): that its subjects not trust one another, that they have no power, and that they think small' (V. 11. 1314ᵃ27–9). This passage is noteworthy because it contrasts the institutions of tyranny (*ta turannika*) with the principles, or *hupotheseis*, of tyranny (see also II. 9. 1269ᵃ32–4), and because none of the three *hupotheseis* appears to be a first, or underived, principle of tyranny. At any rate, none of the three mentions the end, or aim, of tyranny (for the end, or aim, of tyranny see V. 10. 1311ᵃ4, 10; *Rhet.* I. 8. 1366ᵃ4–6).

The passage before us in Book VI can be read either way—as asserting that freedom is *the* fundamental and underived principle of democracy or as asserting that freedom is one among several derived and underived principles (as distinct from institutions) of democracy. There are two considerations favouring the first interpretation. The first is that the only principle of democracy Aristotle actually calls an *hupothesis* mentions the aim of democracy and thus appears to be a first principle (for freedom as the mark, standard, or end of democracy see IV. 8. 1294ᵃ10–11, *EN* V. 3. 1131ᵃ25–9, and *Rhet.* I. 8. 1366ᵃ4). The second is that he implicitly distinguishes between derived and underived principles in the very passage we are discussing. He derives the democratic principle that citizens should rule and be ruled in turn, for example, from the first principle that the aim of democracy is freedom. (See Miller, pp. 156–7.) These two considerations are balanced by two others pointing in the opposite direction. First of all, the chapter as a whole is

structured around the contrast between the principles and the institutions of democracy (*ta dēmotika*, literally, the things that are
democratic). And, secondly, the one occurrence of *hupothesis* is
not preceded by the definite article, as one would expect if Aristotle were referring to the first principle of a constitution (see II. 5.
1263ᵇ30–1, 9. 1269ᵃ32–3, 1271ᵃ41, 11. 1273ᵃ4; VII. 9. 1329ᵃ21–2). The
hupothesis mentioned is presumably just one of the axioms, or
axiōmata, of democracy referred to in the preceding line. On either
interpretation Aristotle is one term short. He needs either a generic term to distinguish the principles of a constitution from its
institutions or a specific term to distinguish the first, or underived,
principles of a constitution from the derived ones.

The first democratic argument is from democratic justice to the
first component of freedom. The first thing we need to understand
is this component. What does it mean to rule and be ruled in turn?
To rule in a democracy is simply to hold a political office; and in
Greek the very same word, *archein*, is used for both. To rule and be
ruled in turn is opposed to ruling continuously (III. 6. 1279ᵃ8–16,
IV. 4. 1291ᵃ36–8, V. 7. 1307ᵇ7–13). Thus, ruling and being ruled in
turn is holding an office in rotation rather than permanently: when
a man holds a given office he is ruling; when the office devolves on
someone else, he is being ruled. The premiss of the argument,
democratic justice, is the principle that political office should be
shared equally on the basis of free status—'number, not worth', as
Aristotle expresses it. The democrat argues, then, that, given this
principle, political offices should be held in rotation.

His conclusion does not follow from his premiss. For, as we have
seen, an office can be distributed equally to all free men without
being rotated among them. The way to do this is to assign it permanently to every free man. This sounds impossible, but Greek democracies did do it with one office. They usually made every free
man a permanent member of the assembly. In Greek democracies
it was normally only the executive and administrative offices that
were held in rotation, not the deliberative, though Aristotle knew
a few in which even the office of assemblyman was held in rotation
(IV. 14. 1298ᵃ9–19). It seems, then, that the conclusion of the democrat's argument is restricted to non-deliberative offices. But the
argument is still not valid. The democrat is relying on two tacit
premisses that rule out the possibility of non-deliberative offices
being held permanently. The first is that such an office must be held

either continuously or in rotation; the second is that it is not possible for everyone to hold the same office at the same time (II. 2. 1261ᵃ32–3). It follows from these two premises that the office in question cannot be held continuously by all free men. But if it is held continuously by some but not by others, it will not be distributed equally to all. Hence, it will violate democratic justice to assign it continuously to anyone. So it should be held in rotation.

Democratic justice, the principle from which the first component of freedom is derived, is not itself a first, or underived, principle for the democrat. For it leaves the connection of free status and the equal distribution of political office unexplained. The explanation, of course, is that all free men *qua* free are equal (III. 9. 1280ᵃ24–5, V. 1. 1301ᵃ30–1). Given that political office should be distributed on the basis of free status and that all free men are equal, it follows that political office should be distributed equally to all free men (III. 8. 1280ᵃ7–25; *EN* V. 3. 1131ᵃ25–8; and see the note to V. 1. 1301ᵃ25–ᵇ4 above).

The argument from free status ignores a considerable portion of the population of a typical Greek city. Women, children, and aliens were free or slave as well as adult male natives (*astoi*). Did the Greek democrat, then, use *eleutheros*, the Greek word for 'free', not only in a broad sense that included women, children, and aliens, but also in a narrow sense that excluded them? This seems unlikely. For what would the antonym of 'free' in the narrow sense be? It could hardly be 'slave'. For there is no broad sense of *doulos*, the Greek word for 'slave', by which Greek women, children, and aliens are all slaves—though in speaking of barbarians a Greek might be willing to apply the word more broadly (I. 2. 1252ᵃ34–ᵇ9). It seems rather that the argument from free status rests on the tacit and undefended assumption that political office should be distributed only among adult male natives. Women, children, and aliens are simply ignored.

The second mark of freedom, living as one wishes, is closely tied to the first. The democrat in fact thinks the second mark entails the first. He thinks that holding office in rotation somehow follows from the demand to live as one wishes. Aristotle gives us only a hint for why the democrat thinks this. He takes the democrat to be at heart an anarchist who reluctantly consents to be ruled only on condition that there be a rotation of ruling and being ruled. The democrat would appear to reason somewhat as follows. He wishes to be free, and he thinks that to be free is to live as one wishes. He tacitly assumes that to be ruled by another is not to live as one wishes, so he concludes that to be ruled by another is to be a slave (see V. 9. 1310ᵃ25–36 and the note thereto). But being a social animal, the democrat wishes to live among other free men. Since he believes it is slavish to be ruled by another, he dreams of a community of free men in which no one is ruled at all. For some reason he gives up this dream. Perhaps he recognizes that the lives different men wish to live are bound to conflict with each other, and this recognition drives him to conclude that free men cannot be parts of one community unless there is ruling and being ruled. Wishing to depart from his dream of anarchism as little as possible, he demands that political office be distributed equally among all the free men in the community—he demands democratic justice. But we saw in the argument from free status how to derive rotation in office from democratic justice. So from this point on in his new argument the democrat simply recapitulates the relevant steps of the old one.

The argument from free living involves two senses of 'free' and 'slave': a strict, or legal, sense and a loose sense. In the strict sense of the words, a slave is one who is owned by another; a free man is one who is not (I. 4. 1254ᵃ8–13). This is 'free' and 'slave' in the juridical sense of free and slave status. In the loose sense of the words, a free man is one who lives as he wishes; and a slave one who does not. This loose sense, which is associated with democracy (V. 9. 1310ᵃ31–2; Her. 3. 83. 3; Thuc. 2. 37. 2; Plato, *Rep.* VIII. 557b4–6; Isoc. *Areop.* 20), expresses what in Aristotle's view is a mistaken conception of freedom and slavery (see the note to V. 9. 1310ᵃ25–36 above). The two senses of 'free' and 'slave' are distinct since a man can be free in one sense while a slave in the other. The democrat thinks he is a slave in the loose sense when he is ruled by another (V. 9. 1310ᵃ31–6), though presumably he does not think he is actually owned by the person by whom he is ruled. Similarly, a legal slave who thinks that a life of slavery is best for him is free in the loose sense. Aristotle thinks this can happen if the legal slave is also a natural slave. The natural slave need only recognize that he would perish without a master to exercise forethought in his behalf (I. 2. 1252ᵃ30–4, 5. 1254ᵇ16–23, 6. 1255ᵇ12–15). The argument from free living clearly involves a slide from the loose sense of 'free' to the strict sense. To see this, one need only ask, With whom does the man who is free in the loose sense wish to take turns ruling and being ruled? The answer, of course, is with men of free status.

Sandwiched between these two arguments of the advocates of democracy is a third argument in which Aristotle, speaking in his own voice, explains why egalitarian democracy is usually proletarian democracy. An egalitarian democracy is one in which political office is distributed on the basis of free status. The primary political institution in a democracy is the assembly, of which every free man is normally a permanent member with one vote; and the assembly usually follows the principle of majority rule (for the principle see IV. 8. 1294ᵃ11–14 and VI. 3. 1318ᵃ28–30). But the majority of free men are normally poor. Consequently, as Aristotle says, 'the needy are more sovereign than the prosperous'. The implication, though Aristotle does not draw it out in the passage before us, is that the poor will use their greater sovereignty to advance their own interests at the expense of the rich (III. 10. 1281ᵃ14–17, VI. 3. 1318ᵃ24–6), making the egalitarian democracy a proletarian democracy (III. 8. 1279ᵇ34–1280ᵃ6).

For a recent discussion of this section see Barnes, pp. 253–6, and Sorabji, pp. 265–6.

1317ᵇ17–1318ᵃ10

Aristotle turns now to the various devices and institutions by which democratic justice is realized, and considers them under three heads: those relating to the offices (items 1 through 6), to the judiciary (item 7), and to the assembly (item 8).

One way of understanding the connection of these various devices and institutions with democrat justice is to see them as attempts to implement one or more of four democratic maxims, the first calling for strict equality, and the others surrendering it bit by bit. By the democratic maxim of strict equality, no free man *at any time* should have more political authority than any other. Thus, it is democratic for every free man to be a continuous, or permanent, member of the assembly, the deliberative element of the constitution. The assembly is the only institution in a Greek city that can be brought under the maxim of strict equality; as a consequence, democrats maximize its power and minimize that of the offices. The

next most important element of the constitution after the deliberative is the judicial. Since it is not practical for every case to be tried
before the entire citizen body, it is democratic to bring the judicial
element under the slightly weaker maxim that no free man should
have more political authority *during his lifetime* than any other free
man during a similar lifetime. This maxim allows for one man to
have more political authority than another on a particular occasion
but not over long periods of time. The office of juror can be parcelled out equally to each free man because of the constant need
for lots of jurors. (Athenian juries consisted of several hundred
jurors.) Since the judicial element can be made almost as egalitarian as the deliberative, it is democratic for it too to have great
power. The greatest challenge for the egalitarian comes with the
offices. It is not possible for every free man to rotate through all the
executive, administrative, and military offices in a city, so there is
bound to be some inequality in their distribution. They fall under
the still weaker maxim that every free man should have an equal
chance of winning any given office and that the odds of winning at
least once during a lifetime should be as high as possible. It is this
third maxim that the democrat is tacitly following when he advocates the use of the lot in selecting officials, short terms of office,
and restrictions on the repeated tenure of the same office. The use
of the lot equalizes the chance of winning any given office, whereas
short terms and restrictions on the repeated tenure of the same
office increase the odds of eventually winning any given office by
increasing the number of times it is filled and decreasing the
number of men eligible for it. There are some important offices,
however, that no Greek democrat would feel it safe to fill with just
any man. The office of general is one such. Even here, the ancient
Greek democrat remains as egalitarian as possible. The fourth and
final maxim is that an office requiring experience or skill should be
filled by election; but the office should be open to any free man, and
the electorate should consist of the entire body of free men. One of
the conditions of all four maxims is that every free man have the
leisure for the political participation they require. Thus, it is democratic to pay jurors and officials and those who attend the assembly
(item 9).

1317^b19–20 The statement that it is democratic 'for all to rule
each, and for each in turn to rule all' is ambiguous. As Aristotle has

pointed out before, the word 'all' can be taken either collectively or distributively (see the note to V. 8. 1307ᵇ30–40 above). Thus, the statement can mean either that the free men rule as a body or rule as individuals. Since Aristotle is discussing the offices rather than the assembly, he must be referring to the democratic practice of rotating offices among all the free men. What he is saying, then, is that it is democratic for every free man, serving as an official during some period of his life, to rule every other free man.

1317ᵇ30–5   That the council is the most democratic of all the offices is perhaps explained by its size. In Athens the council had five hundred members who served for one year and were eligible to serve (after an interval) only once more. This made the odds of being a member of the council at least once during a citizen's life quite high, perhaps as high as one to one or even higher. At any rate the odds were better than for any other office. This may be the reason it is called the most democratic. For more on the council see the note to 8. 1322ᵇ12–17 below.

That the assembly, when the people are paid to attend, draws decisions away from the council was said before at IV. 15. 1299ᵇ38–1300ᵃ4.

1317ᵇ38–41   This sentence is bracketed since it does not fit a list of institutions.

1318ᵃ3–10   This passage implies that there are at least two types of egalitarian democracy. The first type is the proletarian democracy described earlier in the chapter in which the poor use their superior numbers and the principle of majority rule to virtually disenfranchise the rich—in which, as Aristotle says, 'the needy are more sovereign than the prosperous' (1317ᵇ8–9). The second type, 'what is held to be most of all a democracy', is a democracy in which the tyrannic and monolithic majority of the first type is replaced by fluctuating majorities of different ratios of rich and poor, the majority that rules on one issue being different from the majority that rules on another. This second type is evidently the same as the constitution ranked first among the five types of democracy in Chapter 4 of Book IV, which is described in almost exactly the same words. 'The law in this ⟨premier⟩ sort of democracy', Aristotle writes, 'says that to be equal is for the needy to be no more pre-eminent than the prosperous, and for neither to be supreme, but for both to be of the same rank' (IV. 4. 1291ᵇ31–4). It is awarded

the premier place among democracies because to Aristotle's eyes it
is the most truly egalitarian. The problem of its institutional reali-
zation is dealt with in the next chapter. (For more on this passage
see Mulgan, pp. 317–18.)

CHAPTER 3

This chapter addresses the issue of equality. Aristotle is concerned
with the problem, or *aporia*, of devising institutions that will put the
rich and the poor in a democracy on an equal footing and thus
prevent the poor from using their superior numbers and the principle of majority rule to pauperize the rich.

1318ᵃ11–26

Aristotle's proposals for resolving the problem of equality presuppose that the following steps, or something like them, have been
taken: (1) the property of every free man in a given democracy has
been appraised; (2) the values have been entered on a list in order
of magnitude from largest to smallest alongside the men's names;
(3) the total value of all the property has been calculated; and (4) it
has been determined how far down the list one must go to reach
a sum equal to half this total. Aristotle supposes, for the sake of
illustration, that the list contains fifteen hundred names and that
the value of all the property put together of the first five hundred
equals that of the remaining one thousand.
    Aristotle considers two ways to equalize the rich and the poor.
The first way is to 'give the thousand power equal to the five
hundred'. How this is to be done he does not say immediately, but
his explanation is perhaps to be found in the next section. The
second way is for the five hundred and the thousand to each
select—whether by lot or by election is left open—an equal number
of representatives to an assembly. This proposal is particularly
interesting since a representative assembly, as distinct from an
assembly open to all full citizens, would have been an unusual
institution in a Greek city (but see IV. 14. 1298ᵃ40–ᵇ2, 19–23 and
Larsen). What Aristotle means when he says that this assembly is
to be 'supreme over the elections ⟨to the offices⟩ and the courts' is

unclear. Does he mean that officials and jurors are to be selected both from and by this assembly or something weaker?

Aristotle next asks whether 'the justest constitution according to democratic justice' is a balanced constitution that equalizes the rich and the poor in one of the two ways he has just described or rather 'the one based on the quantity (*to plēthos*) ⟨of free men⟩' alone. He does not answer this question explicitly, but argues implicitly for the balanced constitution by arguing against any conception of justice based on a strictly quantitative standard of worth such as the quantity (*to plēthos*) of free men or quantity (*plēthos*) of property, the democratic and oligarchic standards respectively. He claims that oligarchic justice (for which see III. 9. 1280ᵃ25–31) entails the inequality of tyranny; for if political authority is distributed in proportion to wealth and if one man has more property than the other rich men, he should rule alone (see also III. 13. 1283ᵇ16–18). (This argument, it should be noted, is invalid. Oligarchic justice entails one man rule only when one man owns all the property, not when he merely owns more than other property-holders.) Aristotle thinks the democratic conception of justice leads to the injustice of confiscation; for if the assembly follows the principle of majority rule and if every free man has a vote, then the poor, who are many, will have the power to confiscate the property of the rich, who are few (as was said before at III. 10. 1281ᵃ14–17).

The balanced constitution is designed to avoid the inequality and injustice that Aristotle finds in any constitution based on a strictly quantitative standard. But it does not follow from its design alone that the balanced constitution is the justest constitution according to democratic justice. To get this conclusion Aristotle needs two tacit premisses. First of all, he must assume that the justice of the balanced constitution is democratic justice rather than some other sort. And, secondly, he must assume that the balanced constitution does not introduce inequalities of its own that are worse than the ones it is designed to avoid.

Both of these tacit premisses are problematic. It is difficult to see how the justice of the balanced constitution can be democratic justice since the balanced constitution apportions political authority not by the single standard of freedom but by the dual standard of freedom and wealth. The balanced constitution does not seem to be a democracy at all, but the sort of mixed constitution that Aristotle sometimes calls a polity (IV. 8. 1293ᵇ33–4, 1294ᵃ22–3;

Miller, p. 165 n. 46). The truth of the second tacit premiss is also in doubt. For the balanced constitution introduces serious inequalities of its own. It equalizes two groups at the expense of the equality of individuals. Though the rich and the poor are equal, a rich man and a poor man are not. Such an inequality will be especially felt when the political community faces questions of life and death. When the issue is war or peace, why should the vote of a rich man have greater weight than that of a poor man? Is the life of the one worth more than that of the other? No champion of equality will think so.

A version of Aristotle's second way of equalizing the rich and the poor was used in Prussia from 1849 until the end of World War I. In the Prussian version the adult male citizens were divided into three classes of equal voting power on the basis of a list of their names ordered according to the amount of their taxes, the name of the man paying the most heading the list. Each class collectively paid the same amount of taxes, but Class I consisted of those whose names headed the list, Class II of those who names came next, and Class III of the remainder. Roughly 4 per cent of the electorate was in Class I, 16 per cent in Class II, and 80 per cent in Class III. (Seymour and Frary, vol. ii, pp. 14–23.)

1318ᵃ27–ᵇ5

It is not crystal clear how this section relates to the previous one, but it is plausible to suppose that it contains the details of Aristotle's first proposal for equalizing the rich and the poor. For the sake of clarity the numbers he uses to illustrate his ideas—twenty poor men vs. ten rich—are smaller than before and the ratio of poor to rich simpler. Aristotle supposes, as before, that the value of all the property of the ten rich men put together equals that of the twenty poor men; and he appears to envisage one assembly of the ten rich men and another of the twenty poor men. Both assemblies would follow the principle of majority rule, and a measure favoured by both would become effective. But what if a measure favoured by one body is opposed by the other? Aristotle is especially interested in devising a procedure for resolving such a deadlock. He considers the case where a measure is favoured by a majority of the rich (six out of ten) but opposed by a majority of the poor (fifteen out of

twenty), no one abstaining. By the usual rule for bicameral legisla-
tures such as the United States Congress, the measure would
fail. Aristotle is not content with such an outcome, and suggests
melding the two results by a system of weighted voting. There are
various systems of weighted voting, and Aristotle does not make it
clear which he has in mind. Does he mean that each man's vote is
to be weighted according to the value of his assessed property, as in
a joint-stock company (III. 9. 1280ᵃ25–31)? If so, the weight of one
man's vote might be a thousand times greater than the weight of
another man's. Or does he mean that a rich man's vote is to be
weighted according to the ratio of the poor to the rich—two to one
in his example? Following this latter system the vote of a rich man
would have twice the weight of the vote of a poor man, and there
would be seventeen votes—(6 × 2) + 5—favouring the measure
and twenty-three opposing it—(4 × 2) + 15—so the measure
would fail. In describing the method of weighting Aristotle says
simply that 'the side . . . whose property assessment is greater when
both parts are added together should be supreme'. This description
is true of both of the foregoing systems, and hence is not specific
enough to decide between them.

Neither system will settle all disagreements between the two
bodies. Suppose, for example, that the rich vote unanimously for a
given measure and the poor vote unanimously against it. By either
system of weighted voting there will be a deadlock. Since Aristotle
proposed the method of weighted voting to avoid such deadlocks,
he can hardly ignore such a possibility and suggests casting a lot or
'some similar expedient'. What could such a similar expedient be?
Newman suggests (ad loc.) that it might be the rule of modern
parliamentary procedure by which in the case of a tie the side
voting 'No' wins.

1318ᵇ4–5 For the thought see Plato, *Gorgias* 483c5–6 and
Republic II. 359a7–b1.

CHAPTER 4

In this chapter Aristotle divides democracy into four species. There
are two similar divisions in Chapters 4 and 6 of Book IV (1291ᵇ30–
1292ᵃ38, 1292ᵇ22–1293ᵃ10), though in IV. 4 the division is into
five species rather than four. The omission of the first of the five

species—the democracy that equalizes the rich and the poor—from the two fourfold divisions is a puzzle we will need to discuss. In the chapter before us Aristotle distinguishes and ranks the four types of democracy according to the peoples, or *dēmoi*, that are awarded citizenship under them; and he distinguishes and ranks peoples on the basis of their occupations.

There are four principal peoples—farmers, artisans, traders, and labourers (7. 1321ᵃ5–6)—though Aristotle occasionally mentions a few others such as herdsmen (1319ᵃ19–21) and seamen (IV. 4. 1291ᵇ17–26). He always ranks farmers first and labourers last, and with one exception (IV. 3. 1289ᵇ33) artisans ahead of traders (IV. 4. 1290ᵇ38–1291ᵃ6, ᵇ17–28; VI. 7. 1321ᵃ5–6). Farmers are ranked first because their lives, unlike those of artisans, traders, and labourers, have a modicum of virtue (implied by 1319ᵃ24–8). Their virtue is evidently military virtue (*polemikē aretē*). Aristotle says that herdsmen make good soldiers (1319ᵃ22–4) and presumably thinks the same of farmers. Their virtue cannot, at any rate, be higher than military virtue. Otherwise agricultural democracy would rank above polity in Aristotle's hierarchy of constitutions, for military virtue is the highest virtue that he expects of the general run of citizens of a polity (see the note to V. 1. 1301ᵇ9 above). In Aristotle's view the lives of both artisans and traders are 'opposite to virtue' (VII. 9. 1328ᵇ39–41; see also III. 4. 1277ᵃ35–ᵇ7, 5. 1278ᵃ20–1; VIII. 2. 1337ᵇ8–15). He does not tell us why he ranks artisans above traders; but the basis for his ranking is probably his notion that the arts and crafts, or *technai*, are more essential to a city than trade, which is not even listed among the occupations that every city needs (VII. 8. 1328ᵇ2–16).

Aristotle tells us that the first type of democracy extends citizenship to farmers and herdsmen (1318ᵇ11, 1319ᵃ38–9) but not to artisans, traders, and labourers, and that the fourth type extends it to everyone (1319ᵇ2) even bastards and men 'descended from a citizen on only one side' (1319ᵇ6–10). We are left to infer the citizenry of the intermediate types. All he says is that the democracies after the first one 'should deviate in order, and always exclude the worse mass of people' (1319ᵃ40–ᵇ1). This seems to imply that the second type of democracy includes farmers and artisans in the citizen body but excludes traders (and a fortiori labourers) whereas the third type excludes only labourers. But Aristotle might lump two sections of the populace together—artisans and traders, for example—so that all four sections are awarded citizenship in the third type, the fourth type going still farther by awarding it to men rejected under the other types on the score of their birth rather than their occupation. Aristotle is not very interested in the intermediate types, and says practically nothing about them.

1318^{b}6–1319^{b}1

The first and best type of democracy in Aristotle's view is an agricultural democracy that extends citizenship to farmers and herdsmen (who own their own land) but not to the other sections of the populace. It is similar to the constitution that equalizes the rich and the poor described in Chapter 3 in that it too seeks to balance two sections of the free population, though the sections it seeks to balance are different. In agricultural democracy these sections are not the rich and the poor but the notables (*hoi gnōrimoi*) and the populace (*ho dēmos*). Though notability usually connotes wealth (IV. 4. 1291^{b}28), in the section before us Aristotle identifies the notables, not with the wealthy, but with the worthy (*hoi epieikeis*, 1318^{b}35, 1319^{a}3); and the worthy are men of virtue (see the note to V. 10. 1310^{b}12–14) who are sometimes poor (II. 11. 1273^{b}3). Aristotle thinks the offices should be in the hands of the best men rather than the richest (1318^{b}33–4); and to allow for the possibility that the best men may not be wealthy, he suggests that the qualification for the offices should be, not property, but the ability to rule (1318^{b}31–2). Agricultural democracy differs from the constitution of Chapter 3 in seeking to balance quality and quantity (see IV. 12. 1296^{b}17–19) rather than two quantities, that of property and that of free men. And just as the latter constitution is not easily distinguished from polity (see the note to 3. 1318^{a}11–26), so the former is not easily distinguished from so-called aristocracy (see V. 8. 1308^{b}38–1309^{a}9 and note; and for so-called aristocracy see IV. 7. 1293^{b}14–19 and the note to V. 7. 1307^{a}5–33).

The similarity of these two constitutions makes the inclusion of the one that equalizes the rich and the poor as the first of the five types of democracy at IV. 4. 1291^{b}30–1292^{a}38 understandable and its omission from other two divisions a puzzle—a puzzle for which there is not a satisfactory solution. Newman suggests that 'the first two of the five are perhaps treated as virtually one' in the two fourfold divisions (vol. iv, p. xxxvi). But this seems wrong. For the first of the five is evidently the same constitution as the one discussed in the chapter immediately preceding this one (see the note to 2. 1318ᵃ3–10), and we have just seen that that constitution is distinct from the first of the four of the present division. Mulgan thinks the first of the five is dropped from the other classifications because it is not a deviant constitution in which one section of the community rules in its own interest to the complete exclusion of the others and hence is not really a democracy (p. 318). This seems wrong for the opposite reason. The first of the five and agricultural democracy are too similar for one to be deviant and the other not. Either both are really democracies or neither is.

Agricultural democracy is based on the ownership of land, which will need to be thoroughly regulated (1319ᵃ4–19), and grants citizenship only to those owning a certain specified minimum (IV. 6. 1292ᵇ25–6). Those who satisfy the property qualification are eligible to sit in the assembly and to serve on juries and on the boards that review the conduct of officials when their term of office is over. Perhaps they are also eligible to hold the lower offices, and perhaps these offices are filled by lot (see 1318ᵇ30–1). The higher offices at any rate are reserved for men who satisfy a higher property (or personal) qualification and are elective, though every citizen is an elector. It is worth noting that this is exactly the distribution of functions between the populace and the worthy that Aristotle's famous summation argument for democracy leads him to recommend (see III. 11. 1281ᵇ21–38, 1282ᵃ24–41; and for the argument see Keyt 1991, pp. 270–6).

Though Aristotle does not say so explicitly, it is apparent that his reason for ranking agricultural democracy first among democracies is that it comes closest to the constitution that in his view is best without qualification (*haplōs*) (IV. 1. 1288ᵇ21–7)—the constitution of the city of his dreams (*kat' euchēn*, literally, according to one's prayer) described in Books VII and VIII. This ideal city is a true aristocracy (Keyt 1996, p. 141 n. 41) in which citizenship is restricted to men of practical wisdom (VII. 9. 1329ᵃ8–17) and virtue (1329ᵃ22–4) who are wealthy enough to afford the leisure for political activities (1329ᵃ1–2, 17–19) and in which all who must work for a living—farmers, artisans, and traders—are excluded from the political community (1328ᵇ33–1329ᵃ2). The democracy described in the section before us comes as close to this ideal as a democracy can: the offices, or at any rate the higher ones, are reserved for the best men (*hoi beltistoi*), and the only section of the populace awarded citizenship, the one with a modicum of virtue, is given minimal power.

Aristotle's view of the divisions of democracy in Book IV is a bit different. He acknowledges that he is using a standard in his grading of the various types, but the standard he mentions is not the one he appears to be using in Book VI. 'As for the other constitutions,' he says in Book IV, 'since we hold that there are more democracies than one and more oligarchies, what kind should be placed first and second and so on in this way by virtue of one being better and another worse is not difficult to see once the best ⟨constitution for most cities⟩ has been defined' (11. 1296ᵇ3–7 together with 1295ᵃ25–31). The constitution that is best for most cities, which Aristotle calls 'the middle constitution' (1296ᵃ37–8), is the one that is 'through those in the middle' (1295ᵇ35)—those who are neither rich nor poor. The middle constitution may be his standard in Book IV, but it is not visible in the section before us, where his focus is more on virtue than on wealth. He puts little weight on the fact that the farmers in this democracy will own a moderate amount of property, and attempts to strike a balance, not between rich and poor, but between the notables and the populace.

Aristotle's statement that certain institutions are 'customary' in agricultural democracy (1318ᵇ29) indicates that his account of the constitution is based on historical examples, though he does not tell us what they are. It is possible, and perhaps even implied, that some of the cities he refers to in the section before us—Mantinea (1318ᵇ25, 27), Elis (1319ᵃ12), and Aphytis (1319ᵃ14)—were agricultural democracies, but it is never said so explicitly. His prime example may have been the Solonian democracy of early sixth-century Athens (see especially II. 12. 1274ᵃ15–21). A modern example would be American democracy around 1800. The restriction of the franchise to men of landed property combined with an attitude of social deference created something very like the agricultural democracy Aristotle describes. The ideal, as one writer expresses it, was 'of a landed freeholder citizenry and a benign, virtuous patrician leadership' (Wilentz, p. 35)—Aristotle's idea exactly.

1318ᵇ25   On Mantinea see the note to V. 4. 1304ᵃ25–7 above.

$1319^{a}6-19$ In an agricultural democracy it is essential that a man not lose his citizenship by losing all of his land or so large a chunk of it that the remainder does not meet the property qualification. Aristotle lists three laws designed to preserve the citizenship of farmers, and a fourth for rectifying things when problems arise due to the absence of laws of the first three types. The first regulates the maximum amount of land, particularly of the most favourably located land, that one citizen can own. The second forbids the sale 'of the first allotments', that is, the land originally allotted to the settlers of a new colony. The third, the law attributed to Oxylus, forbids a person from pledging his entire estate as security for a loan. The fourth is the rectificatory law of Aphytis, where a large population was crowded into a small territory. Aristotle attributes the fact that the Aphytaeans remained farmers to this law. The law, by setting the property qualification for citizenship low, encouraged even the smallest landholders to cling to their farms in order to remain citizens. The law itself is obscure. It is unclear what function is served by the rigmarole of division. A law that set the property qualification at the amount of land owned by the smallest landholder would seem to be all that is needed.

$1319^{a}12$ The Oxylus to whom Aristotle refers is presumably the mythical founder of Elis. For Elis see the note to V. 6. $1306^{a}12-19$ above.

$1319^{a}14$ Aphytis was a small city on the north-east coast of Pallene, the western prong of Chalcidice.

$1319^{a}19-38$ Aristotle's use of an aristocratic standard is apparent in this section. He thinks herdsmen make a positive contribution to a democracy for two aristocratic reasons. Being physically tough and accustomed to an outdoor life, they are good soldiers (see also Plato, *Laws* III. 695a); and living far from town, they leave politics for the most part to their betters. He thinks artisans, traders, and labourers make a negative contribution for the opposite reasons. Their work is ignoble; and living in town, they are always meddling in politics for which they are unfit.

$1319^{b}1-32$

The discussion of ultimate democracy is in two parts. Aristotle discusses the establishment ($1319^{b}6$) of such a democracy in the section before us and its preservation (1319ᵇ33–5) in Chapter 5. His stance throughout is constructive rather than critical. Though he connects ultimate democracy with tyranny (1319ᵇ27–30, 6. 1320ᵇ30–2), he does not make the connection his motif as he is wont to do elsewhere (IV. 4. 1292ᵃ4–37, 14. 1298ᵃ31–3; V. 10. 1310ᵇ3–4, 1312ᵇ5–6, 34–8, 11. 1313ᵇ32–9).

Ultimate democracy is the democracy with the lowest qualification for citizenship. In characterizing the citizen body of each of the other types of democracy Aristotle tacitly assumes that it will include only the legitimate issue of natives, or *astoi* (III. 5. 1278ᵃ34). He indicates that ultimate democracy calls this assumption into question by offering citizenship even to bastards and those who are in part of slave or alien extraction (1319ᵇ7–10, IV. 4. 1291ᵇ26–7). He does not make it clear whether this is definitive of, or only something that is likely to happen in, an ultimate democracy. His idea may be that ultimate democracy is reached as soon as labourers whose birth is unopen to challenge (*anupeuthunoi kata to genos*) become citizens (IV. 12. 1296ᵇ28–30; for the expression see IV. 6. 1292ᵇ35–6).

Aristotle offers two institutional suggestions. The first is that the qualification for citizenship should be relaxed only to the point where the populace outnumbers the notables and those in the middle (*hoi mesoi*). There are two ideas behind this piece of advice. The first is Aristotle's great elementary principle of constitutional stability that the group that wants a constitution to remain should be stronger than the group that does not (see V. 9. 1309ᵇ14–18 and note). The second is a principle of moderation—the group favouring a constitution should not be so strong that it overwhelms the opposing groups. A democratic lawgiver who followed these two principles would institute an ultimate democracy that falls just short of the middle constitution, the constitution in which the balance of power is held by those in the middle (IV. 11. 1295ᵇ34–9). For this is what an ultimate democracy would turn into if the number of the populace were to drop below that of the notables and those in the middle. Aristotle thus seems to be examining ultimate democracy and agricultural democracy from different perspectives—from that of the middle constitution in the one case and from that of true aristocracy in the other. This is signalled by the fact that the worthy (*hoi epieikeis*) are not mentioned here just as those in the middle (*hoi mesoi*) were not mentioned before. No doubt Aristotle thinks that true aristocracy is too high a standard to apply to a broad-based democracy.

Aristotle's second suggestion for strengthening ultimate democracy is to replace old divisions in the city by new ones and to eliminate private religious rites in favour of a few public ones. The goal, he tells us, is to break up the old intimacies of tribe and brotherhood and to get the citizens to intermingle. The idea presumably is to remove a potential source of faction and to foster social cohesion. In offering this advice Aristotle follows not only in the track of Cleisthenes but also of Plato, who opposed private shrines (*Laws* X. 909d7–910e4) and social isolation (*Laws* V. 738d1–e8).

1319ᵇ4–6 Another reference to Book V.

1319ᵇ17–18, 22–3 Cyrene, a Greek colony on the Libyan coast of Africa, was founded from the island of Thera (modern Santorini) around 630 BC under the leadership of Battus. Herodotus relates the story of Battus and his heirs (4. 150–205) and may be the source of Aristotle's references to faction and tribal reorganization at Cyrene. For he relates that Battus and his heirs ruled as kings until the Cyrenaeans called in a lawgiver named Demonax who restricted their privileges, made the city more democratic, and organized the emigrants into three tribes—the first of Theraeans and their neighbours, the second of Peloponnesians and Cretans, and the third of all the islanders (4. 161. 3). He goes on to report that in the next generation one of the Battiads made a faction because he was dissatisfied with the offices and privileges granted to them under the arrangement of Demonax (4. 162. 2).

1319ᵇ21 Cleisthenes was an Athenian statesman of the late sixth century BC. A member of the noble family of the Alcmaeonidae, he was named after his famous grandfather, the tyrant of Sicyon (see the note to V. 12. 1315ᵇ11–22). The Alcmaeonidae, banished by the tyrant Hippias, combined with Sparta to drive Hippias himself into exile in 510 BC (Thuc. 6. 59. 4; and see the note to V. 10. 1311ᵃ36–9). In the political struggle that followed the restoration of the democracy, Cleisthenes became the people's champion by advancing a programme of reform. There were four parts to his programme. The first was to replace the four original tribes, which were based on kinship, with ten new ones based on domicile, the membership of each of the new tribes being drawn from three localities—the town and surrounding territory, the coast of Attica, and the interior. The importance of this reform lay in the fact that citizenship came through membership in a tribe. The first reform eased the way for the second, weakened the influence of the old families, and increased social cohesion by thoroughly mixing the citizens together. The second reform was to augment the citizen body by enrolling in the new tribes 'many foreigners, and resident aliens who had been slaves' (III. 2. 1275ᵇ35–7). The third reform, a natural consequence of the first two, was to enlarge the council from 400 to 500—50 from each of the ten tribes. The fourth was the institution of ostracism, the object of which was to prevent the restoration of tyranny. (Her. 5. 66, 69–73; *AP* 19–22.)

The mention of Cleisthenes in connection with ultimate democracy raises the question whether Aristotle regards the constitution of Cleisthenes as such a democracy. Cleisthenes is mentioned only one other time in the *Politics*. In the other passage Aristotle reports that Cleisthenes made citizens of men who were not of pure Athenian extraction (III. 2. 1275ᵇ35–7), which is exactly the characterization of ultimate democracy in the section before us. Thus, if he does not regard the constitution of Cleisthenes as an ultimate democracy, we will need to regard this characterization as offering no more than a necessary condition of such a democracy.

Whatever Aristotle thinks of the constitution of Cleisthenes, he signals at least twice that he regards the Athenian democracy of his own day as an ultimate democracy. One signal is the reference in the next chapter, where the topic is still ultimate democracy, to the practice of 'the demagogues nowadays' (1320ᵃ4, 30). If these are not contemporary Athenian demagogues, who are they? Another signal comes in Book II in a passage on Athenian constitutional history. Aristotle says that when the law court grew strong, 'by currying favour with the people as with a tyrant, they changed the constitution to the present democracy' (12. 1274ᵃ5–7). Since 'the present democracy' is a reference to the democracy of Aristotle's own day and since he says elsewhere that it is only in an ultimate democracy that the people, the *dēmos*, are courted as a monarch is courted (IV. 4. 1292ᵃ11–23), he must intend for his reader to conclude that the Athenian democracy under which he was living was an ultimate democracy.

1319ᵇ27–32 For the devices characteristic of tyranny and for the reason the unruliness of slaves is advantageous to ultimate democracy up to a point see V. 11. 1313ᵇ32–1314ᵃ1.

CHAPTER 5

Having discussed the establishment of ultimate democracy, Aristotle turns now to its preservation. The chapter is best read as a subsection of the previous one—as the second half of Aristotle's discussion of ultimate democracy—rather than as a chapter in its own right. Aristotle has two general recommendations for preserving ultimate democracy: protect the property of the wealthy from the depredations of the people, the *dēmos*, and permanently reduce the poverty of the poorest of the people. The political basis of these recommendations is easy to understand. Aristotle thinks that in a democracy faction arises only between the notables and the people, not between one section of the people and another (V. 1. 1302ᵃ11–13). The notables are motivated to form a faction, he believes, when their property is threatened; and their property is likely to be threatened when the people are in need—'poverty', he remarks, 'produces faction and crime' (II. 6. 1265ᵇ12). Thus, his two recommendations are designed to remove both the proximate and the ultimate cause of faction.

Though his focus throughout the chapter is on constitutional stability rather than justice, the measures Aristotle recommends are not simply political stratagems—they also have an ethical dimension. He thinks it unjust for the poor to use their superior numbers to confiscate the property of the rich (III. 10. 1281ᵃ14–17, VI. 3. 1318ᵃ24–6) and consequently must think it just, as well as advantageous, to curb such confiscations. His other recommendation has an ethical basis of a different sort. He wishes to permanently reduce the poverty of the poor, not by a permanent government subsidy, but by giving the poor a start in agriculture or trade. He thinks that simply giving people money is corrupting, since it merely increases their appetites (1320ᵃ30–2; II. 7. 1267ᵃ41–ᵇ5). Giving a man a start in agriculture or trade, on the other hand, helps him to become a better man. For Aristotle thinks that a man's character is affected by his occupation (I. 11. 1258ᵇ35–9, III. 5. 1278ᵃ20–1, VII. 9. 1328ᵇ39–41, VIII. 2. 1337ᵇ8–15) and that hired labour is only a step above slavery (III. 5. 1278^{a}11–13, VIII. 2. 1337^{b}21). Furthermore, he thinks that a city has an ethical goal—the well-being of its citizens (III. 9. 1280^{b}5–8, 1280^{b}40–1281^{a}4). Thus, to give a man a start in agriculture or trade is in his view one way of pursuing the true end of a city.

1319^{b}33–1320^{a}4

1319^{b}40–1320^{a}1 Aristotle speaks of enacting both written and unwritten laws. In Book III he distinguishes 'laws based on writings' from 'laws based on customs' (16. 1287^{b}5–6), and presumably intends the same distinction here (see also Plato, *Rep*. VIII. 563d8; *Stat*. 295a4–7, 298d5–e2, 299a3–4; *Laws* VII. 793a9–d5). Examples of such unwritten laws are the prohibitions against incest and against parading around the market-place unclothed or in women's clothing (Plato, *Laws* VIII. 838a9–b5; D.L. 3. 86). Aristotle does not tell us which of his recommendations would be embodied in written law and which not. He may regard the creation of the custom of the notables giving the poor a start in agriculture or trade as an enactment of an unwritten law.

1320^{a}2–4 See V. 9. 1309^{b}20–1, 1310^{a}19–20, and the note to 1309^{b}18–1310^{a}2.

1320^{a}4–17

Aristotle proposes two measures to protect the wealthy from unjust confiscations of their property. The first would convert confiscated property to sacred rather than public property. This measure goes far beyond the practice in Athens, where only a tenth of confiscated property was allotted to Athena (Xen. *Hell*. 1. 7. 10) and used to pay for such things as sacrifices, the repair and maintenance of the temples, and the common meals of the priests. Aristotle thinks that if confiscated property goes into the public treasury, the jurors will have a personal financial stake in the outcome of any case where the confiscation of the defendant's property is a possible penalty. To understand why this is so one needs to know something about the pay received by an Athenian citizen for serving on a jury and attending the assembly. In the fourth century BC an Athenian juror was paid three obols for each day of jury service

(*AP* 62. 2)—one obol more than the aid granted to the physically incapacitated (*AP* 49. 4). But though trials were short and never exceeded one day (*AP* 67. 1; Plato, *Apol.* 37a7–b1), jurors were members of jury panels, not for a single day, but for an entire year (*AP* 24. 3, 27. 4, 63. 3; Aristoph. *Wasps* 662). We do not know on how many days the courts sat during a year; the best estimate is somewhere between 150 and 200 (Hansen). (In Aristophanes' *Wasps* Bdelycleon claims that each year Athens pays 6,000 jurors a total of one hundred and fifty talents (661–3). One talent being equal to 36,000 obols, his claim implies that the courts sat for a minimum of 300 days a year. Though this figure is inflated, it does indicate that jury service involved more than a few days or weeks of a citizen's life.) Furthermore, during his year of jury service a juror would have the opportunity to attend the assembly forty times (*AP* 43. 3) since the law courts did not sit on any day on which the assembly met (Dem. *Against Timocrates* 80). In Aristotle's time the pay for attending a meeting of the assembly was either six or nine obols depending upon whether it was an ordinary meeting or a principal meeting (*AP* 62. 2)—about a day's pay for an unskilled worker (Rhodes 1981, p. 691). Thus, a juror who never missed a day of jury service and who attended all forty meetings of the assembly would receive on at least one half and perhaps on as many as two-thirds of the days of the year a stipend just large enough to live on (see Aristoph. *Wasps* 291–311) and, consequently, large enough to be anxious about. Such a juror, Aristotle's recommendation implies, might worry that the public treasury, unless buttressed by confiscations, will be depleted before his year of jury service is over. (For more on Athenian juries see MacDowell, pp. 33–40, 247–54.)

Aristotle's second recommendation is to impose a large penalty for frivolous public lawsuits. Public lawsuits (*dēmosiai dikai*) concerned matters that were regarded as affecting the community as a whole such as treason, desertion from the army, and embezzlement of public funds, and could be brought by anyone (that is, any free adult male) who wished (MacDowell, p. 57). (The suit against Socrates was a public suit (Plato, *Euthyphro* 2a).) Private lawsuits (*idiai dikai*) (*AP* 59. 5; Plato, *Laws* VI. 768b1) concerned matters that were regarded as affecting only the individuals involved such as theft, rape, battery, and homicide, and could be brought only by the party claiming to be injured or his family (MacDowell, p. 58). In

Athenian law there was a measure like the one Aristotle proposes. The prosecutor of an unsuccessful public suit was subject to a fine of a thousand drachmas if he failed to obtain one-fifth of the jury's votes (Plato, *Apol.* 36b1–2). The size of the fine can be appreciated when one calculates that, one drachma being worth six obols, the fine would provide one day's pay for two thousand jurors. One reason a man would risk such a fine is that in certain cases a successful prosecutor was awarded a portion of the property confiscated (MacDowell, p. 62). It is unclear whether Aristotle wishes to endorse the Athenian measure or to go beyond it.

<h2 style="text-align:center">1320ᵃ17–ᵇ4</h2>

In this section Aristotle offers some suggestions for easing the financial burden of the assembly and the law courts on the wealthy and for relieving the poverty of the poorest of the poor. His recommendations depend upon whether or not a democracy has what he calls *prosodoi*, or 'revenues'. When used of public revenues, the word *prosodoi* usually signifies revenues in general, including those from property taxes and confiscations, rather than one kind or source of revenue (8. 1321ᵇ31, 1322ᵇ32; *Oec.* II. 1. 1345ᵇ28–1346ᵃ8; *AP* 16. 4). But in the passage before us (as well as at IV. 6. 1292ᵇ33, 38) the word has a narrower sense, for Aristotle tacitly distinguishes *prosodoi* from property taxes (*eisphorai*) and confiscations. He uses *prosodoi* to signify revenues that are (1) surplus and (2) not collected from the notables. In the translation this narrow sense is signalled by the qualification 'special'. Examples of the sort of revenues he has in mind would be those that came to Athens from its silver mines at Laurium (Her. 7. 144. 1; *AP* 22. 7; Plut. *Themistocles* 4. 1) and from customs dues on the trade through its port at the Peiraeus.

Aristotle recommends that a democracy with no special revenues minimize expenditures on the assembly and the law courts by minimizing the number of their meetings and by paying only the needy for jury service. He thinks such a judicial system will be both cheaper and juster than the system in contemporary Athens. Presumably it will be juster because a wealthy defendant will find more of his peers on the jury when jury service requires a smaller sacrifice of a citizen's time. Aristotle does not seem to notice that in another respect the system threatens to be less just. He recommends large courts sitting on only a few days. (Athenian juries ranged in size from 201 to 1,001 or more depending upon the type of case (*AP* 53. 3, 68. 1).) But the more jurors allotted to each jury the fewer juries that can be formed on any given day. How, then, will all the lawsuits of a populous democracy be accommodated if the courts sit on only a few days? Either fewer cases will be tried or the time allowed for each case must be greatly reduced. (In an Athenian trial the plaintiff and the defendant were each allotted a limited period of time to make a speech, and a jury might hear as many as four cases in a single day (*AP* 67 and Rhodes 1981, ad loc.).)

If there are special revenues, Aristotle says that one should not distribute it to the needy, as demagogues do now. But how do they distribute it to the needy now? The implication is that they distribute it, among other ways, as pay to jurors and assemblymen (see also II. 12. 1274^a8–11; Plut. *Pericles* 9. 1). Aristotle recommends instead that the special revenues be distributed to the needy in lump sums large enough for a start in trade or agriculture. From this recommendation we can infer that he regards the needy as those who are neither farmers nor traders (nor presumably artisans). Thus, they must be the lowest of the various peoples, or *dēmoi*, mentioned in the last chapter—the hired labourers, or *thētes*. (He does not suggest helping them to become artisans because a grant or loan of money would not help a man acquire a skill—he needs to serve as an apprentice—and because the arts and crafts were for the most part passed down from father to son (Plato, *Rep.* IV. 421e1, V. 466e4–467a5, X. 599c4–5).) Aristotle's idea, then, is to eliminate, as far as possible, the class of hired labourers. (Their place in the economy would presumably be filled by slaves.) But this would be to change an ultimate democracy into one of the higher types, none of which provides pay for the assembly and law courts (IV. 6. 1292^b41–1293^a6). While the needy are being advanced—'in the meantime'—Aristotle thinks the rich should pay for the 'necessary meetings' but be excused from costly liturgies (1320^b2–4). Newman infers from this that Aristotle wants the special revenues to be used to pay for the assembly and the courts once the needy have been elevated (notes to 1320^a29 and 1320^b2). But this seems wrong. Aristotle does not want the special revenues ever to be so used. For when all the needy have become farmers or traders, no one will need to be paid to attend the assembly or serve as a juror; and until they all become farmers or traders, the special revenues must be used to raise those who are still hired labourers. The 'necessary meetings' to which Aristotle refers are very likely the trimmed down assemblies and courts recommended when there are no special revenues.

1320ᵃ30–2 On the insatiability of appetite and the consequent folly of distributing the special revenues to the many, who live for the satisfaction of it, see II. 7. 1267ᵃ41–ᵇ5.

1320ᵇ4–17

Aristotle says that at Carthage the policy of helping the needy made the people a friend (1320ᵇ5) and that at Taras it made the mass well-disposed (1320ᵇ11). Friendship (*philia*) is a central concept in Aristotle's political philosophy in the sense that it links two of his primary concerns: justice and stability. As enmity (*echthra*) is associated with faction (*stasis*), friendship is associated with concord (*homonoia*) and absence of faction (II. 4. 1262ᵇ7–9; IV. 11. 1295ᵇ13–25; *EN* VIII. 1. 1155ᵃ22–6). Aristotle also thinks that the amount of justice and the amount of friendship under a given constitution are directly proportional to each other (*EN* VIII. 11). It follows from these ideas that the best way to preserve a constitution is to promote friendship both to the constitution and among the various groups structured by it by making the constitution as just as possible. With the deviant constitutions stability and reform march hand in hand.

1320ᵇ7–9 The policy of dividing the needy into as many groups as there are notables and distributing the groups among the notables would have the effect for better or worse of creating a patron–client relationship between a notable and those for whom he is responsible.

1320ᵇ9–11 The policy of the Tarantines of allowing their possessions to be used communally by the needy resembles the policy associated with Sparta and strongly endorsed by Aristotle under the motto 'private property, communal use' (II. 5. 1263ᵃ21–40). He reports that in Sparta they use each other's horses, dogs, and slaves as if they were their own. Taras was a colony of Sparta (see the note to V. 3. 1303^{a}3–6) and probably borrowed the policy from her mother city.

1320^{b}14–16 Selecting some holders of a given office by lot and other holders of the same office by election is an interesting way of mixing representatives of the free population with the putatively more able in a body like the council.

CHAPTER 6

Chapters 6 and 7 discuss the establishment and preservation of oligarchies. The present chapter, mirroring Chapter 4, contains a sketchy division of oligarchy into species. Aristotle writes as if he had two lists before him, a list of the four species of democracy, the better species preceding the worse, and a list of equal length of the species of oligarchy similarly ordered. A species of democracy and a species of oligarchy are opposites if they occupy the same spot on their respective lists. Thus, the dynastic form of oligarchy is opposite to ultimate democracy (1320^{b}30–2). The species of both constitutions get worse as their respective standards of worth—wealth and freedom—are intensified. As a consequence, the species of oligarchy are reverse images of the opposite species of democracy; for the body of citizens expands as the democratic standard is intensified, whereas it contracts as the oligarchic standard is stiffened (see the note to V. 9. 1309^{b}18–1310^{a}2 above). When the various species of oligarchy and democracy are arranged, not as above, but according to the ratio in each of full citizens to free men, they form a continuous spectrum from dynastic oligarchy through the more moderate species of oligarchy and democracy to ultimate democracy, the midpoint of the spectrum being neither democracy nor oligarchy but an ideal mixture of the two that Aristotle sometimes calls 'polity' (IV. 8. 1293^{b}33–4, 1294^{a}22–3; Mulgan, p. 313).

1320^{b}21–9 Since the best kind of democracy and the best kind of oligarchy lie close to each other along this spectrum, they are virtually indistinguishable; and Aristotle describes them in virtually the same words. In the best kind of oligarchy the property qualification is set low enough to qualify the better section of the *dēmos*—the farmers—for full citizenship; anyone who satisfies it qualifies for full citizenship; but only those who satisfy a higher property qualification are eligible to hold the supreme offices. This is precisely Aristotle's description of the best kind of democracy (IV. 4. 1291ᵇ39–41, 6. 1292ᵇ25–31; VI. 4. 1318ᵇ27–31); and some scholars, such as Schütrumpf (p. 117), claim that the two constitutions are identical. This is probably a mistake; for identical species do not belong to different genera. Aristotle gives us two clues to the difference between the two constitutions. In the present chapter he says that in the best kind of oligarchy those who share in the constitution should be stronger (*not* more numerous) than those who do not share (1320ᵇ25–8), and in Book IV he says that the best kind of oligarchy 'is where the offices require a property qualification of such an amount that the needy, *though a majority*, do not share ⟨in the constitution⟩, while it is possible for anyone who acquires the amount to share in the constitution' (5. 1292ª39–41). This latter statement reads like an attempt to distinguish the best kind of oligarchy from every kind of democracy. Aristotle is evidently ignoring the possibility, which he sometimes considers, that the rich might outnumber the poor (III. 8. 1279ᵇ20–3, IV. 4. 1290ª33–7), and basing his divisions of democracy and oligarchy on what generally happens—that the rich are few, and the many poor (III. 8. 1279ᵇ37–8). In the present chapter he seems to be tacitly assuming that oligarchy, the rule of the rich, will always be the rule of a minority, and that democracy, the rule of the free, will always be the rule of a majority (IV. 4. 1290ª40–ᵇ3). Thus, he can use the same words to describe the best kind of oligarchy and the best kind of democracy without fear of conflating the two because he is assuming that the property qualification in an oligarchy will always be set high enough to exclude the majority of free men and that it will always be set low enough in a democracy to include a majority of them.

1320ᵇ30–1321ª1   The similes of the diseased body and the leaky boat with an incompetent crew, familiar from Plato (*Rep.* VI. 487e7–489c7, VIII. 556e3–9; *Stat.* 302a3–b3; *Laws* XII. 945c3–d1), imply that the smallest mistake (*hamartia*) is sufficient to destroy a bad constitution. There are two sorts of mistake according to Aristotle: those concerning universals and those concerning particulars (*EN* VI. 8. 1142ª21–2). Lawgivers make the first sort; office-holders the second. For lawgivers frame laws and constitutions, which are universals, whereas jurors, assemblymen, and officials deal with

particular cases (II. 8. 1269ᵃ16–17 together with III. 11. 1282ᵇ1–6,
15. 1286ᵃ7–28, and *EN* V. 10. 1137ᵇ13). As Aristotle has shown in
Book V, either sort of mistake may destroy a constitution.

1321ᵃ1–4   The idea that populousness (*poluanthrōpia*) preserves
democracy is somewhat at odds with the notion Aristotle has just
advanced that the worst constitutions need the most safeguarding.
For the worst democracies are ultimate democracies; and ultimate
democracies, he claims, are populous (5. 1320ᵃ17). The democracy
he is thinking of when he says that democracies are preserved by
populousness is surely that at Athens, which had existed for almost
two hundred years at the time he penned the sentences before us.
Since the expulsion of the Peisistratids in 510 BC, it had been
overthrown only twice, and then only briefly, being replaced by a
moderate oligarchy in 411 and by an extreme oligarchy in 404–3.
Aristotle seems to have regarded Athenian democracy during all
or most of this period as a democracy of the worst kind (see the
note to 4. 1319ᵇ21).

The oligarchic counterpart of populousness is good structure
(*eutaxia*). But what is good structure? Aristotle says that as law
(*nomos*) is a kind of structure (*taxis*), good law (*eunomia*) is a kind
of good structure (*eutaxia*) (VII. 4. 1326ᵃ29–31). The association
of *nomos* and *eunomia* plays upon the common stem of the two
words, and appears to be almost a pun. For Aristotle indicates
elsewhere that good laws that are not obeyed do not constitute
eunomia, and distinguishes two senses of the word: obedience to
the established laws (whether they be good or bad) and obedience to good laws (IV. 8. 1294ᵃ3–7). The principal signification of
eunomia is thus obedience, or good conduct, rather than good law.
The sense of the word is perhaps best captured by the expression
'law and order', which signifies both the existence and the observ-
ance of law. The *eutaxia*, or good structure, that preserves oligarchy
must be *eunomia* in the broad sense, the law and order that is
consistent with bad laws, since oligarchy is a deviant constitution
and deviant constitutions have bad laws (III. 11. 1282ᵇ8–13).

In Aristotle's view good structure and populousness are incom-
patible. To introduce structure into a great multitude, he says, is
'the work of divine power' (VII. 4. 1326ᵃ25–33). Just as democracy
and oligarchy are opposite, so too are the things that preserve
them.

CHAPTER 7

In the first section of this chapter Aristotle discusses the constitutional implications of the four kinds of military force. In the remaining sections he suggests three ways in which an oligarchy can strengthen its hold on power.

1321ᵃ5–14 That there are four classes of the people reminds Aristotle that there are also four kinds of military force, but he does not claim that there is any correlation between the items of the two fourfold sets. The various kinds of military force are correlated rather with various constitutions, just as the various occupational groups of the populace were previously correlated with various species of democracy. The point of mentioning the two fourfold sets together may be to highlight the similarity of these two correlations.

The two species of oligarchy distinguished in this section—a narrow oligarchy of horsemen and a broader oligarchy of hoplites—are somewhat of an anomaly. They do not correspond in any obvious way to any of the species of the two previous divisions of oligarchy (IV. 5. 1292ᵃ39–ᵇ10, 6. 1293ᵃ12–34). Furthermore, the constitution based on hoplites does not seem to be an oligarchy at all. It is called 'polity' in Book III (7. 1279ᵃ37–ᵇ4), and in the preceding chapter polity is implied to be the constitution from which all the species of oligarchy deviate (1320ᵇ21–2).

Aristotle argues that it is natural to establish a strong (that is, a narrow) oligarchy where the country is suited to horsemen (see also IV. 3. 1289ᵇ35–40, 13. 1297ᵇ16–22). His argument has two explicit premisses. The first is that the safety of a country suited to horsemen (that is, a country with large areas of flat ground) is through cavalry. Thessaly, the country in mainland Greece with the broadest plains, was renowned for its cavalry (Plato, *Hippias Major* 284a4–6, *Meno* 70a5–6, *Laws* I. 625c10–d2). The second explicit premiss is that only the very wealthy can afford to keep horses. The conclusion obviously does not follow from these premisses. Aristotle is making three tacit assumptions. The first is that very few men are very wealthy; the second, a fact about Greek armies, is that soldiers provide their own equipment; and the third, a political principle about the distribution of political rights, is that it is natural for full citizenship to be extended only to those upon whom the safety of a country depends. Given the five tacit and explicit premisses and a definition of oligarchy as the rule of the wealthy (III. 8. 1280ª1–2), it follows that it is natural for there to be a narrow oligarchy where the country is suited to horsemen.

We get an idea of just how expensive it was to be a cavalryman when we consider that, in addition to his horse and his arms and armour, a cavalryman would need a groom, a mount for his groom, and feed for the two mounts (Spence, pp. 272–86). Aristotle assumes that the cavalryman would shoulder most, if not all, of these expenses himself.

In like fashion Aristotle argues that it is natural to establish 'the next kind of oligarchy' where the country is suited to hoplites (see also IV. 13. 1297ᵇ22–8). Country suited to the hoplite phalanx—level ground unbroken by streams or other obstacles (V. 3. 1303ᵇ12–14; Her. 7. 9β1; Plato, *Laws* I. 625c9–d7)—is not unlike country suited to cavalry except that it need not be as wide. Though cheaper than being a cavalryman and hence within the range of a larger number of men, it was still expensive to be a hoplite. In the fourth century BC the hoplite panoply of helmet, breast-plate, greaves, shield, spear, and sword evidently cost several hundred drachmas (Jackson, p. 229). The armour was custom-made to fit the warrior and was sometimes gold-plated (Xen. *Mem.* 3. 10. 9–15). Furthermore, a hoplite needed an attendant (probably a slave) to help carry his arms, armour, and other provisions while on campaign (Thuc. 3. 17. 4, 7. 75. 5; Pritchett, pp. 49–51). One reason he needed an attendant is that his panoply alone weighed nearly seventy pounds (Hanson 1991, p. 78 n. 1; see also Plato, *Laws* VIII. 833b2–5). At the battle of Plataea in 479 BC each Spartan hoplite was attended by seven Helots (Her. 9. 10. 1, 9. 28. 2, 9. 29. 1).

Aristotle completes his survey of the constitutional implications of the various kinds of military force by remarking that light-armed and naval forces are entirely democratic (see also V. 4. 1304ª20–4 and note). The light-armed to whom he refers are presumably peltasts, archers, and slingers, the three other components of a Greek army in addition to cavalry and hoplites (Xen. *An.* 5. 6. 15, *Oec.* 8. 6). (But archers are sometimes distinguished from the light-armed (8. 1322ᵇ1; Plato, *Laws* VI. 756a2).) Peltasts, so-called because of their light shield (*peltē*), were usually armed with a javelin and a short sword. In calling the naval force democratic Aristotle is thinking of the oarsmen aboard a Greek warship. A Greek trireme carried a crew of 200 plus the trierarch, 170 of whom were oarsmen (Morrison and Coates, pp. 107–18). The light-armed and naval forces are democratic since even a poor man can fling a stone or pull an oar.

The empirical principle connecting full citizenship with military importance, upon which Aristotle's argument tacitly rests, and to which he elsewhere alludes (see the note to V. 4. 1304ᵃ20–4), receives additional support from these facts from the twentieth century: that women were given the vote in western democracies around the time that they began to work in munitions factories and to serve in the military, and that in a democracy the age at which a person is eligible to vote tends to be the age at which a person is liable for military service. 'Old enough to fight; old enough to vote' (whatever its merits) is a powerful and usually effective political slogan.

1321ᵃ14–26 The problem Aristotle deals with in this section is how to preserve an oligarchy where there is a large democratic element of light-armed troops and oarsmen. He claims that light-armed troops contend easily against mounted and hoplite forces. This explains why, when faction breaks out, the rich are often defeated by the poor. The solution, he says, is to be found in the example of generals who combine light-armed troops with their mounted and hoplite forces. What Aristotle apparently means is that the oligarchs should not face light-armed democrats with hoplites and cavalry alone, but should have a light-armed force of their own to combine with their hoplites and cavalry. A loyal force of light-armed troops can be formed, he suggests, from the oligarchs' own sons. Their sons can learn the skills of the light-armed while they are still young and can begin serving as light-armed troops as soon as they are taken out of the ranks of the boys— presumably as at Athens at the age of 18 (*AP* 42. 1). They would become hoplites only after a period of such service.

Aristotle's statement that the light-armed contend easily against mounted and hoplite forces is at first glance surprising given the fact that on the battlefield light-armed troops were usually no match for hoplites (for a few exceptions see Thuc. 3. 94–8, 4. 28–40; Xen. *Hell.* 4. 5. 11–18). But Aristotle is thinking of factional fighting within the confines of a city's walls where the advantages of a mount and of heavy arms were effectively negated (see Thuc. 3. 74, 5. 82. 2).

1321ᵃ26–31　Aristotle next recommends that an oligarchy broaden its base—and, hence, become less extreme and more secure—by awarding full citizenship to some of the populace. He suggests three successively more aristocratic ways of doing this. The first, already mentioned at 6. 1320ᵇ25–6, is to allow anyone who satisfies a certain property qualification to become a citizen. The second, or Theban way, is to require in addition that a candidate for citizenship demonstrate that he is unsullied by trade by staying out of it for a certain period—for ten years if the example of Thebes is followed (III. 5. 1278ᵃ25–6). The third, the way of Massalia, goes further still and awards citizenship to everyone, insider or outsider, on the basis of a judgement of the person's worth. (For Massalia see the note to V. 6. 1305ᵇ1–12.)

1321ᵃ31–ᵇ3　Aristotle's third and final recommendation for increasing the durability of oligarchy is to secure the willing non-participation of the many in the most supreme offices by attaching liturgies to them. These liturgies would mark a man's ascent to a supreme office, and would be over and above the usual ones, such as maintaining a trireme or a cavalry horse, which the wealthy would undertake whether they hold a high office or not. (That they are additional liturgies is signalled by the word 'also' in the first sentence of the section.) The liturgies Aristotle has in mind are apparently all religious: sacrifices, votive offerings, and public buildings (presumably temples). His call for magnificent (*megaloprepeis*) sacrifices reminds the reader that these liturgies fall within the sphere of magnificence (*megaloprepeia*) (*EN* IV. 2; *EE* III. 6; *MM* I. 26), the moral virtue governing vast expenditures of money. Indeed, in his account of the virtue in the *Nicomachean Ethics* he specifically mentions expenditures on votive offerings, sacrifices, and buildings (IV. 2. 1122ᵇ19–21). Aristotle's encouragement of expensive liturgies in oligarchies has the same purpose as his discouragement of 'useless' and 'senseless' liturgies in democracies (V. 8. 1309ᵃ14–20, VI. 5. 1320ᵇ2–4)—to secure the acquiescence of those who are disfavoured by the constitution. He complains that oligarchs no longer provide such liturgies, but seek both the profits and the honour of office. This is an impossible goal; for, as he says in the *Ethics*, 'it is not possible at the same time to get

money from the public and to be honoured' (*EN* VIII. 14. 1163ᵇ8–
10). In trying to profit from office they are imitating the many, who
'desire profit more than honour' (4. 1318ᵇ16–17), and make their
oligarchies, as he caustically remarks, 'small democracies'. Aristotle evidently wishes to hold them to an aristocratic standard. For
honour is to aristocracy as wealth is to oligarchy. Men wish to be
honoured for their virtue (*EN* I. 5. 1095ᵇ26–9)—for their magnificence, for example—and virtue is the mark of aristocracy, not
oligarchy (IV. 8. 1294ᵃ10–11). As we have seen, Aristotle's description of agricultural democracy also presupposes an aristocratic
standard (see the note to 4. 1318ᵇ6–1319ᵇ1 above).

CHAPTER 8

1321ᵇ4–12

In spite of its opening words this chapter has no particular connection with the rest of Book VI: as the backward reference at 1321ᵇ5–
6 signals, it is connected rather with the discussion of offices in
Chapter 15 of Book IV (see also IV. 14. 1298ᵃ1–3). In this earlier
chapter Aristotle raises a host of questions but discusses only three.
He considers what it is to be an official (1299ᵃ14–30), discusses
the offices that are peculiar to particular constitutions (1299ᵇ20–
1300ᵃ9), and gives an especially full treatment of the various ways
of filling an office (1300ᵃ9–ᵇ7). In the present chapter he picks up
where he left off. He poses once again several questions that were
left unanswered concerning the number of offices, their identification, and their powers (for the concept of the power, or *dunamis*,
of an office see IV. 15. 1300ᵇ9–12), and reiterates (from IV. 15.
1299ᵃ31–4) his division of offices into two kinds: the kind that are
necessary and the kind that are useful for good structure and order.
Using this division as his organizing principle he then proceeds to
enumerate the various civic offices. The necessary ones are identified first (1321ᵇ12–1322ᵇ37), and then at the very end a paragraph is
devoted to those relating to good structure and order (1322ᵇ37–
1323ᵃ6). Aristotle's survey reflects Athenian practice at some
points (Rhodes 1981, p. 33) and follows in the track of Plato's *Laws*
at others.

The two kinds of office that Aristotle distinguishes are presumably intended to exhaust the field and not to overlap. A necessary office is an office without which a city cannot exist (see also IV. 15. 1299^{a}31); an office relating to good structure and order (if his two kinds do not overlap) is an office without which a city can exist but cannot be well managed. Aristotle seems to have overlooked the possibility that some offices are neither necessary nor related to good structure and order. At any rate he never mentions such offices. It is difficult to think of examples—or at any rate of unproblematic examples—since lawmakers do not usually institute offices they believe to be neither necessary nor related to good structure and order. But since we are only concerned with possibility, such examples are not necessary. All we need show is that it is sometimes an open question whether a given office is either necessary or related to good structure and order. And this is shown by the twentieth-century debate over price controls. Lawmakers are constantly tempted to introduce offices to control the price of one commodity or another. At Athens, for example, the town managers regulated the fees of flute-girls (*AP* 50. 1). But whether such offices are either necessary or good social policy has been hotly debated. (It would probably be premature to suggest that the question has been settled once and for all.) Aristotle seems to tacitly assume that things will go badly unless they are supervised or regulated. He is not alive to the possibility that a city might be well managed precisely because it lacks certain offices. Aristotle's seeming failure to recognize that a given office might fit neither of his kinds may explain the dearth of argument in this chapter. If an office must belong to one of them, it will usually be apparent to which of the two it belongs.

1321^{b}6–8 What is required for a city to be well managed is distinguished from what is required for it to exist not only here but also at III. 12. 1283^{a}20–2. For good structure (*eutaxia*), see the note to 6. 1321^{a}1–4. For the conjunction of structure (*taxis*) and order (*kosmos*) see *Cael*. III. 2. 301^{a}10; *Met*. A. 3. 984^{b}16–17; and Plato, *Gorg*. 504a8.

1321^{b}8–9 The problem faced by small cities of manning all the necessary offices is discussed at IV. 15. 1299^{a}34–^{b}10.

1321ᵇ12–1322ᵃ29

Aristotle begins his survey with six of the 'most necessary' offices. The first three have as their respective spheres the market-place, the rest of the town, and the country (see Plato, *Laws* IX. 881c3–7; XI. 913d5–914a1, 936c3–5). The town is the territory of a city lying within its walls; the country is the territory lying beyond.

1321ᵇ12–18   Market managers (*agoranomoi*)

Aristotle's description of the function of the market managers— to keep an eye on contracts and good order—is a trifle vague. At Athens supervision of the market-place was in the hands of three sorts of official: market managers (*agoranomoi*), who insured that the products being sold were pure and unadulterated; controllers of weights and measures (*metronomoi*); and grain guardians (*sitophulakes*), who regulated the price of grain, meal, and bread (*AP* 51. 1–3). Aristotle presumably means to include the functions of all three under 'supervision of the market-place' and to call all three 'market managers'.

This section contains one of the few arguments of this chapter. From the fact that the inhabitants of a city must buy and sell in order to meet their necessary needs, Aristotle infers that an office that supervises the market-place is a necessary civic office. The tacit premiss upon which this argument appears to rely is that if it is necessary for the inhabitants of a city to buy and sell in order to meet their necessary needs, then a city cannot exist without an office that supervises buying and selling. But this premiss is dubious. For people buy and sell all the time without the sort of supervision that Aristotle seems to envisage—for example, in the underground economy and on the black market. An unsupervised market-place—at whose entry a lawmaker may want to post the warning 'Buyer Beware'—would seem to be perfectly feasible. Whether such a market-place is desirable is a separate question. If it is undesirable, this shows, not that an office to supervise the market-place is a necessary office, but only that it is an office relating to good structure and order.

Perhaps Aristotle's argument should be read in another way. The word 'necessary' occurs in it three times: It is *necessary* for the inhabitants of a city to buy and sell in order to meet their *necessary* needs; therefore, an office to supervise the market-place is a *necessary* office. This focus on the necessary suggests that perhaps Aristotle is not relying on a tacit premiss after all but moving from his explicit premiss to his conclusion by way of a definition. He can do this if, with a little conceptual slippage, he means by a 'necessary' office, not an office no city can exist without, but rather an office that *supervises* those things that no city can exist without. He may have slid from his original definition to this new one without being aware of it.

For more on this argument see Barnes, p. 258; for more on the office itself see Plato, *Laws* VI. 764b1–c4, VIII. 849a3–850a6, XI. 917e2–918a1.

1321^{b}18–27 Town managers (*astunomoi*)

For the office of town management (*astunomia*) see VII. 12. 1331^{b}6–13; *AP* 50. 2, 54. 1; and Plato, *Laws* VI. 759a2–7, 763c3–764c4, 779b7–c7; VIII. 846e3–847b6. The three parts of town management mentioned at the end of the section deal with the maintenance of the city's walls, the care of its water supply, and the guard of its harbour, respectively.

1321^{b}27–30 Country managers (*agronomoi*)

The country managers or forest wardens are responsible for guarding the countryside against foreign enemies and for maintaining order among those who live in the country (VII. 12. 1331^{b}14–17; Plato, *Laws* VI. 760b2–763c2, VIII. 843b7–844d3).

1321^{b}30–3 Revenue officers

The receivers (*apodektai*) or treasurers (*tamiai*) are the transfer agents of the city, receiving money from those from whom it is due and distributing it to the various civic departments. In Athens the receivers distributed the revenue on the same day they received it (*AP* 48. 2), thus obviating the need (mentioned in the passage before us) for guarding it in the interval between receipt and distribution. They evidently performed these functions at regular intervals ten times each year (*AP* 47. 3). (For more on receivers see *AP* 47. 5–48. 2.)

1321^{b}34–40 Sacred recorders (*hieromnēmones*)

In his judicial functions the sacred recorder resembles a court clerk in the American legal system: he receives the charge, brings the case to court, and registers the verdict. His other function is to maintain a register of private contracts.

At Athens there were registers of public, but not of private, contracts (*AP* 47. 2–5). The only law of private contract the Athenians had was that any agreement made voluntarily before witnesses was valid (Plato, *Symp.* 196c2–3; MacDowell, p. 152). The fact that a register of private contracts was not maintained at Athens shows that an office devoted to maintaining such a register would not be a necessary office.

1321ᵇ40–1322ᵃ29 Enforcement officers

Having described the office that records the sentences of the courts, Aristotle turns now to the one charged with carrying them out. He does not give it a name, but it will be convenient to refer to it as 'the office of enforcement' and to those who hold the office as 'enforcement officers'. The office's three functions—to execute the sentences of the law courts, to enforce the penalties against those whose names have been posted as public debtors, and to assume custody of prisoners—resemble those of a county sheriff in the United States.

The names of public debtors would be posted either on the acropolis ([Dem.], *Against Aristogeiton* I. 4) or in the market-place (Plato, *Laws* VI. 762c5, XII. 946d4). At Athens a public debtor was disenfranchised until his debt was paid; he might also be imprisoned or have his property confiscated (MacDowell, pp. 164–7).

Aristotle says that those who exact penalties meet with hostility and enmity, and he implies (1322ᵃ16–18) that those who impose them do too. The reason is obvious. It is natural for a person to hate anyone who imposes or exacts an unfair penalty; and since, as Aristotle says in another context, 'most men are bad judges about their own affairs' (III. 9. 1280ᵃ15–16; see also 16. 1287ᵇ2–3), defendants in lawsuits have a tendency to regard an unfavourable verdict as unjust or, if they concede its justice, to regard the penalty as excessive. This enmity would be difficult for an enforcement officer to bear since in a small city it would be from a neighbour (perhaps even a relative), and since, unlike his modern counterpart, he was not a professional but an ordinary citizen drafted from daily life— the so-called Eleven at Athens to whom Aristotle refers at 1322ᵃ20 were chosen by lot (*AP* 52. 1)—with no special training or experience.

That one of the functions of the office of enforcement was to supervise executions would do nothing to increase its popularity, even though the execution itself was carried out by a professional executioner—the *dēmios*, or 'public man' (*AP* 45. 1. 3; Plato, *Rep.* IV. 439e8, *Laws* IX. 872b6).

Since enforcement is such an odious task, Aristotle feels called upon to demonstrate the necessity of an enforcement office. His demonstration consists of an elaborate chain argument, whose tacit premisses (flagged by asterisks) are easily supplied. (1*) A city cannot exist when it is impossible for men to associate with each other. (2) It is impossible for men to associate with each other when lawsuits do not fulfil their function. (For the foregoing premisses see also Plato, *Crito* 50a2–5.) (3) Lawsuits do not fulfil their function when they do not attain their end. (4) They do not attain their end when penalties are not exacted. (5*) Penalties are not exacted when there is no office concerned with exacting them. (6) Therefore, a city cannot exist unless there is an office concerned with exacting penalties. (7) A civic office is necessary if a city cannot exist without it. (8) Hence, an office concerned with exacting penalties is a necessary civic office. This argument is not only valid but all of its premisses are true. The only one requiring comment is the second, which asserts the impossibility of men associating with each other without lawsuits. Aristotle is thinking of large bodies of men, not of families, friends, or small groups, which often manage quite well without lawsuits. The underlying idea is that men cannot associate with each other without justice and that in large bodies there can be no justice without a legal system.

Aristotle would dilute the hostility and enmity falling upon any particular enforcement officer by multiplying the number of such officers. He has several recommendations. First, different law courts should have different enforcement officers. Secondly, enforcement should not be the province of enforcement officers alone; other officials should share the burden—with the proviso, however, that an official who imposes a penalty should not also exact it. Thirdly and finally, the officials who supervise the custody of prisoners should be different from those who exact penalties.

This last recommendation leads Aristotle to reflect on the problem of securing the right jailers. Good men shun the office, and bad men cannot be trusted. So he recommends eliminating detention officers altogether and having the prisoners guarded by cadets or civic guards and by officials in some sort of rotation. At Athens the cadets, or *ephēboi*, were the young men who were receiving the two years of compulsory military training that began at the age of 18 when they were registered as citizens (*AP* 42). For civic guards see Plato, *Laws* VI. 760a6–e3. For the idea of using cadets or civic guards in law enforcement see Xen. *Cyr.* 1. 2. 12.

1322ᵃ29–ᵇ37

1322ᵃ29–ᵇ6 Military officers

In this section Aristotle describes the command structure of the armed forces of a good-sized Greek city. In this structure the hoplites are under the command of a general (*stratēgos*) or warlord (*polemarchos*), who is also the commander of the entire army. The cavalry is divided into squadrons commanded by squadron commanders (*phularchoi*: literally, tribal commanders), who are subordinate to the cavalry commander (*hipparchos*). (For *phularchoi* as horsemen see Aristoph. *Lysistrata* 561; Plato, *Laws* VI. 756a1–2, VIII. 834c5.) The light-armed troops and the archers are divided into companies commanded by company commanders (*lochagoi*: literally, leaders of armed bands), who are subordinate to a corps commander (*taxiarchos*). In the Athenian army a *taxiarchos* commanded hoplites (*AP* 61. 5) but here apparently, as at Xenophon, *Anabasis* 4. 1. 28, he commands light-armed troops. In the navy the triremes are commanded by trireme commanders (*triērarchoi*), and the fleet is commanded by a naval commander (*nauarchos*), or admiral.

Aristotle says that these offices are ranked higher in dignity than the necessary offices mentioned previously because they require experience and trustworthiness. These two requirements call to mind the discussion in V. 9 of the three qualities desired in those who hold the supreme offices: friendliness toward the established constitution, ability (tacitly equated with experience at 1309ᵇ4–5), and virtue. Since a city must trust its military officers not to betray the constitution or to falter in battle, it is plausible to suppose that in the passage before us Aristotle intends the concept of trustworthiness (*pistis*) to cover both the first and the last of these, both loyalty and bravery. (For these two kinds of trustworthiness see Plato, *Rep.* VI. 503c9–d2, VIII. 567d5–e7.) Friendliness toward the established constitution is important because the military officers are charged among other things with guarding the city against domestic enemies (which Aristotle distinguishes from military needs).

In listing some of the duties of the military officers Aristotle mentions inspecting and marshalling the citizens. What he is referring to is a military review in which the hoplites are drawn up in order of battle (IV. 13. 1297^{b}19–20; Xen. *Cyr.* 2. 41. 1).

1322^{b}6–12   Auditors and accountants

At Athens every official was subject to an examination, or *euthyna*, when his term of office came to an end. The examination had two parts. The first part was financial and was conducted by a board of ten accountants (*logistai*), who looked for evidence that the official was guilty of embezzlement, bribery, or misdemeanour in his handling of public money. The second part dealt with other kinds of misconduct in office and was carried out by a board of ten auditors (*euthunoi*: literally, straighteners). (*AP* 54. 2; MacDowell, pp. 170–2; Plato, *Laws* XII. 945b3–946e4.)

1322^{b}12–17   The council (*boulē*)

Aristotle claims that where the many rule—that is to say, in a democracy (III. 8. 1279^{b}21–2, V. 7. 1307^{a}16)—the council 'is most supreme in all things'. He does not mean that the council is the supreme element in a democracy; for he says in this very passage that the council 'convenes the supreme element in the constitution', which in a democracy is the assembly (2. 1317^{b}28–9). What he means is that the council plays the lead role in the political life of the city in so far as it prepares the business for the assembly, presides over its meetings, and implements its decisions. The council of five hundred at Athens, which met every day except holidays, did all of these things and more (*AP* 43. 2–49). For Plato's views on the central role of this institution see *Laws* VI. 756b7–758d9.

Aristotle discusses pre-councillors in more detail in Book IV (14. 1298^{b}26–32, 15. 1299^{b}30–8).

1322^{b}17–29   Religious officials

Aristotle distinguishes religious offices from political ones on the straightforward ground that religious offices deal with the affairs of the gods, not with citizens (IV. 15. 1299ᵃ17–23). He devotes a paragraph to religious offices because he regards the supervision of religious affairs as a prime function of a city (VII. 8. 1328ᵇ12), though he does not explain why.

The qualifications for holding a religious office are not much different from those for holding a political one. The office-holder must be a citizen (VII. 9. 1329ᵃ29–30) and must be unstained by homicide or similar pollutions (Plato, *Laws* VI. 759c3–6). Other than that, a religious office, as Isocrates says, is one that any man can fill (*To Nicocles* 6); and it was often filled by lot (*AP* 47. 1, 50. 1, 54. 6–8)—perhaps to allow for divine intervention (Plato, *Laws* VI. 759c1).

We get a glimpse of the organization of a temple from the various religious officials that Aristotle claims are to be found everywhere except in small cities. In addition to priests (*hiereis*), there are, he says, (1) masters of the sacrifices (*hieropoioi*), who organize the sacrifices for the priests, buying the animals, maintaining order at the sacrifice, and after the sacrifice selling the skins (Burkert, pp. 95–6), (2) guardians of the shrines (*naophulakes*), who presumably have the responsibility referred to at the beginning of the section for the preservation and restoration of the temple buildings, and (3) treasurers (*tamiai*) of the sacred funds, who oversee the finances of the temple and disperse the funds that the two preceding kinds of official need to fulfil their functions.

As Aristotle indicates, not all the public sacrifices are assigned to the priests; some are performed by political officials. At Athens, for example, there was an official called *basileus* ('king'), another called *archōn* ('official'), and members of the council called *prutaneis* ('presidents'), all of whom performed sacrifices (*AP* 3. 3, 56. 2–5, 57. 1; Rhodes 1972, p. 132; Burkert, p. 95).

1322ᵇ29–37 Summary

In his recapitulation, Aristotle organizes the necessary offices into three groups: (1) those concerned with the gods, war, and finance; (2) those that deal with a particular region of the city; and (3) those connected with the law courts and those concerned with deliberation.

Aristotle sometimes distinguishes the element that deliberates (*to bouleuomenon*) from the offices and implicitly identifies it with the assembly (IV. 14. 1297^{b}41–1298^{a}9); but in the passage before us, which is a summary of offices, he must be thinking of the council (*boulē*) as the deliberative element.

1322^{b}37–1323^{a}10

1322^{b}37–1323^{a}1 Having completed his survey of the necessary offices, Aristotle turns now to the offices directed to good structure (*eutaxia*) and order (*kosmos*) (1321^{b}7–8), the offices peculiar to prosperous and leisured cities that care for good order (*eukosmia*). He says that some of these offices—in particular, the aristocratic superintendent of women (*gunaikonomos*) and superintendent of children (*paidonomos*) (IV. 15. 1300^{a}4–6)—are clearly (*phanerōs*) not democratic. What about the other offices mentioned? Does Aristotle think that they too are not democratic, only less clearly not? Or does he mean to imply that they, or some of them, *are* democratic? It is difficult to see how he could think any office directed to good structure and order is democratic given his regular association of democracy with disorder (*ataxia*), unruliness (*anarchia*), and living as one wishes (V. 3. 1302^{b}28–9, 31, 9. 1310^{a}32–4; VI. 2. 1317^{b}11–12, 4. 1319^{b}27–32). He claims that this last feature of democracy, living as one wishes, makes the democrat loath to be ruled by anyone (2. 1317^{b}11–17). But if he thinks the democrat is reluctant to accept even the necessary offices, how could he regard an unnecessary office as democratic?

Aristotle's reason for claiming that the superintendent of women and the superintendent of children are not democratic is that a poor man, lacking slaves, must use his wife and children as attendants (*akolouthoi*, literally 'followers'). One function of a slave was to serve as an attendant (Aristoph. *Eccles.* 593) and to carry the purchases when his master went shopping in the market-place. (The cheapskate sketched by Theophrastus carries his purchases of meat and vegetables himself in the folds of his gown, and when his wife needs an attendant, hires one merely for the occasion (*Characters* 22).) But if the poor must use their wives as attendants, then, as Aristotle explains elsewhere (IV. 15. 1300^{a}4–7), it will be impossible to prevent the women of the poor from going out. The conclusion that the office of superintendent of women is not democratic now follows with the addition of two tacit premisses: first, that a superintendent of women would see that female citizens stay indoors where they belong, and, second, that an office is inappropriate to a given constitution if it is designed to enforce regulations that presuppose material resources beyond the reach of a large portion of those who are citizens under that constitution. The argument that a superintendent of children is not democratic is evidently intended to be similar, though it is not so clear how the poverty of the poor would interfere with the function of this office.

Aristotle's ideal city has a superintendent of children, who among other things supervises the stories they are told and takes special care that they associate as little as possible with slaves (VII. 17. 1336ᵃ30–2, 39–41). Whether his ideal city is to have a superintendent of women he does not say. But to insure that pregnant women get enough exercise he suggests that the lawgiver require them to take a daily walk to the temple connected with childbirth (VII. 16. 1335ᵇ12–16)—the temple of Eileithyia (Plato, *Symp.* 206d2–3) or of Artemis (Plato, *Theaet.* 149b9–10)—and this would seem to imply a supervisor of women to see that they actually do take their walks (see also Plato, *Laws* VI. 783d8–784e1).

1323ᵃ1–3 The gymnastic and Dionysiac contests (*agōnes*) referred to here are the dramatic, musical, and athletic contests in honour of the gods that were such a prominent feature of Greek life (see VIII. 6. 1341ᵃ9–12; *Rhet.* III. 15. 1416ᵃ28–34; *AP* 56. 5, 57. 1, 60. 1, 3; Plato, *Laws* VI. 764c5–765d3).

1323ᵃ6–10 This section seems like an afterthought. Aristotle has been discussing several offices that are found under some constitutions but not under others. This leads him to reflect that there is one political function—supervising elections—that is assigned to different offices under different constitutions. He does not explain why guardians of the law are aristocratic; indeed, in an earlier passage they are connected, not with aristocracy, but with oligarchy (IV. 14. 1298ᵇ26–9). Pre-councillors (*probuloi*) are oligarchic because they are few in number (IV. 15. 1299ᵇ34–6), oligarchy being literally rule of the few (III. 6. 1278ᵇ11–13, V. 7. 1306ᵇ24–6). The committee of pre-councillors appointed at Athens in the wake of the Sicilian disaster consisted of just ten members (*AP* 29. 1–2; Thuc. 8. 1). The large size of a council, on the other hand, makes it a democratic institution. At Athens, however, the elections of high officials were supervised, not by the whole council of five hundred, but by a subcommittee (*AP* 44. 4).

BIBLIOGRAPHY

1. Texts, Translations, and Commentaries

AUBONNET, JEAN, *Aristote, Politique*, vol. ii (Books V and VI) (Paris, 1973).
BARKER, ERNEST, *The Politics of Aristotle* (Oxford, 1946).
DREIZEHNTER, ALOIS, *Aristoteles' Politik* (Munich, 1970).
JOWETT, B., *The Politics of Aristotle,* 2 vols. (Oxford, 1885).
NEWMAN, W. L., *The Politics of Aristotle*, 4 vols. (Oxford, 1887–1902; repr. 1973).
ROSS, W. D., *Aristotelis Politica* (Oxford, 1957).
SCHÜTRUMPF, ECKART, and GEHRKE, HANS-JOACHIM, *Aristoteles Politik*, vol. iii (Books IV–VI) (Berlin, 1996).

2. Books and Articles Cited in this Work

ANDREWES, A., *The Greek Tyrants* (London, 1956).
BARNES, JONATHAN, 'Aristotle and Political Liberty', in Patzig, 250–63.
BULLOCK, ALAN, *Hitler and Stalin: Parallel Lives* (London, 1991).
BURKERT, WALTER, *Greek Religion*, trans. John Raffan (Cambridge, Mass., 1985).
CONQUEST, ROBERT, *Inside Stalin's Secret Police* (London, 1985).
——*The Great Terror: A Reassessment* (Oxford, 1990).
DOVER, K. J., *Greek Homosexuality* (Cambridge, Mass., 1978).
DUNBABIN, T. J., *The Western Greeks* (Oxford, 1948).
EASTERLING, P. E., and KNOX, B. M. W. (edd.), *The Cambridge History of Classical Literature* (Cambridge, 1985).
EHRENBERG, VICTOR, 'The Foundation of Thurii', *American Journal of Philology*, 69 (1948), 149–70.
GOMME, A. W., ANDREWES, A., and DOVER, K. J., *A Historical Commentary on Thucydides*, 5 vols. (Oxford, 1956–81).
HALBROOK, STEPHEN P., *That Every Man Be Armed: The Evolution of a Constitutional Right* (Albuquerque, 1984).
HALLIDAY, W. R., *The Greek Questions of Plutarch* (Oxford, 1928; repr. 1975).
HAMILTON, ALEXANDER, MADISON, JAMES, and JAY, JOHN, *The Federalist Papers* (Cutchogue, NY, 1992).
HAMMOND, N. G. L., *A History of Greece to 322 B.C.*, 3rd edn. (Oxford, 1986).
——*Philip of Macedon* (London, 1994).

——and GRIFFITH, G. T., *A History of Macedonia*, vol. ii (Oxford, 1979).

HANSEN, MOGENS HERMAN, 'How Often Did the Athenian *Dicasteria* Meet?', *Greek, Roman, and Byzantine Studies*, 20 (1979), 243–6.

HANSON, VICTOR DAVIS (ed.), *Hoplites: The Classical Greek Battle Experience* (London, 1991).

——'Hoplite Technology in Phalanx Battle', in Hanson (1991), 63–84.

HOBBES, THOMAS, *Leviathan* (London, 1651).

HOFFMANN, PETER, *Stauffenberg: A Family History, 1905–1944* (Cambridge, 1995).

IRWIN, TERENCE, *Aristotle's First Principles* (Oxford, 1988).

JACKSON, A. H., 'Hoplites and the Gods: The Dedication of Captured Arms and Armour', in Hanson (1991), 228–49.

KEYT, DAVID, 'Aristotle's Theory of Distributive Justice', in Keyt and Miller, 238–78.

——'Aristotle and the Ancient Roots of Anarchism', *Topoi*, 15 (1996), 129–42.

——and MILLER, FRED D., Jr. (edd.), *A Companion to Aristotle's* Politics (Oxford, 1991).

KHRUSHCHEV, NIKITA, *Khrushchev Remembers*, trans. and ed. Strobe Talbott (Boston, 1970).

KNIGHT, AMY, *Beria: Stalin's First Lieutenant* (Princeton, 1993).

LARSEN, J. A. O., *Representative Government in Greek and Roman History* (Berkeley, 1955).

MACDOWELL, DOUGLAS M., *The Law in Classical Athens* (Ithaca, NY, 1978).

MACHIAVELLI, NICCOLÒ, *The Discourses*, trans. Leslie J. Walker, SJ, with revisions by Brian Richardson (London, 1970).

——*The Prince*, trans. and ed. Robert M. Adams (New York, 1977).

MICHELL, H., *Sparta* (Cambridge, 1952; paperback, 1964).

MILLER, FRED D., *Nature, Justice, and Rights in Aristotle's* Politics (Oxford, 1995).

MOLL, CHRISTIANE, 'Acts of Resistance: The White Rose in the Light of New Archival Evidence', in Michael Geyer and John W. Boyer (edd.), *Resistance Against the Third Reich: 1933–1990* (Chicago, 1994), 173–200.

MORRISON, J. S., and COATES, J. F., *The Athenian Trireme* (Cambridge, 1986).

MULGAN, RICHARD, 'Aristotle's Analysis of Oligarchy and Democracy', in Keyt and Miller, 307–22.

PATZIG, GÜNTHER, *Aristoteles' 'Politik': Akten des XI. Symposium Aristotelicum* (Göttingen, 1990).

PICARD, GILBERT CHARLES, and PICARD, COLETTE, *The Life and Death of Carthage* (London, 1968).

POLANSKY, RONALD, 'Aristotle on Political Change', in Keyt and Miller, 322–45.

PRITCHETT, W. KENDRICK, *The Greek State at War, Part I* (Berkeley, 1971).

RAWLS, JOHN, *A Theory of Justice* (Cambridge, Mass., 1971).

RHODES, P. J., *The Athenian Boule* (Oxford, 1972).

——*A Commentary on the Aristotelian* Athenaion Politeia (Oxford, 1981).

ROSS, W. D., 'The Development of Aristotle's Thought', in Jonathan Barnes, Malcolm Schofield, and Richard Sorabji (edd.), *Articles on Aristotle*, vol. i (London, 1975).

ROWE, CHRISTOPHER, 'Aims and Methods in Aristotle's *Politics*', in Keyt and Miller, 57–74.

SCHOLL, INGE, *The White Rose: Munich 1942–1943* (Middletown, Conn., 1983).

SEYMOUR, CHARLES, and FRARY, DONALD PAIGE, *How the World Votes*, 2 vols. (Springfield, Mass., 1918).

SHERWIN-WHITE, SUSAN M., *Ancient Cos: An Historical Study from the Dorian Settlement to the Imperial Period* (Hypomnemata, 51; Göttingen, 1978).

SORABJI, RICHARD, 'Comments on J. Barnes: State Power: Aristotle and Fourth Century Philosophy', in Patzig, 264–76.

SPENCE, I. G., *The Cavalry of Classical Greece* (Oxford, 1993).

WHITE, STEPHEN A., 'Thrasymachus the Diplomat', *Classical Philology*, 90 (1995), 307–27.

WILENTZ, SEAN, 'Property and Power: Suffrage Reform in the United States, 1787–1860', in Donald W. Rogers (ed.), *Voting and the Spirit of American Democracy* (Urbana, 1992), 31–41.

ZELLER, EDUARD, *Aristotle and the Earlier Peripatetics*, vol. ii, trans. B. F. C. Costelloe and J. H. Muirhead (London, 1897).

GLOSSARY

αἵρεσις	hairesis	choice, election
αἰτία	aitia	cause, reason
ἀκρασία	akrasia	weakness of will
ἀξία	axia	worth
ἁπλῶς	haplōs	without qualification, simply, generally
οἱ ἄποροι	hoi aporoi	the needy
ἀρετή	aretē	virtue
ἄρχειν	archein	to start, to rule, to hold office
ἀρχή	archē	beginning, origin, start, starting point, principle, office, rule, *in plural*: office-holders, officials
ἀρχόμενος	archomenos	one who is ruled, a subject
ἄρχων	archōn	ruler, officer, official
ἄστυ	astu	town
βουλή	boulē	council
γένος	genos	family, kinship, class, type
οἱ γνώριμοι	hoi gnōrimoi	the notables
δεσποτικός	despotikos	despotic, mastery (1314[a]8)
δημαγωγός	dēmagōgos	demagogue, popular leader (1319[b]11)
(ὁ) δῆμος	(ho) dēmos	(the) people, democracy
δημόσιος	dēmosios	public
δημοτικός	dēmotikos	of the people, democratic
δίκαιος	dikaios	just
δικαστήριον	dikastērion	(law) court
δίκη	dikē	lawsuit
διόρθωσις	diorthōsis	rectification
δύναμις	dunamis	power, force, ability
ἔθνος	ethnos	nation
εἶδος	eidos	kind
ἐκκλησία	ekklēsia	assembly
ἑκών	hekōn	willing
ἐλευθερία	eleutheria	freedom
ἕξις	hexis	disposition
ἐξουσία	exousia	authority, licence
ἐπιβουλεύειν	epibouleuein	to conspire against
ἐπιείκεια	epieikeia	goodness
οἱ ἐπιεικεῖς	hoi epieikeis	the worthy

243

ἐπιθυμία	epithumia	desire
ἔργον	ergon	work, task, function, occupation (1321ᵃ29), fact (1308ᵃ2)
εὐγενής	eugenēs	well-born
εὔθυνα	euthuna	audit
εὐκοσμία	eukosmia	good order
οἱ εὔποροι	hoi euporoi	the prosperous
εὐταξία	eutaxia	good structure
εὐτυχία	eutuchia	good fortune
ἔχθρα	echthra	enmity
ἡγεμών	hēgemōn	leader
τὸ θητικόν	to thētikon	the labouring class
θυμός	thumos	spirit, spiritedness; *in plural*: violent feelings
ἴδιος	idios	private, individual, distinctive, peculiar
καινοτομεῖν	kainotomein	to make innovations
καλός	kalos	beautiful, noble
κατάλυσις	katalusis	overthrow
κινεῖν	kinein	to alter, to stir up
κίνησις	kinēsis	alteration
κληρωτός	klērōtos	filled (*or* selected) by lot
τὸ κοινόν	to koinon	the community
κοινός	koinos	common, communal, public, general
κύριος	kurios	supreme, sovereign, highest (1323ᵃ7), absolutist (1306ᵇ20)
οἱ μέσοι	hoi mesoi	those in the middle
τὸ μέσον	to meson	the middle class, the mean (1309ᵇ19)
μεταβάλλειν	metaballein	to change
μεταβολή	metabolē	change
μικρὰ φρονεῖν	mikra phronein	to think small
μικρόψυχος	mikropsuchos	small-minded
μοχθηρία	mochthēria	vileness
μοχθηρός	mochthēros	bad
νεωτερίζειν	neōterizein	to make (*or* to seek) a new order
νόμιμα	nomima	legal system
νομοθετεῖν	nomothetein	to pass a law
νομοθέτημα	nomothetēma	institution
νομοθέτης	nomothetēs	lawgiver
νόμος	nomos	law
οἱ ὅμοιοι	hoi homoioi	those who are alike (*or* similar in quality), the Equals (1306ᵇ30)
οὐσία	ousia	property

ὄχλος	ochlos	rabble
παρέκβασις	parekbasis	deviation
οἱ πένητες	hoi penētes	the poor
πλεονεκτεῖν	pleonektein	to get (*or* take) more (and more)
τὸ πλῆθος	to plēthos	the mass (*or* multitude)
οἱ πλούσιοι	hoi plousioi	the wealthy (*or* rich)
πολίς	polis	city
πολιτεία	politeia	constitution, polity
πολιτεύεσθαι	politeuesthai	*as passive*: to be governed; *as middle*: to engage in politics, to be active politically, to govern (oneself)
πολίτευμα	politeuma	governing class
πολίτης	politēs	citizen
πολιτικός	politikos	of a citizen, political
ὁ πολιτικός	ho politikos	the statesman
πρόβουλος	proboulos	pre-councillor
πρύτανις	prutanis	president
σόφισμα	sophisma	chicanery, strategem (1322^{a}21)
σπουδαῖος	spoudaios	good
στάσις	stasis	faction
στοιχεῖον	stoicheion	elementary principle
σωτηρία	sōtēria	preservation
τελευταῖος	teleutaios	ultimate
τέλος	telos	implementation, end, property tax
τυχή	tuchē	chance
ὕβρίς	hubris	insolence
ὑπόθεσις	hupothesis	fundamental principle
φθορά	phthora	destruction
χώρα	chōra	country, land, territory

INDEX LOCORUM

(Excluding Politics *V and VI)*

GENERAL INDEX

Boldface numerals refer to pages in the translation.

Erythrae **12**, 108, 111
Euboea 88, 113
Euripides **23**, **26**, 159–60, 161
Eurypon 149
Eurytion **14**, 113
Euthycrates **8**
Evagoras **25**, 159

faction 63–5
farmers **43**, **44**, 74, 195, 207, 208–11
Ferdinand, Archduke Francis 94
flatterers **31**, 102, 174
force **9**, **29**, 100, 149
freedom **38**, **40**, 58–63, 141–2, 195–200
    badly defined **23**, 142
    two marks of **40–1**, 195, 197–9
    two senses of 199–200
free status **1**, 58, 138, 197–8
friends, friendship **20–1**, **31**, 64, 102,
    134–5, 171, 173, 220

Gela **37**, 84, 188
Gelon **5**, **28**, **36**, **37**, 84, 91, 165, 173
general(s) **10**, **21**, **52**, 104, 134, 201, 234
    with supreme power 105, 110, 146,
    166
Gomme, A. W. 92
good structure **49**, **50**, 223, 228–9, 237–
    9
Gorgus **35**, 88
Göring, Hermann 151
Griffith, G. T. 111, 112
guardian(s) **21**, **24**, **33**, 149, 184
    of the city **12**, 110
    of the harbours **51**, 231
    of the laws **54**, 238
    of the shrines **53**, 236
guard(s) **16**, **24**, **30**, **33**, **52**, 104, 112,
    124–5, 149, 172, 234; *see also*
    bodyguards

Hadrian 173
Halbrook, Stephen P. 153
Hamilcar 165
Hamilton, Alexander 64
Hammond, N. G. L. 89, 111, 112, 158,
    160
Hanno **15**, 119–20
Hansen, Mogens Herman 217
Hanson, Victor Davis 225
haplōs, see without qualification
Harmodius **25**, 157
hatred **28**, 167

heiresses **8**, 97
Hellanocrates **26**, 160
Heraclea **11**, **12**, **14**, 103, 107–8, 113
Heracleides **26**
Heracleodorus **6**, 88
Heraclitus **34**, 180
Heraea **6**, 87–8
herdsmen **44–5**, 62, 207, 208, 211
Hesiod **28**
Hestiaea-Oreus, Hestiaeans **7**, 88
Hieron **28**, **30**, **36**, 91, 165
Hipparchus 157
Hipparinus **13**, 110
Hippias 157, 183, 213
Hippodamus 89–90
Hitler, Adolph 146, 150, 151, 154, 164
Hobbes, Thomas 152
Hoffmann, Peter 154
honour(s) **4**, **15**, **20**, **24**, **25**, **29**, **34**, 79,
    80, 179, 227–8
    lovers of **17**, **27**, **34**, **43**, 118, 163–4
    office of **24**, **38**, 146
    of office **14**, **15**, **50**, 80, 118
hoplite(s) **49**, 68, 87, 99, 100, 153, 224–
    7, 234–5
    expense of being a 225
Horse and Rider, fable of 146
Huber, Kurt 164
hubris, see insolence
hupothesis, see principle, fundamental

Ialysus 82
Iapygia, Iapygians **5**, 86
inequality **1**, **2**, **3–4**, **19**, **42**, 60–1, 71–2,
    204–5
inheritances **20**, 133
insolence **4**, **8**, **20**, **25–6**, **28**, **33**, **34**, 79–
    80, 155, 156–7, 159–60, 178, 179–80
    kinds of 156–7
Iphiades **13**, 113
Irwin, Terence xvi, **66**, 142
Istrus **11–12**, 108

Jackson, A. H. 225
Jowett, Benjamin 75, 77, 94, 125
jurors **14**, **47**, 58, 201, 216–17, 218–20
justice:
    democratic **42**, 59
    distributive 56–62, 63, 71–2
    natural or absolute 59–62, 139, 148
    oligarchic **42**, 59, 204

Kasmenē 83